EVOLUTIONARY ASTROLOGY

Pluto and your Karmic Mission

Deva Green

The Wessex Astrologer

Published in 2012 by
The Wessex Astrologer Ltd
4A Woodside Road
Bournemouth
BH5 2AZ
England

www.wessexastrologer.com

ISBN 9781902405780

Previously published by Llewellyn Worldwide 9780738714516

A catalogue record of this book is available at The British Library

Cover design by Tania at Creative Byte, Poole, Dorset

Dedication

I would like to dedicate this book to my beloved father, Jeffrey Wolf Green, and my family. Without their love and support I would have not found the determination or faith to write this book. My father has helped many, many people through his years of counseling service using Evolutionary Astrology. His presence in my life has been an inspiration. I would also like to dedicate this book to the divine blessings of the great Master Yogananda.

Acknowledgments

Special thanks to: Kristin Fontana, who has been the editor of this book—her devotion to Evolutionary Astrology and grateful service has been a deep personal blessing; Rose Marcus, who has been an invaluable source of support; and all those who I have crossed paths with and who have motivated me to continue on in this line of work (you know who you are).

About the Author

Deva Green is the daughter of Jeffrey Wolf Green, who was the founder of Evolutionary Astrology, and author of the books, *Pluto: The Evolutionary Journey of the Soul* (usually referred to as Volume 1), and *Pluto: The Soul's Evolution through Relationships* (Volume 2), both published by The Wessex Astrologer. Deva has also edited a collection of her father's previously unpublished notes and seminars in *Essays in Evolutionary Astrology: The Evolutionary Journey of the Soul* (The Wessex Astrologer). She is a graduate of the evolutionary astrology correspondence course designed to create certified evolutionary astrologers. In addition, she co-taught an introductory course for evolutionary astrology with Kim-Marie Weimer. Deva has lectured at the annual Evolutionary Astrology Conferences in 2005 and 2006, and at NORWAC 2007.

Contents

Foreword

Jeffrey Wolf Green

It seems so many lifetimes ago now that I first began to lecture and write about evolutionary astrology. The first lecture occurred in 1978 in Seattle, Washington. From that lecture onward, wherever I went to lecture on the evolution of the Soul, its evolutionary journey from life to life that could empirically be measured and understood through the symbolism of astrology, the lecture halls would be packed and overflowing. The hunger and thirst for this information is simply overwhelming. When the first volume of *Pluto: The Evolutionary Journey of the Soul* was first published by Llewellyn in 1985, it became an immediate best seller. Along the way, many foreign publishers have printed it in many, many different languages. In 1994, I established the School of Evolutionary Astrology which had teaching centers in the United States, Canada, Europe, and Israel. This included a video correspondence course that offered certification as an evolutionary astrologer, utilizing this system of understanding the Soul's evolution through time. In 1998, work was completed on the second volume, *Pluto, Volume II: The Soul's Evolution Through Relationships*, which dealt with the Soul's relationship to other people, and why we attract the kinds of people that we attract to ourselves for our ongoing evolutionary purposes and intentions through time. God willing, I will soon begin work on the final volume to the Pluto trilogy.

Evolutionary astrology is based on the evolution of the Soul. The Soul in astrology correlates to Pluto. The evolution of the Soul, from life to life, is simply based on a core dynamic that exists in all Souls: Desire. Within all Souls there are two root desires that serve as determinants for its evolution. One desire is to separate from that which created the Soul in the first place. For many that can be called God. For others it can simply be called the Source of All Things. The other desire is to return to that which created the Soul. The evolution of the Soul is thus a function of a progressive exhaustion of all separating desires that can leave only one desire remaining. And that is to return, or reunite, with that which has created it in the first place. This simple natural law or truth can be validated by all peoples independent of beliefs or cosmologies. All of us have whatever separating desires: the new possession, the new career position, the new lover, and so on. We may, in fact, have the ability to actualize those desires, and once we do, we do indeed have a temporary sense of satisfaction—but what soon replaces that satisfaction: dissatisfaction. It is this dissatisfaction that echoes the ultimate desire to return to that which created the Soul in the first place, and it is only that desire that leads to a state of permanent satisfaction. All peoples on Earth have this experience that only requires that you validate your own experience. It does not require any beliefs at all. It is this simple and natural law or truth that is the core of Evolutionary Astrology.

The entire paradigm that is used in evolutionary astrology is provable by anyone who uses it. It can be proved by your own life experience, and it can be proved through the clients that you work with if you are a practicing evolutionary astrologer. It is proved by one's life. The entire paradigm that is used by evolutionary astrology is Pluto, it's polarity point, the South Node and North Node of the Moon, and the location of their planetary rulers with all the aspects therein. This paradigm does reflect where the Soul has been before the current life, where the life was left off, where it picked up from, and where it was going. It does answer the underlying questions that are so deep in the heart of many: why am I here, and what are my lessons. Again, this evolutionary paradigm is provable by anyone who chooses to do so. I say this because there have been certain voices in astrology who have attempted to undermine evolutionary astrology without ever making the actual effort to use the paradigm itself.

When I first began lecturing on evolutionary astrology in 1978 there was no one else doing so. For many, many years I was the only voice who did so. Indeed, no astrologer had ever dealt with the evolution of the Soul at all. No astrologer even dealt with the obvious and natural law of evolution either. Today there are many who have read the Pluto books, many who have attended or taken the correspondence course in evolutionary astrology, and of course all the people who have attended my lectures on this subject over a twenty-five-year career. As a result, there are new voices and teachers in this vital work.

And now I have the privilege of introducing to you my daughter, Deva Green who has written this necessary and deep work on evolutionary astrology, a how-to, hands-on guide to the right use and practice of the underlying principles of evolutionary astrology. It offers concrete, step-by-step examples of how to apply the evolutionary paradigm to the birth chart. In so doing you can prove to yourself the paradigm of evolutionary astrology. It simply requires that you validate your own actual life experiences as viewed through this paradigm. Deva has studied my work for many, many years now, and of course had many conversations with me about it. As such, she is uniquely qualified to teach this work as reflected in her first book, *Evolutionary Astrology,* which is now in your hands.

God Bless,
Jeffrey Wolf Green

Foreword

Mark Jones

I have had the privilege both of studying with Jeffrey Wolf Green the first and only time he taught an astrology school in the United Kingdom, and of teaching evolutionary astrology alongside Deva Green at the Norwac Conference in Seatlle. Through my own teaching and speaking on evolutionary astrology in the U.K. and America, I have seen firsthand the power of this material to transform people's lives.

Here, Deva Green draws a blueprint for the methodology of evolutionary astrology, leading on from the pioneering work of her father, Jeffrey Wolf Green, described in his books *Pluto: The Evolutionary Journey of the Soul* and *Pluto: the Soul's Evolution through Relationships*. This approach will enlighten both beginners to the subject and more advanced students or practitioners, through its clarity and breadth of focus.

Deva begins with an expression of the fundamental philosophy underlying evolutionary astrology, identifying it as springing from natural laws which guide our evolution in nature. The author shows that this approach to astrology can reconnect the subject to an evolving sense of purpose or meaning here on earth. That beyond the materialistic emphasis of our culture, and its obsessions with appearance, longevity, and lifestyle, astrology can have a place in the discussion of our deepest need. The need to belong or enjoy a felt connection with our life; a connection which extends to the very source of that life, the source of the earth and the heavens also.

Having established this context, the understanding of astrology within the journey of the Soul back to the source of all things, Deva outlines a methodology that utilizes the natal chart in understanding the nature of the path any individual is on in this journey; the nature of the road, of the vehicle, any roadside amenities, the obstacles that might lie ahead.

This methodology takes as its starting point the seminal and incredibly indepth analysis of Pluto begun by Deva's father in his first Pluto book, and builds on it through analysis of the nodal axis and its rulers. From this evolutionary axis at the heart of the natal chart, Deva shows the core evolutionary concerns of the individual as revealed by the natal chart. With Pluto as the deepest point of unconscious security and orientation from the individual, the notes open up the nature of the past development of that orientation and the probable future direction such a development might take. In this way the natal chart can be seen as an incredible opportunity—a window into the core concerns of any given individual as they enter into this life—born into it over and over again.

Even materialistic thinkers acknowledge ideas can have a life beyond the individual brain. I think of Richard Dawkins and Daniel Dennett, and the exploration of the idea of *memes*, ideas that expand rapidly beyond and independent of the host thinker, or of the morphogenetic field research of the biologist Rupert Sheldrake. Within a less materialist philosophy, we can talk of intuited *wholes*, of meanings left by more evolved consciousness in the very fabric of the earth's energy, for individuals to pick up and run with, or certain astrological transits that influence the collective mind—such as the culmination of Pluto in Sagittarius, under which archetype this book was written. More simply, we can say that there are certain ideas whose time has come. It feels to me like the idea of evolutionary astrology, which can give such valuable insight into the nature of the human condition and journey, is an idea whose time has come. Deva Green has given a brilliant introduction to the nature of that idea. May it benefit all who read it.

God Bless,
Mark Jones

Introduction:
What Is Evolutionary Astrology?

The purpose of this book is to synthesize and apply the main principles of evolutionary astrology described in Jeffrey Green's *Pluto: The Evolutionary Journey of the Soul* (volume 1 of Green's Pluto series). This book is intended to aid and facilitate the study and integration of the material in the *Pluto* volume. Because the Soul correlates with Pluto in the natal birth chart, it is critical to deeply and thoroughly understand the meaning of Pluto when practicing this type of astrology. Pluto, or the Soul, then becomes the starting point and bottom line upon which all other factors in the birth chart are interpreted and given meaning.

The polarity point of Pluto by house and sign reflects the person's next evolutionary steps for this life, and correlates to the evolutionary cause, or intentions, of the life itself. The main principles of evolutionary astrology will be described and then applied, using real-life case studies. This is to be done through specific, in-depth illustrations of each central principle that is described in each chapter. This handbook is structured to operate as a "how-to book," from A–Z, in the context of demonstrating how to apply the principles of evolutional astrology. The illustrations in this book are also meant to help the individual accurately analyze a birth chart in full detail, and gain a deep understanding of the core principles of evolutional astrology. In this way the individual will have a very solid foundation of these core principles.

The challenge when learning evolutionary astrology is to synthesize all the various principles and astrological correlations that we learn. For example, we have the planet Venus in a specific house and sign, and this planet may be making aspects to other planets. How do we begin to correctly interpret this isolated factor in the birth chart? What steps do we take to correctly interpret any symbol in the birth chart? We will describe the procedure to synthesize all the various factors in a birth chart in this handbook. This process culminates in the ability to fully and precisely interpret any natal birth chart. In order to develop the ability to interpret a birth chart we must break down all the main principles of evolutionary astrology in a linear, step-by-step process. In this book, we will discuss and analyze the meaning of Pluto, its polarity point, the four main evolutionary conditions of the Soul, how to determine the main evolutionary/karmic dynamic in the birth chart, the archetypes (signs) of the natural zodiac, and apply the planetary method of chart interpretation.

Another critical factor that will be included in this book is the four main ways the Soul effects its evolution. Within this, we will describe how our own choices and responses to our evolutionary growth needs will be the causative factor in the types of life experiences we have. Again, we will break down each principle in a succinct, yet thorough, explanation of each principle, and then apply them in full illustrations. Thus, this handbook serves to create a comprehensive understanding and integration of the main principles of evolutionary astrology.

The Principles of Evolutionary Astrology

If we are to accurately practice this type of astrology we must first understand its philosophy and belief system. Evolutionary astrology is based upon observation and correlation. It is founded upon natural laws and truths. Natural laws are laws that are self-evident in nature, and are not dependent on a specific belief system in any way. Evolutional astrology reflects the natural truth that every Soul is in on an evolutionary journey, so to speak, to reunite or merge with the Source or the Creator. The very principles of evolutionary astrology teach the essence of natural laws that explain, and govern the operation of the totality of the manifested Creation itself. In other words, by the sheer fact that Creation exists in the first place, there must be intrinsic, natural laws that explain and govern the operation of the manifested Creation. These natural laws and truths are in sharp contrast to man-made laws or doctrine. It should be clear, then, that evolutional astrology does not require any specific belief system to validate the truth of the principles and natural laws it teaches, incorporates, and utilizes as we interpret a birth chart. Any individual can validate these natural laws by simply validating his or her own life experience.

What does the zodiac symbolize in the first place? The symbols used in the zodiac represent the totality of human consciousness in its natural form. The naturally existing functions within consciousness are represented by each of the archetypes, or signs of the zodiac. We will discuss the difference between these archetypes when they are expressed naturally, guided by natural law, and when they are distorted relative to the conditioning of man-made laws. The natal birth chart, in all its totality, reflects the Soul's specific psychological make-up, and structure of consciousness. The planets correlate to the specific psychological make-up of the Soul. The houses and signs which these planets are in will reflect how the planets are conditioned, and how they are operating within any person's consciousness. Thus, the birth chart will symbolize the person's intrinsic energetic pattern and vibration coming into the life. Evolutionary astrology gives us a precise tool to determine the exact degree of any Soul's evolution or awareness because it includes the four stages of human evolution. In addition we have a very thorough understanding of the past behavioral dynamics of the Soul because of the symbolic meaning of Pluto and its correlation to the Soul. Pluto's polarity point, then, gives us an objective, yet detailed, understanding of the person's next evolutionary steps in this life.

The four natural evolutionary conditions, or states, of humankind are: the Dimly Evolved condition, the Consensus condition, the Individual condition, and the Spiritual condition (there is a chapter devoted to describing and applying the evolutionary states. The reader will be able to determine their evolutionary state by the descriptions given in that chapter). The dimly evolved state is, most commonly, Souls that are just evolving into human consciousness from other life forms (animal and plant life forms). Another reason a Soul may be in this state is relative to his or her own actions in the past leading to de-evolution. Two to three percent of all Souls on the planet are in this condition. The consensus state is when the Soul simply agrees and conforms to dictates of the majority of his or her culture, or society. Roughly 75 percent of all Souls are in this evolutionary state. The individuated state is when the Soul desires to become a unique individual, independent from the conditioning of the consensus society. Roughly 20 percent of all Souls are in this evolutionary state. The spiritual state is when the Soul desires to know, merge, and serve God. The Soul will naturally align with timeless, natural laws of the Universe. Roughly 2–3 percent of all Souls are in this evolutionary condition. Other mitigating factors to include when analyzing a birth chart are the person's gender, cultural/religious conditioning, and economic status.

The methods given to us in evolutional astrology are dramatically different and unique from any other astrological practice that is known today. Again, we now have scientific tool within our grasp to determine the exact degree of evolution of any individual relative to the four natural evolutionary conditions. We have a detailed understanding of the specific nature of individual's past behavioral dynamics and orientation to life that have created the current moment and reality for the client (Pluto). We can then accurately determine the person's next evolutionary steps because of our understanding of the current operative dynamics within any individual (Pluto's polarity point). We can now embrace that everybody has unique and specialized lessons in life, and we can objectively guide clients and friends toward these goals. Now that we have described and introduced the main principals of evolutionary astrology we can discuss Pluto and its correlation with the Soul.

I

Pluto and Pluto's Polarity Point

The Soul: What Is a Soul And How Does It Evolve?

Before we discuss the Soul and its evolution, we must first understand the phenomenon of evolution. What is evolution in the first place, and how can we objectively validate that we are all evolving? The simplest way to validate the natural law of evolution is based on the universal human experience in which all of us know that we are in a continuous state of becoming. This is not a function of beliefs, or needing to believe it. It is simply a fact. In addition to the universal experience of becoming, we can observe the natural law of evolution in countless ways, as applied to the totality of Creation. We can observe it in the context of human life, plant and animal life, and the fundamental changes to the Earth itself as an evolving planet.

Evolution, simply defined, is the process of one form leading to the next in such a way that the form is completely and unalterably changed. A good analogy of this process is a caterpillar that makes a cocoon and then changes into a butterfly. Evolution can be the changing of energy, the changing of a pre-existing structure into a totally new structure, or the change of anything. The word *change* implies evolution. Another aspect of evolution that we must address is involution. This is a simple principle that describes the death of the old patterns, or a pre-existing something. That which pre-exists can be energy patterns, a structure or any old form that is preventing further growth and causing stagnation.

Involution, or the natural law of the death of a pre-existing structure, must proceed evolution. The death of the old behavioral patterns, or pre-existing form must occur before evolution, or change, can occur.

When evolution becomes necessary, it always implies that stagnation has occurred, and no further growth can manifest. In all life forms there exists a natural law called survival. When this natural law is ignited, or stimulated, for whatever reasons, it will always cause the natural law of involution and evolution to occur so the survival of the life form or structure can be sustained. There are two main ways that evolution and involution manifest. One form of evolution is cataclysmic and the other form is uniform, or slow, yet progressive, change. These, obviously, are two distinctly different manifestations of evolution. Cataclysmic evolution correlates with intense, sudden, and abrupt changes in which the pre-existing structure is fundamentally altered in a short period of time. In uniform evolution, the structure, or pre-existing form, changes gradually over time, whereas cataclysmic evolution creates stark and immediate changes. These two types of evolution can be objectively validated by any of us, and do not require beliefs or philosophies of any nature. Astrologically, Pluto correlates with the natural laws of evolution and involution.

The Soul

Because Pluto correlates with the Soul, we will briefly discuss the Soul and the ego that each Soul creates, before we describe and illustrate the meaning of Pluto in the birth chart. What is a Soul? How can we know that we do indeed have a Soul, or become aware of our Soul?

We can experience and validate our Soul outside the testament of enlightened beings, and specific beliefs of any kind. The definition of the Soul given to us by all the great avatars and gurus of our time, and applied in the Pluto material, is this: The Soul is an immutable consciousness, or energy, which has its own identity that remains intact from lifetime to lifetime. It is naturally a part of the Universal Consciousness that created it in the first place. Immutable means that this consciousness cannot be destroyed, because energy cannot be destroyed, and can only change form. Clearly, when we discuss the Soul, we are describing the nature of energy that is no different than the energy of consciousness itself. Astrologically, consciousness correlates with Neptune. The most important question to ask and answer in our discussion of the Soul is how can we all objectively validate and experience our Soul independent from belief systems of any kind. In other words, how can we inwardly prove to ourselves that we have a Soul, and in this way experience our own Soul? Again, the Soul is the energy of consciousness. We cannot open up the brain and find the Soul. However, we cannot open up the body and find emotions either, but we all know that we have them. We cannot open up the brain and find the Soul because it is consciousness. Consciousness, again, is energy.

Consciousness, itself, exists everywhere on earth in all forms of life. The existence of consciousness has been, and still is, one of the greatest mysteries posed to scientists because science has not been able to explain the origin of consciousness or even how it came to be. Yet, an origin or universal source of consciousness must exist because of the sheer fact that consciousness exists in the first place. This is exactly the starting point for the creation of religions and philosophies; the human need to contemplate and consider, within the desire to know, where we come from, and why. Such contemplation and reflection of this nature becomes the causative factor of beliefs. These beliefs are the result of human pondering upon the origin of life itself. I think we can all agree that there is a fundamental difference between actual knowing and the need to believe in an answer. The point here is to emphasize that there is a way to know the answers to the big cosmic questions, versus the need to believe in any given answer. The sheer fact that there is a manifested Creation implies that there must also be truths that inherently exist because of the fact that manifested Creation exists in the first place. In other words, there must be an origin of Creation by the sheer fact of its existence. In generic terms, this origin is called the Creator, the Source, or the Origin of All Things. In religious terminology this is called God, or the Goddess.

It is an observable fact that consciousness exists in all forms of life. That which is the Source of consciousness, of itself, must also be consciousness. Thus, the totality of consciousness emanates from this Source. All life forms have the appearance of being separate from other life forms, yet are simultaneously connected to one another. Take the example of two plants that are next to one another. These two planes appear separate, yet are simultaneously connected to one another by the sheer facts of being plants. The point of this illustration is to demonstrate that there is an individualized aspect to consciousness, yet there is also a universal aspect to consciousness that binds all the individualized aspects of consciousness together.

Another way to illustrate this point is the wave upon the ocean. The ocean is certainly the origin of the wave. However, from the point of view of the wave, if the individualizing aspect of consciousness is centered there, the wave appears and seems separate. In other words, if the center of gravity of consciousness is centered in the wave, then the wave appears and is experienced as something separate from its own source: the ocean. On the other hand, if the center of gravity within consciousness is in the ocean, then the ocean simultaneously experiences its totality, while at the same time experiencing the individualizing aspect of itself as manifested in the waves that emanate from it.

In the very same way, then, the universal consciousness, which is the origin of all consciousness, has created and manifested the totality of the manifested Creation. This, of course, includes the human being and the consciousness within the human being. Within human consciousness, there exists a natural, individualizing aspect. This occurs as a natural result of the human life form as a seed that produces many other branches that is no different than the ocean and the wave. Thus, each human being has its own individualizing consciousness that is called the Soul. Remember that the Soul is an immutable consciousness that remains intact from lifetime to lifetime, and is naturally a part of the Universal Consciousness that created It in the first place.

How can we know independent from belief systems that a Universal Creator, or Source, exists? Long ago, before the development of religion, philosophies, and complicated cosmologies, the human being learned through inner looking, or contemplation, that a light appeared on the interior of consciousness as breath became very shallow, and even stopped. This light appeared as a natural result of breath shallow-ing or stopping. Much later in human history, this became known as the third eye. It is this very light that symbolized and connected the individual consciousness reflected in the Soul to the Universal Consciousness that is the Universal Source, or the Origin of All Things. The human being also learned long ago that by merging its own individualized consciousness, or Soul, with that light, its consciousness would expand in such a way that the individual consciousness itself then becomes Universal and was then able to consciously experience the Ultimate Source of All Things: The wave returned to the ocean. These fundamental principles are all based on natural laws. Natural laws are truths that are self-evident in nature, and will be true for all times, whether the human being inhabits the planet or not.

The Evolution of the Soul

The Soul undergoes a continual metamorphic process that allows all Its limitations, points of stagnation, and blocks to be transmuted and purged. The analogy of the caterpillar who makes a cocoon and then changes into a butterfly applies to describe the metamorphosis of the Soul as well as the general phenomena of evolution. How does the Soul evolve? How can we consciously understand, or experience, the Soul's evolution? In the Soul there are two co-existing, antithetical desires. One desire is to return to the Source that created it, and the other is to separate from the Source. It is exactly the interaction of these two antithetical desires that create and determine not only our past in all its totality, but the nature of our current reality. This is true on an individual as well as collective level. The past has a reason for being, just as the present has a reason for being. It should be clear, then, that the Soul evolves by exhausting all its separating desires. Desire is the determinate of evolution. As we evolve, the desire to know and merge with God, or the Source, becomes ever stronger.

At some point in our evolutionary journey, the desire to return to God, or the Creator, is the only desire left in our Soul. Over a great period of evolutionary time, this creates Creation-realized masters such as Yogananda, Sri Yuketswar, Jesus, and Babaji. The point to embrace is that the Soul is on a natural evolutionary journey back to the Creator. Every great master and spiritual teacher that spoke with truth and wisdom validated that he or she too had to evolve, and that every Soul must undergo the same evolution as the Masters to reach the same high state of God-realization. It is important to understand that the Soul and its metamorphic process is typically unconscious in the vast majority of people. The influence of the two antithetical desires within the Soul are commonly not consciously understood. The desire to return to the Source, or Creator is the stronger of the two desires, even if an individual is not conscious of this desire in his or her life. Of course, as we evolve we become more conscious and aware of our Soul. We begin to perceive our lives and understand our own desire nature in the context of the two opposing, antithetical desires within our Soul. It is exactly this process of eliminating separating desires and simultaneously acting upon the desire to return to the Creator that stimulates, or ignites, such an evolution.

A very simple way to experience, and objectively validate, these two desires within the Soul is the universal experience of satisfaction and dissatisfaction. We can have separating desires of any nature—for example, we may desire a new possession, a new lover, or a new career, and so on. There is a sense of temporary satisfaction soon after we actualize our separating desires, but what soon replaces that temporary sense of satisfaction? Is there not a very intense feeling within our being that there must be more than the actualization of that separating desire, and a very strong sense of dissatisfaction? The feeling of dissatisfaction is an echo of the desire to return to God, or the Creator, even though many people do not consciously recognize it as such. It is critical to understand, or perceive, these emotions and experiences in this light, because the intense sensation of dissatisfaction commonly fuels yet another separating desire. At some point in our evolutionary journey we will realize that only the desire to return and merge with the Creator will provide true and lasting satisfaction. This is exactly the process and realization that all great masters and gurus experienced, and emphasize within their teachings. In spiritual terminology, this is what has been termed "nette." This describes the process of purging separating desires that triggers the realization within of the Soul of "not this, "not that" in the context of seeking ultimate satisfaction. There are many people that could not care less about cosmologies, the Soul, or understanding life in holistic context, yet they still want to know what they should be doing in their life. Individuals may desire to make the inherently right choices in their life, and ask questions regarding the correct life choices. Some people may want to know what their specific life lessons are, and in that context the purpose of the life itself. We can help guide and objectively answer such holistic questions through understanding of evolutionary astrology, and specifically, Pluto's correlation to the Soul.

The Ego

In each life, the Soul creates an ego. The ego, astrologically, correlates with the Moon. The ego is pure energy, just like the Soul. We cannot open up the brain and find it. Simply stated, the ego serves as an integrating function within subjective consciousness. The ego reflects our own self-image. Without the ego we could not speak our own name. A common and destructive myth that many of us have been subjected to in spiritual life is that, somehow, we must rid ourselves of the ego. Evolution is effected, again, by the Soul purging its separating desires. As this process occurs, the center of gravity within consciousness shifts from the ego to the Soul. Thus, the ultimate goal within spiritual life is to shift the center of gravity from the ego to the Soul, not ridding ourselves of our ego.

A metamorphosis of the egocentric structure occurs as this shift in consciousness is made. The individual progressively learns to view himself or herself (the self-image), as well as every other life form in manifested Creation, as an aspect or reflection of the Creator. In other words, when the center of gravity within an individual is centered in the Soul, then the egocentric structure of that person will naturally reflect a unity and identification with the Creator. The person's self-image will be founded upon such unity and connection with the Source. The perception of separation, or of being a separate entity (from an egocentric point of view) from the Source and other life forms in the manifested creation, will dissolve as such an evolution is made. The water triad of the Zodiac of Cancer (Moon),

Scorpio (Pluto), and Pisces (Neptune) correlates with the metamorphosis (Scorpio) of the individualized ego (Cancer) as the person develops a direct connection and identifies with God, or the Source (Pisces).

Unlike the energy of the Soul, which is sustained from lifetime to lifetime until the final merging with the Creator occurs, the energy of wave upon the sea again serves to illustrate this point. The Soul, or ocean, manifests different egos—or waves—life after life. Even though the waves rise and fall in any given life that the Soul creates, the ocean is sustained. In other words, the egos that the Soul manifests in each life rise from birth, but dissolve back into the ocean (Soul) upon completion of each life. Their energy is not destroyed, but simply absorbed back into the energy that created it in the first place. The ego created by the Soul allows for the individualizing aspect of the Soul in each life, and serves as the vehicle through which the evolutionary intentions of the Soul in any given life occur. Each ego that the Soul creates is oriented to reality so that the very nature of the orientation serves as a vehicle through which the life lessons occur and are understood by the Soul.

Again, in each life the ego allows for a self-image of the Soul to occur relative to the individualizing aspect of the Soul. The analogy of a movie projector and the lens on the projector clearly illustrates this point. If I have a movie projector with no lens on it, then all the screen will show is diffused images of light. Without the lens on the projector there is no distinct or clear images generated from the light of the movie projector. Thus, the lens serves as a vehicle through which the inherent images on the film can be focused and given distinct shape, form, and images. In the very same way the ego that the Soul generates in each life operates as a vehicle, or lens, through which the inherent images that exist within our Soul take form. This natural law of consciousness is the cause of that allows for individual self-perception and the word "I" itself.

The Soul, or Pluto, astrologically speaking, correlates to the genetic code, RNA, DNA, chromosomes, and enzymes. In each life the Soul is the determinant for the entire genetic code of the life, or human form, that it is being born into. Each life that the Soul creates is a continuation of what had come before, where each new life correlates to the ongoing evolutionary lessons or intentions of any given Soul. Thus, the body type—which includes the race to be born into, the appearance of it, the culture being born into, the parents of origin, the specific and individual nature of emotions, feelings, psychology, desires and so on— correlates to the Soul's intentions reflected in the genetic code in each life. This is all given individual form in each life via the egocentric structure, or Moon, that the Soul creates in each life. Thus, any person can make such statements as "this is who I am," "this is what I need," "this is what I am feeling," "this is what I am learning," and so on. The ego that the Soul creates in any life correlates with the individualizing aspect of human consciousness in this way.

When death occurs in any given life, as mentioned before, the ego that the Soul had created for that life dissolves back into its origin: the Soul. Since both are energy, and energy cannot be destroyed, where does the Soul go upon physical death of the body; where is it on an energetic level? Most of us have heard of the words "astral plane," or "heaven and hell." Obviously, what these words refer to are other realities, or planes of existence. Simply speaking, the astral plane is an energetic plane of existence that all Souls go to after completion of physical lives on places like Earth. Energetically, this plane of existence is much less materially dense than places like Earth. After physical death, the Soul goes to the astral plane in order to review the life that has just been lived, and to prepare for yet another birth on places like Earth. Upon the completion of a life on Earth, the ego dissolves back into the Soul in such a way that the center of gravity within consciousness, when in the astral plane, is the Soul itself. For the vast majority of people living lives in the material plane, we call Earth the center of gravity of consciousness—the ego itself. This is why these individuals feel within themselves that they are separate from everything else: the center of gravity being the egocentric "I."

In the astral plane, the center of gravity shifts from the ego to the Soul, so that when death occurs in any life the memory of the ego of that life is sustained. This is necessary for the Soul, for it is the memory of the ego that allows the Soul to not only review the life that has just been lived, but also serves as the basis for the next life to be lived relative to the continuation of the evolution of the Soul itself. In each life we pick up where we left off before. Thus, the memory of the ego in each life is the causative factor in determining the type of egocentric structure the Soul needs to create in the next life. In essence, it is the memory of the ego that the Soul draws upon, the images contained therein, that serve as the basis of the next egocentric structure that the Soul needs to generate in each successive life that promotes its ongoing evolution.

Astrologically speaking, this dynamic is symbolized by Pluto (Soul), and the South and North Nodes of the Moon. The South Node of the Moon correlates to the prior egocentric memories of the Soul, its prior egocentric structure, and the South Node determines the placement of the Moon in each life. The natal Moon, then, correlates with the current egocentric structure of the Soul, and how the transition from past to present will be experienced in every moment of life. The North Node of the Moon correlates with the evolving, or forming, egocentric structure of the Soul, and the nature and types of inner and outer experiences that the Soul needs and desires in order to facilitate its ongoing evolution. In turn, this will then constitute the new egocentric memories and images that the Soul will draw upon when a life has been lived and terminated at physical death.

The Moon also correlates to one's family of origin in any given life. It should be clear that, upon the death of the physical body, the Soul goes to the astral plane and meets again important family members, and others close to the Soul. This is the reason we continue to meet again those same family members upon re-birth into yet another physical life. It is the memory of the ego, now combined with the memory of family, that is the source of this phenomenon, and which continues until there is no longer any evolutionary or karmic need to sustain such relationships.

Pluto in the Natal Birth Chart

In the natal birth chart, Pluto correlates to Soul. Pluto, then, will correlate with the pre-existing patterns of identity association, desires, and bottom-line orientation of an individual coming into the life. The current evolutionary intentions for the current life are symbolized by the polarity point of Pluto. Pluto correlates with the deepest unconscious emotional security patterns that any of us can have because of the tremendous personal identification with the area symbolized in the natal position of Pluto. Most of us automatically gravitate to these patterns of behavior because they are familiar, and represent such a deep sense of emotional security. Emotional security is rooted in the need to be self-consistent, which is a function of the past, or what has come before. The natal position of Pluto is the path of least resistance in this context. In volume 1 of his *Pluto* series, Jeff Green observes that roughly 75 to 80 percent of our behavior is influenced by unconscious forces that are directly linked to such past patterns in identity association. These past patterns are tied to the cumulative evolutionary forces rooted in our desires. However, not many of us are aware of the influence of these past desires and identity associations in the present moment in time.

These past patterns create limitations and points of stagnation in the context of further evolution. There is a reliance upon these past patterns for emotional security reasons, which create obvious evolutionary blocks. Pluto's polarity point symbolizes how these limitations can be overcome, and transmuted. The potential for conflict and confrontation at the current time is very high, because of evolutionary pressure to transform old patterns and the emotional security that is linked with these past behavioral patterns (Pluto) into new patterns of behavior (polarity point of Pluto). We must consider the two co-existing desires within the Soul, and the impact these desires have on the choices we make to transform our old patterns of behavior (desire to return to the Source) or to stay stuck in the past patterns of behavior that are inhibiting further growth (desire to separate from the Source). Desire is the determinate to evolution. These choices will be the causative factor to the degree of conflict and tension that we experience in our current reality. As we evolve by embracing the evolutionary necessities of the life reflected in Pluto's polarity point, the natal position of Pluto will automatically regenerate into higher levels of expression. The old patterns, desires, and identity associations symbolized by the natal position of Pluto will die, or be purged, within the person—only for new patterns to be born into consciousness. Generally speaking, this describes the metamorphic process of evolution as the Soul exhausts its separating desires; a type of death and re-birth is experienced by all of us as we evolve in this way.

Succinctly put, the desires, past patterns of behavior, and patterns of identity association reflected in the natal position of Pluto by house and sign are those of the evolutionary past. The natal position of Pluto will describe any individual's specific individualized lessons, past patterns of identity association, and desires. We all pick up where we left off, and the natal position of Pluto symbolizes where an individual will pick up in this life. Yet, millions of people are born with Pluto in the same sign. What does this mean from an evolutionary point of view? Those that are born with Pluto in the same sign are within the same generation. All those born with Pluto in Libra, for example, are in the same generation. Pluto was in the sign of Libra from approximately 1971 to 1983. The archetype of Libra, generally speaking, correlates with extremities, and the need to learn balance relative to such extremities. Is it only a coincidence that this generation is labeled as Generation X, or extreme? The natal sign of Pluto correlates to the general vibration of the entire generation that the person is born into, and the past desires, intentions, and patterns of identity association of the individual's generation. Why does this phenomenon occur? From an evolutionary point of view, this occurs to accomplish the evolutionary needs of the planet. However, Pluto is always to be put in an individualized context. The house that Pluto occupies indicates the specific and individualized lessons, desires, intentions, and past patterns of identity association of each person. Thus, the sign conditions the house of Pluto in this way. Many people are born with Pluto in the same sign, yet all have specific natal horoscopes that will drastically alter how Pluto is expressed and is operating within an individual's consciousness. The four natural conditions of human evolution further magnify this point.

Pluto correlates with the generalized phenomenon of karma, or action leading to reaction, because it contains all the desires and intentions of the evolutionary past. The two co-existing desires within the Soul reflect that we all have free choice, or free will, in terms of the choices and decisions that we make. It is through accepting the responsibility in our own desires, and accepting that we are all personally responsible for our evolution, that we can grow to greater heights. It is important to understand that karma can be 100 percent positive or 100 percent negative—it is not inherently negative. The interaction of the two co-existing desires within our Soul is the causative factor of the perception of that which we think we need. That which we think we need is the determinate to the choices we make. The choices we make determine the actions we initiate. These actions have reactions, which lead to more actions, and so on, ad infinitum.

Our own cooperation or resistance to the evolutionary necessities of the Soul determines the types of evolutionary experiences we will have, and for what reasons we have these experiences. Remember that there are two distinctly different types of evolutionary growth described as cataclysmic and non-cataclysmic, or uniform. If we resist the evolutionary intentions of the Soul to such a point that no further growth can occur, then we will experience a cataclysmic evolution in some form, in order to enforce the necessary changes. The experiences that are associated with cataclysmic change are stressful and traumatic in nature. If we cooperate with the evolutionary intentions of the Soul then we can integrate traumatic events of this nature in a positive manner through understanding the evolutionary reasons why the event occurred. In this way, the old behavioral patterns that were previously inhibiting growth will be allowed to die, and new patterns will emerge within consciousness. Uniform evolution correlates with evolutionary events that are nontraumatic in nature. These events will manifest as smooth, gradual, yet progressive, evolution as we continually transmute areas of limitations within ourselves.

A critical question to address is why do any of us resist the evolutionary growth of the Soul in the first place? What psychological dynamics create resistance to evolution? Again, there is a tremendous degree of personal identification and emotional security associated with the natal position of Pluto, or the Soul. The Soul and its previous identity and behavioral patterns are the deepest source of unconscious emotional security that any of us can have. The desire for self-consistency is based upon the desire to maintain the past, and the old and familiar ways of operating in life. The resistance to change, or evolution, becomes compulsive in the worst case scenarios. However, the Soul in all of us does desire to grow, which is re-flected in the stronger of the two desires within our Soul to return to the Source.

The dynamic of attraction and repulsion is another universal phe-nomenon that connects with the two co-existing desires in the Soul, and will be experienced in the natal position of Pluto. We can be attracted to the very thing we are repulsed by, and conversely, we can be repulsed by—the very thing we are attracted to. Ultimately, repulsion manifests toward any desire or attraction to anything other than the desire to re-turn to the Source. This dynamic will manifest in the natal position of Pluto. An important psychological dynamic that correlates with Pluto is attraction and repulsion to cultural taboos, or that which is shunned or forbidden by a culture. What is considered taboo can be anything: val-ues, beliefs, ways of operating, and experiences of all kinds. Why is this phenomena specifically connected to Pluto? As stated in *Pluto, Volume I,*

> Taboos represent a potentially powerful experience or association through which the individual may discover an aspect or dimen-sion of him- or herself. In addition, that which is considered taboo can be very attractive because of the potential to transform exist-ing behavioral limitations through experiencing it.

Taboos can be positive or negative in nature. An attraction of any na-ture to an inherently negative taboo is a reflection of the desire to sepa-rate from the Source. A growth process can still occur, even if such nega-tive experiences manifest because the person is now in touch with the nature of his or her separating desires, and can use positive will power to purge these attractions to negative taboos from the Soul. Positive taboos are taboos that allow a transmutation of our pre-existing limitations in behavior and identity associations. Attractions to positive taboos are a re-flection of the desire to return to the Source. Sometimes, the consensus in any culture can judge something negatively and create a taboo even if it is intrinsically positive in nature. The example used to illustrate this point in *Pluto, Volume I,* is when Jesus ate with the "outcasts," or "unde-sirables" in society. He ate with those he was not supposed to associate with, whom others shunned. Up until the point when Jesus acted in this way, such an action, even though it was clearly very positive and pure in nature, was labeled taboo by the consensus culture of that time. Another example of a cultural taboo is astrology itself. The consensus does judge astrology as a "bogus science." Some individuals even view astrology as a dark, or evil, practice. The point of these statements is that there is a natural attraction to positive taboos, because such taboos allow growth to occur—yet the culture may not allow the necessary experience of positive taboos in order for personal evolution to continue.

What forces are in control from an ultimate point of view relative to the two antithetical desires of the Soul? The universal forces of good and evil—or from a spiritual point of view, God and Satan—are in control. The two desires are contained, or originate, within our own Soul, yet the influence of God and evil manifest through these desires. The force of God, or good, manifests through our desire to return to the Source. The Satanic force, or evil, manifests through maintaining and exhibiting separating desires. Evil is dependent on human delusion, and the desire for maintaining a separate existence from the Creator. We can now perceive the dynamics of cooperation and resistance, and attraction and repulsion, as reflections of these two universal forces that are inherently positive and negative in nature.

All the negative characteristics associated with Pluto, such as defensiveness, vindictiveness, jealousy, spitefulness, possessiveness, manipulation, suspicion, and compulsion, manifest as any individual resists his or her evolutionary growth needs. This psychology manifests because emotional security is threatened, or challenged, at the deepest possible level; the Soul. The individual experiences deep insecurities in the context of change and further evolution, because these past patterns constitute the person's unconscious emotional security. Conversely, positive attributes of Pluto such as motivation of self and others, strength of will, rebirth and regeneration, and willingness to change as necessary will manifest as an individual cooperates with his or her evolutionary intentions. In this context, the natal Pluto can represent an area of great strength within our Soul. Pluto's polarity point, as mentioned before, describes how the limitations and weaknesses within the Soul can be transmuted, and thus the evolution of the Soul can take place. A continual death and re-birth is experienced in this way as the Soul in all of us evolves.

Applying Pluto's Correlations in the Natal Birth Chart

To illustrate the principles of Pluto and its correlations in the natal birth chart, let's put Pluto in a specific house first, then add a specific sign. These brief examples will demonstrate how to effectively synthesize the archetypes of the zodiac, and the meaning of Pluto in the natal birth chart. The natal position of Pluto serves as the bottom line and starting point from which all other factors in the birth chart will be interpreted and given meaning. We now understand the specific current, or present, operative dynamics within any individual at the deepest level; the Soul level. We understand the evolutionary cause, or intentions, for any life reflected by Pluto's polarity point.

As a simple example, let's put Pluto in the 6th house. To do this, we must first understand the archetype of the 6th house, or Virgo. The core psychology of the 6th house archetype is the need for self-improvement, to learn humility, to be of service to the Whole, or society, and learn to inwardly adjust whatever is needed in order for evolution to proceed. Humility and the need for self-improvement induces the awareness of all the person's shortcomings and imperfections. This is why the 6th house correlates to feelings of inferiority, inadequacy, and lacks which leads to self-doubt. There can also be a need for self-punishment related to feelings of inferiority and lack. This awareness of what is lacking, deficient, or needs to be improved within the person creates guilt, and the need to atone for that guilt in some manner. The need to self-improve creates a very self-analytical focus. Essentially, we are analyzing our own ego. However, it usually requires the formation of a crisis to induce an analysis that leads to self-knowledge. A common distortion that manifests within the 6th house archetype is the creation of a compulsive crisis because of feelings of inferiority and the need for self-punishment. Crisis is a very painful way to learn.

The 6th house, or Virgo, has a direct correlation with the Garden of Eden myth because of the dynamic of guilt linked with inferiority and superiority, leading to a psychology of dominance and submission. In the myth, women are presented as the "spiritual downfall" of men, and the temptation of the senses. Women are thus made to feel guilty and inferior, and there is a need to atone for this guilt. Men are presented as the embodiment of spirit who "gave in" to the temptation, and are made to feel guilty, yet angry, because of the guilt related to feeling superior to women. Dominance and submission creates the psychological distortions of sado-masochism. Typically the woman's psychology reflects the distortion of masochism, and the man reflects the distortion of sadism. In some cases these distortions operate simultaneously within a person's consciousness. (These distortions are very clearly and thoroughly described in *Pluto, Volume II: The Soul's Evolution Through Relationships,* and will be more deeply explored in the chapter describing the natural archetypes.)

In essence, in this archetype, the person experiences an inverted pyramid effect, specifically in the context of learning to be of service to society, or the Whole. The work function is a vehicle through which the individual achieves self-improvement, and self-perfection. The inverted pyramid describes a situation wherein everybody else's needs are on the top, and the individual's needs are on the bottom. In the 5th house, or Leo, subjective development is at its maximum which leads to the creative actualization of the special purpose. In the 5th house, we are creatively actualizing everything that we are. Now, in the 6th house, the person is learning what he or she is not, and this awareness pierces the inflated ego like a balloon. All delusions of self-grandeur are purged as a result. The 6th house correlates to eliminating any behavioral dynamic that is linked to a self-oriented or narcissistic world. It is a transitional archetype from subjective awareness and development (which began in Aries and culminated in Leo) to objective awareness and development (which begins in Libra and culminates in Pisces).

Pluto in the 6th house, then, correlates with the past desires to learn lessons of humility, self-purification, self-improvement, and learning to be of service to the Whole, or society. Pluto in the 6th house correlates with an intense degree of self-analysis (usually triggered by excessive crisis) in order to induce the awareness of what needs to be improved or adjusted within the individual. Most commonly, such a deep awareness of what needs to be improved and adjusted within the person creates a compulsive negative or critical self-focus. In this condition, the person, somehow, never feels good enough, or is never ready to perform the tasks that he or she is being inwardly directed to do from the Source. This leads to the person not developing his or her total capacity, or abilities, and creates yet another source of guilt. Of course, this self-critical and negative vibration is then projected into the outer environment, and the person compulsively focuses on lacks and imperfections in the environment, and in others. There is a deep, existential void that cannot be filled—expect through a relationship with the Creator (Pisces polarity point). Commonly, this psychology creates behavioral distortions by attempting to fill this void in a variety of denial or avoidance type activities. The "busy bee" syndrome is a well-known distortion of the 6th house archetype. This behavior consists of making excuses, which appear to be perfectly valid arguments, for why the Soul will not do what it knows it should do, when it knows it should do it. This psychology manifests because of resistance to facing the deep existential void within, and the need for self-punishment relative to that intense inner critical focus. Victimization of this inner reality, or of always pointing to the outer reality as the cause of the problem, is another distortion that correlates with this archetype. Pluto in the 6th house, then, symbolizes the need to purge victimization from the psyche.

Now let's put Pluto in Libra in the 6th house. To do this we must first describe the archetype of Libra, and then synthesize this archetype with the meaning of Pluto, and the archetype of the 6th house. Libra correlates with the initiation of a diversity of relationships with others, in order to learn personal and social equality, and inner balance. There is a need to objectively understand the sense of individuality, or identity, in a social context. Libra symbolizes that an extremity has been reached, and that the person is trying to create, or learn, balance within him or herself. Libra evaluates its own individuality through comparison and contrast with others in relationships, and in the outer environment in general. This is why this archetype correlates to the initiation of a diversity of relationships. There is a distorted need to be needed within this archetype that dictates the creation and the formation of relationships. There are projected needs, leading to expectations, because of the dynamic of the need to be needed. In other words, the person is looking externally for the partner to fulfill some displaced needs, or expectations that have not been met within.

Another distortion of this archetype is when a person unconsciously turns the partner into a defacto God/Goddess because of extremity of projected needs of the individual. The other extreme is when a person unconsciously desires to be turned into a defacto God/Goddess in the partner's life. This clearly creates codependencies, imbalances, and extremes within relationships. One partner may dominate the other partner, and expect to have his or her needs constantly meet by the partner, to the exclusion of the partner's needs. Naturally, at some point, the partner who is being dominated will assert his or her own needs. These dynamics create, in the worst extremes, an alter-ego affect. This describes a situation wherein the person who is being dominated is simply an extension of the dominating partner's needs and expectations. The roles of dominator and dominated can alternate within the same relationship, or within different relationships. Pluto in Libra is learning how and when to objectively give to others what is needed from the other person's reality, not their own. The key to this is objectively listening to others in such a way as to identify what another truly needs, and not what the person thinks the other needs, or is projecting that the partner needs from a self-centered reality based on his or her own needs. In this way personal and social equality is achieved within relationships. A state of inner and outer balance is developed, and the awareness of the relativity of personal needs, values, and beliefs is learned as well.

When we put Pluto in Libra in the 6th house, the 6th house orientation and desires are approached by initiating relationships with others symbolized in the archetype of Libra. The need for self-improvement, self-purification, humility, and to be of service to society has become a part of the individual's process of initiating relationships with others (the 6th house Pluto in conditioned by the sign of Libra). In other words, service to the Whole, self-improvement, self-purification, and humility are all learned through initiating a diversity of relationships with others in order to achieve balance, and personal and social equality. It is through the process of comparison and contrast with others that Pluto in Libra evaluates its own individuality. These comparisons will be made in the context of the needs and desires of the 6th house Pluto. For example, the individual may compare him or herself to others based upon the specific work that the individual performs, or desires to perform. The person may feel inferior because the type of work he or she performs is not as good as others from a societal point of view, and then project this critical vibration upon others. The person will use the work function to compensate in some manner for deep feelings of inferiority and lack. For example, the person may desire a work function of high social status in order to fill the existential void and face the deep feelings of inferiority and lack. In another extreme, the individual will deny him- or herself any relevant and meaningful work. In all cases, the person will form or initiate relationships with others in order to effect self-improvement, learn to be of service to the Whole and others, and purge the Soul of delusions of grandeur. The desires, lessons, and intentions of the 6th house are the foundation upon which the individual initiates relationships.

In addition, the person may attempt to use relationships to fill a deep existential void within him or herself. There is a compulsion to be in relationships because of this dynamic. The person is looking outward in the relationship for the partner to "fix" him or her in the context of the need for self-improvement and self-purification. The person is unconsciously turning the partner into a defacto God/Goddess. (Most commonly it would be a woman who acted in this way, because of the previously described conditioning patterns of masochism linked to the 6th house.) In this condition, the person will experience constant demoralizing treatment by the partner in the relationship as a reflection of his or her own inner undermining activity, feelings of inferiority, and the need for self-punishment. In this case, the person cannot help but attract a partner who reinforces such deep feelings of inferiority and inadequacy. The individual's inner reality is outpictured in a relationship of this nature. Clearly, excessive crises will be experienced within relationships if this inner orientation is in place.

In the other extreme that can manifest within this natal Pluto placement, is a person who is always focusing on the partner and the relationship in a very critical manner, and is unconsciously humiliating the partner because of this orientation. The partner may unconsciously desire to be a defacto God/Goddess in the partner's life. (Typically, a man will act in this manner relative to the conditioning patterns of sadism linked with the 6th house.) In the first scenario the person who is being constantly criticized will be dominated by the partner. The partner expects the individual to fulfill his or her projected needs. There is always a crisis that the dominated person must attend to, just like putting out a brush fire, which creates a "fix it" person. In the other extreme, the individual will expect the partner to always be the "fix it" person, and will constantly create crises that he or she expects the partner to resolve.

From our understanding of the symbolic meaning of Pluto, and the archetypes of Virgo and Libra, we can now fully interpret the core, archetypal meaning and desires of a person who has Pluto in Libra in the 6th house as we have just demonstrated. We have a clear picture of the inherent limitations symbolized in the natal position of Pluto, as well.

Let's put Pluto in Libra in the 5th house. The core archetype of the 5th house, or Leo, is creative actualization. Individual's with natal Pluto in the 5th house or Leo have needed and desired to be in control of their own special destiny, and to shape it out of the strength of their will. Creative actualization of the special purpose, or special destiny, occurred in this way. It is because of the need for creative actualization of the special purpose that the Leo archetype creates a pyramid reality structure where the individual's needs are at the very top. This dynamic leads to a more or less narcissistic orientation to life. Delusions of self- grandeur correlate with the 5th house, as well. There is a distorted need to be outwardly recognized as special in some way, and to have constant external feedback of this nature. This creates a virtual bottomless pit in the context of the need for attention, flattery, and recognition. Whatever is given is never enough, and the individual compulsively looks outward for such recognition. The person may unconsciously manipulate people and situations in order to receive this attention, or recognition. The person may feel threatened or defensive if another individual is given love, attention, or recognition.

Another problem of the 5th house is overly identifying with the creative principle of the universe, and the special purpose or destiny from an egocentric point of view. The individual will consider him or herself the source of their own creativity, which creates obvious limitations from an evolutionary standpoint. The creative purpose will totally define and shape the person's sense of identity in a negative expression of this archetype. The individual will commonly only give to others when it suits some personal, self-centered need, and he or she does not truly give what the other person needs according to their reality. It is important to understand that the person may truly desire to give to another even though this dynamic is operative within the Soul. Previous to the current life, there has been an intense degree of subjective self-focus, symbolized by Pluto in Leo in the 5th house.

Now, again, we synthesize the archetype of Libra and Pluto in the 5th house. This symbol reflects that creative actualization occurs through relationships with others in order for the same lessons of balance and equality to be learned. The special destiny and purpose is now linked with the initiation of relationships. A diversity of relationships were initiated prior to the current life, and creative actualization took place in the context of those relationships. The creative actualization process became the foundation upon which the individual initiated relationships with others. (The 5th house Pluto is conditioned by the sign of Libra.) These individuals will have the distorted need to be constantly, outwardly validated by the partner as special, and will unconsciously seek to form relationships of this nature. In a negative expression, the person will be dependent on the relationship and the partner to creatively actualize. In this case, the individual is expecting that the partner creatively actualize his or her special destiny instead of the person independently acting to actualize him- or herself. In another extreme, the person will expect the partner to act in this way, and that creative actualization only occurs vicariously through the partner and the relationship. The person may form many relationships in order to receive the required acknowledgment that he or she desires, yet leave the relationship if the required attention or recognition is not given, or the need that created the relationship is no longer in place. This creates another projected need, and the formation of yet another relationship. Comparison and contrast with others occurs in the context of the individual's special purpose and destiny, and how the other person is creatively actualizing that destiny. In other words, the special purpose and creative actualization process is the determinate of the comparisons and contrasts with others relative to Pluto in Libra. Again, by synthesizing the archetypes of Pluto, Libra, and Leo we come to a very thorough understanding of the past dynamics and desires of the Soul.

These generalized descriptions of the natal position of Pluto are meant to illustrate the symbolic meaning of Pluto in the natal birth chart. Clearly, there are a diverse number of expressions Pluto can have, even if it is in the same sign relative to specific house Pluto occupies, and the person's natal birth chart. The critical principle to remember is that the same bottom-line, or core, archetypes apply in all cases, no matter what other mitigating factors in a birth chart we must include. When we grasp the core underlying archetypes in this way and, of course, the symbolic meaning of Pluto, we can adjust these archetypes to reflect the person's natural evolutionary condition, and the other mitigating factors of the birth chart.

Pluto's Polarity Point

Pluto's polarity point, by house and sign, correlates to the specific evolutionary intentions for this life of any individual. It symbolizes the evolutionary cause, or intentions, of the life itself. The entire generation of those that have Pluto in Libra is thus learning the evolutionary lessons and intentions reflected in the polarity sign of Aries. The house Pluto's polarity point is in reflects the Soul's specific, individualized evolutionary lessons and intentions. The lessons and intentions of the sign of Pluto's polarity point will be approached and learned through the house it is in. The limitations of the past, reflected in the natal Pluto, will be transmuted by embracing the current evolutionary intentions described by Pluto's polarity point. In this way, there is an automatic re-expression, or metamorphosis, of the natal Pluto. A death of the old patterns of behavior associated with the natal Pluto leads to a rebirth of new patterns of behavior in those areas via the polarity point. The polarity point of Pluto is the unknown, the unfamiliar or uncharted ways of being. Yet, the Soul in each of us desires to embrace these new patterns and ways of being because the Soul in each of us desires to grow. Pluto's polarity point describes the psychological metamorphosis that must occur in any person in order for evolution to occur.

Let's use the same example of the natal Pluto described earlier to demonstrate the principle of Pluto's polarity point. The inherent limitations, generally speaking, that correlate with natal Pluto in Libra are codependent relationship formations based upon the need to be needed, an identity crisis because of this orientation, and being dominated, or dominating others in relationships. Extremes of all sorts will be purged and a state of inner and outer balance will manifest as the person consciously acts to implement the evolutionary intentions of the Aries polarity point. The limitations of the 6th house Pluto are an excessive critical focus, compulsive inner crisis, and a very deep inner emptiness, or an existential void, that creates a variety of avoidance and denial oriented behavior. This void cannot be filled except through a relationship with the Divine, which is a lesson of the 12th house polarity point. Victimization of this inner reality must also be eliminated from the psyche if evolutionary growth is going to occur.

Pluto in the 6th house has the polarity point of the 12th house. The 12th house polarity point, generally speaking, symbolizes the need for self-forgiveness, to align with the Source, purge delusions, learn faith in the Divine, and dissolve all old mental/spiritual/physical patterns of behavior that are preventing a direct connection to God. An entire cycle of evolution is being brought to culmination in the archetype of Pisces, or the 12th house. Now let's discuss the polarity of Pluto in Libra, which is Aries. The Aries polarity point symbolizes the need to initiate a new direction, or a new cycle of evolutionary becoming. There is an essential need to have the courage to strike out on the individual's own in order to discover what this new cycle of becoming is about. This occurs on an instinctual basis. The person will learn through action and reaction, relative to the reactions to his or her actions that have been generated, or initiated. In this way, an intense sense of self-discovery and continual state of becoming is felt within the Soul. This is why the Soul will need freedom and independence to create the necessary experiences that lead to self-discovery, and perpetual growth in the context of developing individuality. In other words, experience is a vehicle through which self-discovery occurs, which requires an essential freedom and independence. The need to initiate a self-motivated direction in life without the consent of another, and independent from the impact of relationships in this context, is reflected in the Aries polarity point. The Soul's intrinsic individuality is acted upon and developed as such actions are put into motion. The person is no longer dependent on others or relationships to provide a sense of their own individuality. These individuals must learn to choose to be in relationships only with others who have the capacity to initiate their own self-motivated life direction, by their own means. In addition, the individual will know when and how to give to others, and learn to withhold giving in certain situations where the partner is not applying what was given before, yet is continually asking for more giving. In this way, the person stops the creation of dependencies, and is actually practicing a supreme form of giving. The individual must learn to perceive the withholding of giving from others in the same light. In this way, relationships of co-equality, mutual independence, and balance can be formed. These individuals will realize that by giving first to others what is needed, their own needs will be met ten-fold. This is how balance and equality is achieved personally, and in relationships.

We can now synthesize these two archetypes of Aries and the 12th house, and determine the evolutionary intentions of a Soul with this polarity point. The polarity point of Aries and the associated evolutionary requirements are learned through the lessons and needs of the 12th house. Simply stated, as the person acts to purge delusions from his or her Soul, and merge with God, new relationship patterns will be born. These new patterns will emerge as the person initiates his or her own direction in life, and acts to establish the intrinsic identity. This polarity point symbolizes that the development of the identity must be in alignment with the Creator's will, and occurs simultaneously with spiritual development. In other words, the individual must use the Creator as a guiding light to develop his or her own identity, and decide what actions to put into motion. The Source will be used as a reflection point of the Soul's true identity. The person will gain the courage to strike out on his or her own, and initiate their own direction in life through dissolving all egocentric barriers that are preventing a direct and conscious merging with the Creator. The relationship to the Creator becomes the primary source of independence, and courage. The necessary new relationship patterns will emerge into consciousness in this way.

Self-forgiveness of the faults and imperfections of the individual and others will eliminate an excessively critical focus, and replace constant crisis. The deep inner void will be replaced with a relationship with the Creator. This evolution will create obvious changes to the types of relationships that the person forms. The inner negative and critical focus is no longer projected outward. The compulsive need for relationships is purged from the Soul. The 12th house polarity point reflects that such lessons manifest as the person dissolves all egocentric barriers that are preventing a direct and conscious merging with the Creator, and acts to spiritually develop. In this way an entire cycle of evolution is brought to culmination, or completion.

To further demonstrate the principle of Pluto's polarity point, let's apply the polarity point of Pluto in Libra in the 5th house. Pluto in Libra in the 5th house has the same polarity sign of Aries, but in the 11th house. The same evolutionary necessities of Aries still apply, except that they will be learned through 11th house types of experiences. Limitations reflected in Pluto in the 5th house are an excessive self-oriented, or narcissistic, approach to life; over-identification with the creative principle of the universe and special purpose from an egocentric point of view; the compulsive need for constant external feedback in the context of being considered special and important; and only giving to others when it suits a personal need from a self-centered reality.

The 11th house reflects the need to detach from a narcissistic, self-oriented world. Detachment leads to objective awareness of the individual and of life in general. True generosity will then manifest. The special purpose, or destiny, of the 5th house must now be linked with a socially relevant need. Often, these individuals will be blocked, in varying degrees of magnitude, from actualizing the true potential of the special purpose, or destiny, in order to enforce this lesson. The blocking force is the societal structure itself, because it is apparently not recognizing the individual as special, according to the amount of external feedback he or she requires. Frustration and emotional implosion will occur if the creative actualization is not linked with a relevant societal need. Liberation from past forms of behavior specifically linked with the 5th house and its correlation to excessive self-orientation occurs through such detachment and objectification. The creative actualization process will be fundamentally changed as a result. The need to be considered special or important through constant external feedback is removed. The person learns to acknowledge him- or herself in this manner from within, and is no longer insecure. Liberation and objectification of all delusions of grandeur occur through linking the special purpose to a societal need. The person now has the awareness that he or she is part of a whole, or society, and is not just focused on him- or herself. The person is now able to objectively validate and appreciate other people's special capacities, and creativity without feeling insecure or threatened. In addition, over-identification with the creative principle of the Universe from an egocentric point of view will be purged. These individuals will realize that they are just a channel for the creative energy of the universe to flow through. The person will identify the Creator as the source of his or her creativity. As the creative purpose is linked to a socially relevant need an objective awareness of self will be developed, and detachment from the pyramid reality structure will take hold within consciousness. The special destiny or purpose does not define or shape the person's sense of identity as it had in the past.

These 11th house lessons will become a vehicle through which the intentions and needs of the Aries polarity point will manifest. The intrinsic individuality of the Soul will be developed as the person learns the necessary evolutionary lessons of detachment and objectivity, and links his or her special destiny to a socially relevant need. The person will gain an objective awareness of his or her identity, and initiate actions to develop this identity in an objective manner. The Soul will have the courage to strike out on Its own and implement these actions in order for self-discovery to occur. The necessary objectivity and detachment from an excessively self-centered orientation to life will create the courage to act in this way because there is no longer a need for external validation. The person will only be in relationships with those who can objectively reflect his or her true identity and who also have the capacity to implement their own self-initiated actions. The need for constant positive external feedback in relationships will be eliminated. Creative actualization will occur in relationships based on mutual independence. The person will have the courage to be a group of one if necessary, a very deep need symbolized in the polarity point of Aries in the 11th house. The person will creatively actualize a destiny that allows his or her true uniqueness to shine, and will be oriented to helping others actualize in the same way.

These illustrations demonstrate the principle's of Pluto and its polarity point. The evolution of Pluto through its polarity point will be the main theme throughout the individual's entire life. We can now identify the core dynamics of any individual's Soul program from an evolutionary point of view

Pluto Retrograde

Another factor to include in our discussion of Pluto is Pluto retrograde. Retrograde as an archetype, or function, within consciousness symbolizes that an acceleration of evolution must now occur. This evolution will occur through rejecting or rebelling against the consensus or status quo's conditioning patterns relative to the planetary function that is retrograde. The person must now experience and define the planet that is retrograde on a personal or individual level, independent from the prevailing consensus conditioning patterns. Any planet that is retrograde will be inwardly felt as a strong feeling of disconnection for the consensus. This experience of disconnection triggers, or ignites, a psychological withdrawal from the consensus, and a sense of isolation results. Most commonly, the need to rebel against or reject the status quo has not been fully resolved. This is why the retrograde symbol typically correlates to reliving past experiences and circumstances. In this way, the necessary resolution of such dynamics can occur. The individual may have initiated actions in the past to individualize and rebel from his or her past conditioning patterns of the status quo, yet those actions were not fully followed through. The specific lessons and dynamics that are being repeated are reflected in the planet by house and sign locality, and aspects the planet is making to other planets. The intention of this type of life circumstance is to resolve these dynamics in order for evolution to continue.

There is an individualizing impulse in the retrograde function which instigates personal evolution. The status quo, or consensus conditioning patterns of the past, cannot be gravitated to, relative to the need for growth. This individuating impulse takes hold as the person withdraws from the impact of societal conditioning in order to effect this evolution in his or her own way. Internalization of consciousness occurs. A good analogy to describe this process is peeling away the layers of an onion to arrive at its core. There is a smooth, continual evolution of the planetary function that is retrograde. In other words, the planet that is retrograde must be acted upon in a very unique, individualized manner, and in this way, given personal meaning. The person may outwardly manifest conformity patterns in this area, or not act on the evolutionary impulse symbolized by Pluto retrograde because of resistance to his or her evolutionary requirements. However, on some level the person will not be able to relate to such behavioral patterns. The person may seek to act on the retrograde impulse at some later point in his or her evolutionary journey, as stagnation and non-growth occurs.

When Pluto is retrograde in the natal birth chart, it reflects a tremendous desire to throw off past conditioning patterns of society or culture at all four levels of evolutionary development. The individualizing impulse of the retrograde archetype is now experienced at the deepest possible level relative to Pluto's correlation to the Soul. The sense of dissatisfaction is more deeply and constantly felt in people who have Pluto retrograde than in those who do not. The sense of dissatisfaction, again, is an echo of the desire to return to the Source. Separating desires within the Soul are purged at an accelerated manner in order to achieve evolution.

It is exactly this need to accelerate the elimination of separating desires within the Soul that creates the psychological effect of intense and constant dissatisfaction. An individual who has Pluto retrograde will feel inwardly that he or she cannot relate to the prevailing consensus orientation and expectations, even if the desire to transform or purge these past limitations is not consciously acted upon. The person will inwardly distance him- or herself from the prevailing consensus because of this feeling, even if this feeling is not outwardly expressed. This withdrawal serves to instigate the evolutionary intention of Pluto retrograde. Pluto retrograde tends to emphasize the desire to return to the Source because of the intensified experience of dissatisfaction relative to the mainstream orientation and attitude toward life in general. (The specific patterns that are being purged and eliminated from the Soul are described by the house and sign locality of the natal Pluto that is retrograde.) Half the people on earth have this placement in their natal birth chart because Pluto is retrograde six out of twelve months in each year. From an evolutionary standpoint, this phenomena occurs in order to ensure the evolution of the human-being as a species. The evolution takes place via those who will not conform to the status quo. These Souls will help others in society evolve the status quo to greater heights when society's conditioning patterns have become crystallized, outdated, and are preventing further growth. Thus, Pluto retrograde enforces evolutionary growth at all four levels of evolution on a personal and collective level.

To clarify the principle of Pluto retrograde, let's use another brief example, comparing and contrasting Pluto in Libra/6th house ℞ and Pluto in Libra in the 6th house. The 6th house Pluto, as described earlier, correlates with past-life desires and intentions to learn humility, self-improvement, and to be of service to the Whole, or society. Pluto in Libra desires to learn personal and social equality, and inner balance. These lessons are learned through initiating a diversity of relationships with others. In this way the individual evaluates his or her individuality through comparison and contrast with others.

If Pluto is retrograde, then the individual is at an evolutionary juncture where he or she cannot relate to the consensus conformity patterns
in the context of the dynamics associated in the natal position of Pluto.
Most likely, these specific conditions and conformity patterns reflected
in the natal Pluto have been experienced in the past, and the person
is re-living such dynamics in order to resolve them. The evolutionary
pressure of the Soul to purge past limitations of the areas reflected in
the natal Pluto will be quite intense, because the person has experienced the limitations of the prior behavioral dynamics linked with this
area prior to the current life. The person would actively withdraw and
retreat from the impact of society in order to effect the necessary evolution. Stagnation, limitations, and blocks are deeply felt relative to the
individual's desire to transmute such limitations and purge unconscious
conditioning patterns of the status quo. Generally speaking, Pluto in
Libra in the 6th house ℞ reflects that such limitations are conforming
to society's conditioning patterns regarding how to be of service, self-
improve, and how to be in relationships with others.

If Pluto is not retrograde, then the person will not necessarily need to
rebel or reject the consensus conditioning patterns of this nature. The evolutionary pressure to purge conformity patterns and transmute limitations
of this nature is not as intense, because the individual is not necessarily in
a re-live situation relative to his or her past. The Soul is not necessarily at a
point where it intensely desires this transformation, as will the individual
with Pluto retrograde. Of course, we must consider the person's natural
evolutionary and karmic condition in order to fully understand the level at
which Pluto is operating, but these examples do clarify the basic principles
of Pluto retrograde. The key difference to grasp is how natal Pluto is experienced and expressed by the individual depending on the natal position of
Pluto (direct or retrograde).

The four types of evolution are discussed below, and are described
in *Pluto Vol. I* (p 27–29):

1. When we become overly identified with some area in our lives,
   either on an emotional level or from an egocentric point of view,

to such an extent that an emotional shock of some nature must occur to enforce the necessary change. Often, this is linked with a traumatic or cataclysmic event. Cataclysmic events occur when the Soul has resisted the necessary evolutionary growth to such an extent that the event must manifest in order for growth to continue. There are two reasons for experiencing any kind of cataclysmic or traumatic change. One is evolutionary necessity, and the other is karmic retribution. These two reasons for experiencing a traumatic event are vastly different from one another, and we will describe the difference between them more thoroughly when we describe this type of evolution.

2. Through forming a relationship with something that we perceive we need, but feel that we don't currently have, an evolution takes place as we encounter our personal strength and weaknesses. Through this merging, a Plutonian osmosis occurs and we extract the essence of the relationship we have formed inside ourselves. In this way we can create a positive and healthy evolutionary experience and grow past our evolutionary blocks and limitations. This inner metamorphosis is linked with noncataclysmic, or uniform change—a slow, yet progressive, change.

3. When we encounter times in our lives in which we experience an intense personal stagnation, we become aware that we are, in fact, not growing anymore. The frustration point with this type of evolution is that we are aware of only the symptom(s), not the causes(s), and we tend to tune out everything else in our lives as we try to uncover the cause of this block. This process is similar to a dormant volcano that suddenly turns active because, as we uncover the source of the block, unconscious content suddenly pours into conscious awareness, and we finally become aware of the source of the block. This process is analogous to the volcano that suddenly turns active. The Soul evolves through this process of overcoming psychological blocks and allowing necessary changes to take hold.

4. There are times in our lives when we become aware of a latent or dormant capacity within the Soul that was previously not conscious. We suddenly become aware, or conscious, of this hidden capability, and it now requires strength and perseverance to actualize the capacity. This is exactly how evolution takes place—the Soul deepens into greater development as its capacity is actualized.

An important point to remember is that these evolutionary processes do not occur as isolated events, but can, in fact, occur simultaneously.

Another vital factor to incorporate is that the three main reactions to our evolutionary growth described in *Pluto Vol. I* directly impact the types of Plutonian experiences that we will have. The three reactions are: (1) totally resisting growth, which is uncommon, (2) changing in some ways and not in others. This is by far the most common choice, and (3) totally embracing the necessary changes and evolutionary growth in an open and non-threatening way. This, of course, is an uncommon choice. It is our response to our evolutionary growth needs that creates the types of experiences we will have. If my Soul desires to change/purge certain negative dynamics, yet I am resisting the necessary change, then the possibility of a cataclysmic event will be very likely. In this case the desire to change overrides the resistance, and the change will happen after the cataclysmic event. This will teach us to stop resisting necessary growth, and to try our best to maintain a positive and open attitude toward change. The key word here is desire. If the desire to change, to return and merge with the Source is strong enough, then it will happen. Unfortunately, if the resistance or desire to stay separate from the Source is strong enough, then that will happen as well.

2

Pluto and the Nodal Axis: The Main Evolutionary/Karmic Dynamic in the Birth Chart

Pluto and Its Relationship to the Nodal Axis

The relationship between Pluto and the nodal axis is an important one to understand. The nodal axis, the planetary rulers of each node, Pluto, and its polarity point all make up the main/evolutionary karmic dynamic in the birth chart. The nodal axis itself describes the placement of the North and South Nodes of the natal Moon. As mentioned before the Moon correlates with the current egocentric structure of the Soul, which is the reason the nodal axis plays such a significant role in the natal birth chart. A planetary ruler is the planet that rules the sign of North and South Nodes. For example, if the South Node is in Aries, then the planetary ruler would be Mars. The North Node would be in Libra, and its planetary ruler would be Venus. We must include the aspects to other planets that Pluto, the North and South Nodes, and the planetary rulers are making when determining the main/evolutionary karmic dynamic of a birth chart. All other symbols in the natal chart will be conditioned by, or put in the context of, this main evolutionary/karmic dynamic.

Pluto, the South Node, and its planetary ruler is termed the trinity of past because these symbols specifically describe the core, bottom-line dynamics that have been operative in the Soul's past, and will be the natural point of gravitation for the Soul coming into this life relative to emotional security. We can now understand the current operative dynamics of the Soul in the present moment in time. The polarity point of Pluto, the North Node, and its planetary ruler is termed the trinity of the future because these symbols correlate with the core evolutionary intentions for the life, and how the Soul is going to actualize those evolutionary intentions throughout the lifetime. If we understand how to correctly interpret these symbols, then we can determine what the next steps are for any individual, from an evolutionary point of view, and how to actualize those next steps.

The nodes of the moon act as the modes of operation to actualize the intentions of either the past reflected in the natal Pluto, or the evolutionary intentions of this life represented by Pluto's polarity point. The South Node of the moon acts as the mode of operation of the past, and describes how the desires and intentions of the natal Pluto were actualized. The South Node represents the past egocentric structure, including the self-image, of the Soul. The South Node symbolizes how the evolutionary desires and intentions of the past were consciously actualized and integrated from an emotional standpoint on a daily basis. The North Node, in turn, represents the developing or forming egocentric structure that the individual will use to consciously integrate and actualize the evolutionary lessons for this life, as described by Pluto's polarity point.

The Moon, again, reflects the person's current egocentric structure, and how the transition from the past to the future, represented by the North and South Nodes, will take place in the present moment in time. The planetary rulers of the nodes will act as facilitators to develop the North and South Nodes. In other words, just as Pluto and its polarity point use the nodes to actualize themselves, so, too, do the nodes use the planetary rulers to actualize themselves.

The Nodal Axis: Modes of Operation

Let's briefly illustrate the principles of the North and South Nodes and their correlation with the modes of operation of the past and future before we include the planetary rulers of the nodes. For example, let's put the natal Pluto in the 8th house, and the South Node in the 3rd house. Pluto's polarity point is the 2nd house, and North Node in the 9th house. The core, or bottom line, orientation of such a Soul coming into the life is to create a metamorphosis of its current limitations in the context of evolution. This is done through intense internal and external confrontations in order to expose these limitations, and for growth to occur. The 8th house correlates to the entire field of psychology in general. Clearly, a Soul with Pluto in the 8th house will naturally be psychologically oriented. The individual will penetrate to the core of his or her own desire nature, in order to purge all limitations, and create a metamorphosis beyond those limitations.

This desire of the 8th house is exactly what leads to the psychology of the Soul always asking the question "why?" "Why do I operate in this way, and this person in another way?" "Why do I desire this?" "Why am I reacting in this way right now?" and so on. Such inner questioning leads to a penetration of the Soul's motivations, intentions, desires, and psychology (psychoanalysis). The 8th house correlates with focusing upon the famous bottom line of any problem. Growth can then occur because the person understands the root cause of his or her limitations, and can create a metamorphosis beyond such limitations. The individual with an 8th house Pluto naturally desires to penetrate others in this way, and will have natural psychological skills that can be used to motivate others to overcome their own limitations. Evolution occurs as the individual penetrates him or herself and others, and transmutes compulsive and degenerative patterns of behavior into new patterns that facilitate the Souls' growth.

How would these confrontations, metamorphoses, and psychological penetration have occurred, or been actualized, in the past in the context of the 3rd house South Node? The 3rd house, or Gemini archetype, correlates with the collection of a variety of facts, data, and information in order to rationally explain our connection to the universe. This function in consciousness gives labels and classifications to the physical world; i.e., we give an object a specific label such as a cup, or a book, or a table, and so on. The 3rd house correlates with our ability and need to communicate our ideas, facts, and points of views with others, and the need to take in this type of information, from others in the environment. The collection of facts, information and data allows growth to continue because the generation of new ideas and thoughts creates a natural expansion of the mental mind.

Negatively expressed, this archetype correlates to opinions, biases, and superficial information in general. In addition, the information may not be fully assimilated. A very common distortion of this archetype is to buy this book or that, take this class and that class—yet the books go unread, and the classes are not integrated. This archetype correlates with the mental structure within consciousness relative to the type of information and facts that are collected from the external environment. The third house, or Gemini, correlates with the linear function within our brain, or the left brain, that is logical and empirical. It symbolizes how we are inwardly thinking, and thus how we communicate with others.

In the case of the 8th house Pluto and South Node in the 3rd house, generally speaking, the person collected a diversity of information and facts in the outer environment that allowed the transmutation and penetration of the person's psychology and desire nature to take place. Intense dialogues of an intellectual nature would most commonly occur with others to generate the necessary information of this nature, as well as to penetrate to the bottom line of the person's own psychological make-up. The person's prior self-image is based on the intellectual understanding and orientation that was created by the nature of the information that was absorbed into the psyche (South Node in the third). The person will psychologically penetrate others based on the type of information that he or she collected of this nature.

The limitations in this case are the potential of manipulation (Pluto 8th house) of the information the individual collected in order to rationalize some negative characteristic, or to resist the necessary evolution (3rd house South Node). The information that has been collected is not necessarily wrong, or invalid, but it is limited in some manner. The individual could rationalize manipulating or using others in this way, as well as experience being used and manipulated by others in this manner. It would not be uncommon that a person with this signature had experienced manipulation, betrayal, and use by another based on the type of information that was being communicated which was not honest. The individual would then have experienced intense emotional shocks as the other person's actual intentions and agenda was revealed. The core point to remember is that the nature of the pre-existing intellectual structure and psychology will constitute the individual's unconscious security at the deepest possible level. This dynamic could then create resistance in the context of embracing information that does not validate the individual's own pre-existing psychological orientation and point of view (Pluto/8th house, South Node in the 3rd house). In this context the person will feel threatened or challenged when his or her ideas and point of view are not supported by new information that is taken in from the external environment.

Another distortion of the 3rd house that creates limitations is collecting an excessive amount of information that appears to logically connect in many ways, yet a true assimilation of those facts cannot occur. There is no consistent reference point to interpret all the facts. In other words, the person creates a revolving door of perspectives in which there is no consistent viewpoint. Mental implosion occurs if too many facts are collected in this manner without a consistent or holistic foundation. Positively expressed, this individual will use information to re-empower him- or herself (Pluto in the 8th house), and to create a true metamorphosis of his or her psychology through the type of information and facts that are collected and absorbed into the psyche.

Pluto's polarity point is the 2nd house, and the North Node is in the 9th house. In this example, then, the lessons of the 2nd house polarity point will be actualized through the 9th house North Node. The generalized lessons of the 2nd house polarity point are self-reliance, self-sustainment, and inner simplicity. There is a need to withdraw from the impact of others in the external world in order that the Soul identify from within what intrinsic capacities it has to sustain itself. An aware-ness of the person's intrinsic capacities leads to a natural self-reliance, as well as the awareness of the person's own identity, or essence, in contrast to aspects that the individual has absorbed internally through osmosis of others. Commonly, the need to learn these lessons has necessitated con-frontations with others in order to expose all limitations that are prevent-ing evolution (8th house Pluto).

Confrontations of this nature serve to trigger the required inner withdrawal and internalization symbolized in the 2nd house polarity point. Withdrawal from the impact of society and internalization of consciousness and termination of interaction with those who do not re-flect or support this evolutionary growth is critical. This is why so many of these individuals have experienced, or will experience, the shock of having the rug of emotional security pulled out from underneath their feet. These internal and external confrontations will revolve around the need to become self-reliant and self-sufficient (2nd house polarity point).

How, specifically, will this self-reliance manifest, or be actualized, rela-tive to the 9th house North Node? The 9th house North Node reflects the need to expand consciousness to include a holistic belief system that ex-plains our connection to the cosmos in a philosophical, cosmological, or metaphysical manner. This archetype correlates to our intuitive faculty, which is guided by the right brain. There is a correlation to natural law, or laws that exist naturally (independent from any belief system) and are self-evident in nature. Our belief system is the determinate to how any of us will interpret life itself. The forming egocentric structure of the in-dividual and the resulting self-image should be based on embracing natu-ral law. The need to understand life in metaphysical, cosmological, and philosophical context will be fulfilled through an alignment with natural law. In all cases, the beliefs that individuals take in will constitute the basis of the forming egocentric structure and self-image.

Embracement and absorption of the differing belief systems and philosophies in the environment, and then picking one that intuitively felt right to the individual, will allow the necessary self-reliance to take hold (Polarity point 2nd house, North Node in the 9th house).

A synthesis of all the facts, data, and information that the person has collected must occur in order to create a cohesive system, or body of knowledge. Such intellectual synthesis creates a holistic interpretation and understanding of these facts. There is a focus in the 9th house on the bigger picture, or central concept, of facts, rather than putting facts together in a linear, logical way. The individual must learn to first intuitively grasp the whole of any concept that he or she is trying to learn, and then allow all the different parts of the whole to naturally reveal themselves. The person will then be able to interpret all the facts, information, and data in the environment in a consistent manner, versus experiencing a revolving door of perspectives. The belief system that the individual will align with in this case must be orientated to, and include, specific natural laws that teach the individual how to establish self-reliance from within him- or herself (Pluto in the 2nd house, North Node in the 9th house).

An evolution of the 8th house Pluto is accomplished as the person acts to learn the evolutionary lessons described in the 2nd house polarity point. The evolution of the 3rd house South Node and how it acts to actualize the 8th house Pluto is automatically reflected in the regeneration of the natal Pluto. This evolution will manifest as the person's approach to change, growth, and metamorphosis is completely transformed. The person will perceive change as a positive and necessary aspect of life, and desire to cooperate with his or her evolutionary lessons of this nature. The person's previous psychological orientation and understanding of life in general will be completely transformed as well. The information and facts that the person collects will reflect this psychological metamorphosis. The person will come to the realization that truth is relative, which is reflected in the South Node in the 3rd house, and North Node in the 9th house. The person will now be able to create an ongoing, continual transmutation of his or her inner limitations as stagnation is experienced. The ability to change, or grow, as necessary will replace the experience of a loss of emotional security. Intense internal or external confrontations of a negative nature will subside as well. This individual will not promote a dependency upon him- or herself, or be involved with anybody who operates in this manner.

The person will no longer need to defend his or her opinions or viewpoints as right and others as wrong that do not agree with such facts, and information. Biases, opinions, and information based on cultural conditioning will be purged (Pluto in the 8th house, South Node in the 3rd). The person will perceive this type of information as shallow, and lacking in the depth that he or she desires. The person now has the ability to determine the difference between facts and opinions, and natural law versus indoctrination (North Node in the 9th house). The alignment with natural law and a holistic belief system allows the synthesis of all the facts to occur.

This brief illustration is meant to apply the meaning of the nodal axis in the birth chart, and demonstrate how the nodes act as modes of operation to actualize Pluto and its polarity point. In addition, the metamorphosis of the natal position of Pluto and the South Node is seen as the Soul embraces the evolutionary lessons of Pluto's polarity point and the North Node.

To further clarify the principle of Pluto and its relationship to the nodal axis, let's use another simple example, but put the nodes in the opposite houses to the previous example. The 8th house Pluto has now actualized itself through a 9th house South Node. The 2nd house polarity point will be actualized through a 3rd house North Node. How would the 9th house South Node actualize the desires and intentions of the 8th house Pluto desires already discussed?

In the case of the 8th house Pluto and South Node in the 9th house, the Soul would have used the belief system to create, or actualize, the penetration and transmutation reflected in the 8th house Pluto. These beliefs will determine the individual's orientation and attitude to change, evolution, and transmuting his or her own limitations. The past egocentric structure of the Soul will be based on the specific beliefs of the individual (South Node in the 9th).

In this case, it is the belief structure of the individual that will create the limitations toward growth and evolution because the person may use such beliefs to thwart, or resist, the necessary evolution that must occur. Just as the person with the South Node in the 3rd house only absorbed information that supported the pre-existing psychological orientation and point of view, the person with the South Node in the 9th house runs the risk of only absorbing beliefs that support the pre-existing psychological orientation. The belief structure has become rigid and outdated because of this psychology. (These beliefs, most commonly, will reflect mainstream, or consensus religious conditioning patterns, even if the person is not conscious of the influence of such religious conditioning. There is a vast difference between religious indoctrination and natural law.)

The pre-existing psychological orientation and the beliefs that reflect this orientation constitute the individual's deepest sense of emotional security. Evolution cannot proceed if the psychological orientation of the individual does not change, and allow a transmutation of the belief structure of the individual to manifest. Positively expressed, the person will be in alignment with natural truths and use natural laws to actualize the necessary evolution and metamorphosis of the 8th house Pluto. The person will perceive change and evolution as a necessary part of life, and his or her belief system will reflect this psychological understanding. The beliefs of the individual may not be wrong, or invalid, but are limited in some manner.

An inherent distortion of the 9th house is to orientate to a portion of the truth, and yet the person will feel that this is the total truth. In this way, the person will attempt to convert others to his or her own beliefs, stating that these are the only valid beliefs, the only valid truth. This encourages generalizations, or projecting that the person's own personal beliefs should be true for all people. This dynamic, of course, is not conscious. The need to convince and convert others to conform to the individual's own beliefs would be very common relative to the South Node in the 9th house, because such beliefs constitute the person's emotional security.

How would the 2nd house polarity point actualize itself through the 3rd house North Node? The generalized evolutionary intentions of the 2nd house polarity point will be actualized through the collection of a diversity of information, data, and facts in the environment. This information will promote a self-reliant attitude, and facilitate the individual's lessons in identifying his or her own inherent capacities and abilities. The forming egocentric structure of the individual is based on the information, facts, and data that the person collects in the environment of this nature.

There will be dialogues with others of a philosophical/intellectual nature (South Node in the 3rd house, North Node in the 9th house) that would expose the person's inner limitations and force the individual back in on him- or herself. The information, facts that the person collects, and dialogues with others will promote self-reliance because the nature of the information and the dialogues will force the person inward. This would occur as the individual attempted to convince and convert others to his or her beliefs, and they will experience others who are just as strong, or powerful, in their beliefs who will not allow this conversion to take place. The individual will then take in the information of the other person who is perceived in this way, and will be forced inward in order to learn self-reliance. It is very likely in this scenario that information that a person received would directly undermine his or her existing psychological understanding, orientation, and belief structure. In other words, through the effect of these intellectual dialogues and experiences, the person will be forced to acknowledge his or her own limitations, and the rigidity of the beliefs that are preventing further growth.

As the person becomes increasingly more self-reliant, the evolution of all his or her past limitations takes hold. The rigid, outdated belief structure of the individual will naturally be transmuted as this evolution manifests. Conditioned beliefs that are preventing further growth will be purged. Through such intense dialogues with others and the information that such dialogues generate, the individual will realize that truth is relative, and be inwardly secure in his or her own intellectual framework and viewpoints (Pluto in the 2nd house, North Node in the 3rd house). The person will only collect facts, information, and ideas that reflect natural laws (South Node in the 9th house), and support the actualization of self-reliance, and self-sustainment. The need to convince and convert others reflected in the South Node in the 9th house is eliminated because the individual is secure in his or her beliefs. This is an identical process as the person with the South Node in 3rd house. The key difference to emphasize is how these specific lessons symbolized in the natal Pluto and its polarity point are learned relative to the nodal axis's correlation with the modes of operation of the past and the future.

In the first example of the 8th house Pluto and South Node in the 3rd house, the lessons of self-reliance and sufficiency symbolized in the 2nd house polarity point were learned and actualized through the person's belief structure and alignment with natural laws, because the 9th house reflects the lessons of the future. In this example, where the nodal axis was put in the opposite house of the previous example using the South Node in the 3rd house, the lessons of self-reliance and sufficiency are learned through the individual's intellectual structure, intellectual/philosophical dialogues with others, and collecting a diversity of knowledge that allowed self-reliance to manifest (2nd house polarity point, North Node in the 3rd house). Intellectual/philosophical confrontations through dialogue with others are typically experienced in order to induce the lessons of the 2nd house Pluto by forcing the individual back in on him- or herself through such confrontations.

These brief illustrations are meant to clarify and apply the meaning of the North and South Nodes and how the nodes act as modes of operation to actualize the evolutionary intentions and desires of the past and the future, and the relationship of Pluto and the nodal axis. In summary of the main principles of this section, the desires of the past and how they were actualized are symbolized by the natal placement by house and sign locality of Pluto and the South Node. The evolutionary intentions of the future and how these lessons will be actualized are symbolized by the placement of Pluto's polarity point, and the North Node. We must include aspects that these symbols are making to arrive at the full and total analysis of the main/evolutionary dynamic in the birth chart, but the central principles just described will demonstrate how to correctly interpret Pluto and the nodal axis in the natal birth chart.

Applying the Planetary Rulers of the Nodes

Now that we have illustrated the principles of Pluto, its polarity point, and the nodal axis, we can add the last factor that we need to include in order to determine the main evolutionary/karmic dynamic in a birth chart. As mentioned before, the planetary rulers of the nodes will act as facilitators to the North and South Nodes to actualize themselves. The house and sign locality of the planetary rulers of the nodes will describe how the Soul will actualize or develop the lessons and intentions reflected in the North and South Nodes. We must include the aspects that the planetary rulers form to other planets in order to fully interpret how they will operate within consciousness, and contribute to the main evolutionary/karmic dynamic. However, we must first know how to interpret the planetary rulers themselves, and understand how they function to facilitate, or actualize, the North and South Nodes.

Let's use the same example as before to illustrate principles of the planetary rulers of the nodes. Pluto is in Leo in the 8th house, and South Node is in Pisces in the 3rd house. The planetary ruler of the South Node is Neptune in Libra in the 10th house. The polarity point of Pluto is Aquarius in the 2nd house, and the North Node is in Virgo in the 9th house. The planetary ruler of the North Node is Mercury in Cancer in the 7th house.

Pluto in the 8th house, as described before, correlates with the desire and intention to penetrate the psychological make-up, motivations, and desires of the Soul in order to evolve past, or create a metamorphosis of, internal limitations. Pluto in Leo reflects that this penetration and transmutation has been used to creatively actualize the person's special purpose, or destiny. The person has used knowledge of a psychological nature to shape his or her special destiny out of the strength of the will. The desire to create an ongoing metamorphosis and transmutation of existing limitations is linked with the special destiny, and the process of creative actualization.

Delusions of grandeur often correlate to Pluto in Leo, because the Soul has overly identified with the special purpose and creative energy from an egocentric point of view, and also as a compensation for deep insecurities within the Soul. Thus, the individual expects to be acknowledged as special or important in some way. A pyramid reality structure is created where the individual's needs are at the very top, and other people's needs are at the bottom. Intense internal and external confrontations have or will occur in order to expose all the limitations clearly seen in this orientation. Specifically, these confrontations would have occurred in the context of the creation of the pyramid reality structure and how this psychology manifests within the creative actualization process. These are the core desires and intentions of the evolutionary past reflected in the natal Pluto in Leo in the 8th house.

Keeping in mind the core dynamics previously discussed, how would the South Node have actualized these desires and intentions of the natal Pluto? The South Node in Pisces in the 3rd house symbolizes that the individual is extremely susceptible and impressionable to the ideas, opinions, and intellectual viewpoints of those in his or her environment. The person's self-image is founded on the type of information and facts that he or she collected, and the need to merge with the Creator. The person will be hyper-sensitive to his or her environment.

In some cases, a revolving door of perspectives will be experienced because the person has and will absorb an excess of information that merely reflects the mainstream, or consensus understanding in that environment. The person's intellectual viewpoint is fixed or stuck in this pattern because it is always based on prevailing consensus viewpoints. In all cases, the person has collected many facts that appear to logically connect in many ways, but there is no holistic foundation to create a consistent interpretation or understanding of all these facts. The person will attempt to defend his or her own viewpoints and opinions as right, and others as wrong, if others do not agree with the individual. The information that the individual absorbs will support the existing psychological orientation. However, relative to the South Node in Pisces, the person will unconsciously, or subconsciously, desire to take in information that will allow mental expansion to occur, and dissolve past intellectual conditioning patterns that are inhibiting further growth. The individual may take in information of this nature on an unconscious level, even if growth is resisted (8th house Pluto).

There is a need to dissolve an entire past cycle of evolution reflected in the South Node in Pisces, and to dissolve all egocentric barriers that are preventing a direct conscious merging with the Creator. It would be very common in this case for the person to take in information of a consensus nature in the context of the need for spiritual development.

(The religious conditioning of the individual, e.g., Catholic, Christian, Buddhist, and so forth, will determine the type of information that he or she absorbs in a spiritual context.) This type of intellectual susceptibility creates the limitations intrinsic to the 8th house Pluto, and will condition the Soul's approach and attitude toward creating continual evolution. In addition, this dynamic creates mental confusion and suffocation. In all cases, the Soul's pre-existing psychological orientation and development will determine the type of information that is collected from the environment. Specifically, the behavior that needs to be dissolved is the absorption of information based upon rationalizing resistance to change, growth, and transmuting pre-existing limitations within the Soul.

The person will experience disillusionment relative to information, facts, and viewpoints of others that does not provide the ultimate meaning that he or she is seeking, nor allows evolution to occur. At some point in time the information, facts, and intellectual patterns that reflect such conditioning patterns will be perceived as superficial, and lacking in the depth that person desires and needs (8th house Pluto, South Node in Pisces / 3rd house). Positively expressed, this natal signature will reflect the ability to use information of a universal, transcendent, and spiritual nature to dissolve these past patterns, and to culminate in an entire cycle of evolution. The information can then be used to affect the necessary metamorphosis of the person's inner limitations and the resulting psychological patterns that these limitations create. Again, the information that the individual takes in is not necessarily wrong, but limited in some way. Creative actualization of the special purpose will reflect this inner psychology.

The person would not experience intense stagnation and implosions, but would instead achieve a state of continual metamorphosis of his or her limitations by changing whenever change becomes necessary. The process of creative actualization would mirror this on-going metamorphosis. The person will not be looking to others to acknowledge him or her as special, or the environment to outwardly acknowledge the person in this manner. In any of these cases, these core dynamics describe how the South Node in Pisces in the 3rd house has actualized the past desires and intentions of the natal Pluto in Leo in the 8th house.

How would the planetary ruler of the South Node have actualized the desires and lessons of the South Node in Pisces in the 3rd house? Neptune in Libra in the 10th house, the planetary ruler of the South Node, reflects that there has been an authority figure in the individual's life, most likely the individual's father (10th house), who attempted to control the formation of the person's intellectual development. There was a repression of what could be spoken, or communicated, and what could not (South Node in Pisces/3rd house, planetary ruler Neptune in Libra/10th house). This was based on the father's own pre-existing intellectual structure as it was conditioned by the consensus society (Planetary ruler Neptune in Libra/10th house). The person experienced domination by this authority figure, who expected him or her to simply conform to the conditioning patterns of society. The type of information that the person absorbed reflects the repression and conditioning of the father, or key authority figure in his or her life.

There is a need to establish the individual's own voice of authority in society symbolized in the planetary ruler of Neptune in the 10th house. However, most commonly, the person conformed to consensus and societal conditioning in the context of how to express authority, and was again dominated by the expectations of others in society (Neptune in Libra/10th house). The person was looking outward in society to express individual authority instead of establishing this authority from within him- or herself. The need for social status to provide emotional security is symbolized in Neptune in the 10th house.

The individual typically brought this orientation into his or her adult life. The work function or social career will reflect these distortions, based upon such past conditioning patterns, if the person does not act to purge them (Neptune in the 10th house). Neptune in Libra symbolizes that this individual has initiated a diversity of relationships with others in order to establish the person's authority in society, and to take in the necessary information that he or she desired, reflected in the South Node in the 3rd house. Yet, in a majority of cases this had led to a situation where the individual attracted a partner who psychologically mirrored the father or the key authority figure in the person's life in the context of the 8th house Pluto. These types of relationship are initiated from an unconscious emotional standpoint of looking for a teacher type. In actual reality, this teacher type would be very authoritarian in nature, and would tell the individual what to think, and how to think about it. The authority figure may be perceived as possessing a spiritual knowledge that the person feels he or she is lacking. This dynamic is reflected in the South Node in Pisces/3rd house, and the planetary ruler of Neptune in Libra/10th house.

This current orientation led to an identity crisis because such partners did not reflect back to the individual his or her true identity, or essence. In this way relationships of codependency, and inequality were put in place. Extremes of all sorts are experienced (planetary ruler in Neptune in Libra/10th house). A situation could have been created where the person acted just as the father figure had done, and attracted others into his or her life that permitted such emotional/psychological control and domination.

With Neptune in Libra, the need to experience diversity of relationship types is vital for the Soul. The need for diversity is re-emphasized by the South Node in the 3rd house. This need conflicts with the pre-existing psychological orientation to fit in with others in the environment by conforming to mainstream society in the context of intellectual and spiritual development. The partner(s) that the person attracts will reflect these dynamics in the ways that were previously described. In the vast majority of cases, this signature indicates that the Soul is attracting the same types of relationships with the same types of people over and over again, no matter how many times the person terminates relationships, and initiates a new relationship with a different partner, hoping that the relationship will somehow be different.

The need for diversity in relationships and intake of a variety of information in the outer environment reflects the Soul's need to evolve past its current limitations (which have been previously discussed). The 3rd house placement of the South Node correlates with the intake of a diversity of information that allows spiritualization to manifest. As mentioned earlier the person would subconsciously, or unconsciously, desire to take in information of truly universal, transcendent, and spiritual nature, which will allow the past intellectual conditioning patterns to dissolve. The person naturally desires to initiate relationships with others that are founded upon equality, balance, and mutual independence (Neptune in Libra/10th). The person will, at some point, desire to establish his or her own voice of authority within society and within relationships. Such relationships would allow the necessary intake of transcendent and spiritual information to be absorbed into the Soul. The basis of the relationship will be founded upon mutually supporting and motivating the continual growth in each partner, and allowing the necessary intellectual exploration to occur.

How is evolution going to proceed in this case? Pluto's polarity point is Aquarius in the 2nd house, and the North Node is in Virgo in the 9th house. The planetary ruler of the North Node is Mercury in Cancer in the 7th house.

Simply stated, the 2nd house polarity point and the generalized need to develop a self-reliant and self-sufficient orientation to life will allow the necessary objectivity and detachment from a self-oriented world which is required by the Aquarius polarity point to be brought to fruition. The awareness of the Soul's intrinsic and unique capacities will emerge into consciousness, and then be linked to a socially relevant need. All egocentric delusions of grandeur will be purged in this way, and detachment from the pyramid reality structure will manifest. The person will become self-reliant, and from that standpoint will not need others in the environment to acknowledge him or her as special. The person's psychological orientation and creative actualization process will be fundamentally changed for the better through this type of evolution and awareness.

The North Node in the 9th house symbolizes that the belief system, and philosophical information that the individual takes in, will serve as the guiding light to establish self-reliance and link the special purpose with a socially relevant need. The person will need to align with natural laws in order to establish the evolutionary lessons of Pluto's polarity point in Aquarius in the 2nd house. The North Node in Virgo correlates with the need for inner purification, discrimination, and service to the Whole, or society. The elimination of victimization is vital, and the ability to discriminate between delusions and actual reality must manifest. The person's evolving egocentric structure is based on his or her beliefs, the need for self-improvement, and to be of service to others in general. Choosing what information to take in and what to leave out will occur naturally.

Such discrimination will be based upon discerning facts that reflect truth versus opinions and biases which do not. The revolving door of perspectives can be eliminated in this way, because a holistic foundation based on the individual's belief system has been established. The specific type of service to society will be guided by an alignment with natural laws, and reflect the individual's inherent and natural capacities. With this natal signature, it is very possible for the individual to be involved in some way in teaching (North Node in Virgo/9th house) that includes emotional/psychological knowledge. This is reflected in Pluto in Leo in the 8th house relative to its Aquarius/2nd house polarity point. This emotional/psychological wisdom is based on natural laws and truth, which is symbolized in the North Node in the 9th house. Teaching would also allow development of the necessary objectivity and detachment required in the Aquarius polarity point.

How are the lessons of the North Node in Virgo in the 9th house going to be developed? The planetary ruler of the North Node is Mercury in Cancer in the 7th house. Generally speaking, the individual will need to learn inner balance and equality, choosing relationships with others who support and encouraged the individual's growth. Mutual independence and co-equality can then be realized. Balancing the individual's own needs with the needs of others is a critical lesson symbolized in the planetary ruler. Emotional stability, security, and a positive self-image can manifest through such relationships (Mercury in Cancer). True emotional giving and nurturing can take place. These lessons will occur within the family environment, and with others who are in a close, and personal relationship with the individual (Mercury in Cancer). The need for self-purification, self-improvement, and to be of service to society will be learned through forming relationships of this nature.

This example demonstrates how the planetary rulers of the nodes will act as facilitators to actualize the mode of operation of the past, and the mode of operation of the future. Again, there is now an automatic rebirth, or regeneration, of Pluto, the South Node, and its planetary ruler to higher levels of expression as the person embraces his or her evolutionary growth needs. The main evolutionary/karmic dynamic in the birth chart serves as the foundation, or bottom line, upon which every other factor in the birth chart will be interpreted and given meaning.

Pluto in Aspect to the Nodal Axis

As described by Jeffrey Wolf Green, "When Pluto forms a direct aspect to the nodal axis it symbolizes that specific and unique evolutionary and karmic dynamics exist. The specific nature of the aspect determines what those factors are" (*Pluto, Vol. I,* 16). The core meaning and evolutionary intentions of all Pluto aspects to the nodal axis have been taken from *Pluto Vol. 1* (p 16–23). We will use in depth illustrations in order to apply, or demonstrate, these central principles.

Pluto Conjunct the South Node

Pluto conjunct the South Node indicates one of three possible evolutionary conditions:

1. The individual is in an evolutionary and karmic state of reliving past conditions because of a failure to deal with, or resolve successfully, issues described by the house and sign that Pluto and the South Node are in. The planetary ruler of the South Node provides additional information concerning this issue and necessity.

2. The individual is in a state of evolutionary and karmic fruition. In the past so much sincere effort has been put into the area in question, with such pure intentions, that the individual is reaping what was sown before. The individual has some kind of special destiny to fulfill. Look to the planet ruling the South Node, its sign, and house locality, to supply additional information concerning this condition.

3. The individual is in a simultaneous evolutionary and karmic condition in which certain conditions from the past are being relived,

while other conditions are in a fruition state. The house and sign positions of Pluto and the South Node will describe these issues and conditions. Check the locality, by sign and house, of the planet ruling the South Node for additional information.

The first two conditions are rare; the third is the most common condition when Pluto conjuncts the South Node. (It is interesting to note that former president John F. Kennedy had Pluto conjunct the South Node.) How can we know which condition exists for any individual? The best way to determine this is to observe, or ask questions about the individual's life. It is difficult to understand what condition exists merely by looking at the birth chart alone. If you do ask questions about the individual's life, then those questions should revolve around the areas and experiences symbolized by the polarity point of Pluto and the North Node. If you know the individual, then your own observations should revolve around the same areas. If there seems to be a total blockage from being able to realize these polarity points then condition one exists. If there seems to be something unique and special about the individual's life relative to the house and sign that Pluto and the South Node are in, then condition two exists. If there are elements of both then condition three exists.

On the other hand there are factors in the birth chart that can help us understand the probability of karmic conditions. In general, nonstressful aspects to Pluto conjunct the South Node tend to indicate a fruition condition. Stressful aspects tend to indicate a relive condition. A combination of both types of aspects tend to indicate a dual condition. The nonstressful aspects formed by other planets to Pluto and the South Node would indicate, by house and sign locality, those conditions that are in a state of karmic fruition. The stressful aspects formed by other planets to Pluto would indicate, by house and sign locality, those dynamics that are in a relive condition.

To demonstrate the principles of stressful and nonstressful aspects to Pluto conjunct the South Node, let's use a brief example. Let's use the planet Venus, and illustrate how it would manifest within consciousness in the context of an inconjunction to Pluto and the South Node.

An inconjunction is a stressful aspect. Generally speaking, the planet Venus correlates with our inner relationship and the external relationships we form based on our inner relationship. An inconjunction will always symbolize that some type of crisis is being experienced in the context of actualizing the evolutionary intentions for the life. In this example, then, the crisis will pertain to unresolved dynamics relative to the Soul's external relationships that are blocking further growth, and the inner relationship patterns that create relationships of this nature. The Soul will meet again with key people from the past, and continue to form relationships with them until all old dynamics that are blocking evolution are resolved. The realization that our inner relationship creates, or is the determinant to, our external relationships is crucial from an evolutionary point of view. The house and sign position of Venus will describe the nature of the crisis relative to the specific external relationship patterns that must be purged, and the Soul's inner relationship patterns that are causing negative and degenerative relationships to be formed. We must put these core correlations in the context of dynamics symbolized by Pluto's conjunction to the South Node.

If Venus formed a nonstressful aspect to Pluto and the South Node then those areas symbolized by Venus will most likely be in a state of karmic fruition. For the sake of an example, let's use a trine. A trine symbolizes that the Soul has the ability to consciously understand the entire evolutionary process—the past that led to the current moment in time. This creates an ease of integration that is reflected in nonstressful aspects. The Soul will easily understand what steps to take in order to establish the evolutionary intentions for the life in general (either on a personal or social level). The Soul's inner relationship and external relationship patterns will be experienced positively in this case, because the individual has worked to resolve issues pertaining to the past of this nature. In other words, the trine symbolizes that the necessary dynamics have been resolved relative to Soul's internal and external relationships, and will operate in a positive and integrated manner toward the actualization of Pluto's polarity point.

In addition to the above, there are other contributing factors and principles to consider when Pluto is conjunct the South Node. In all three conditions, unless there are mitigating factors, the individual will be blocked from being able to realize fully the evolutionary issues described by the North Node until the second Saturn return which occurs at fifty-six years of age. The first Saturn return, which occurs at twenty-eight years of age, symbolizes the normal amount of time we spend living out, or fulfilling, the evolutionary and karmic conditions of the past. The mitigating factors that can reduce the amount of time spent fulfilling these past conditions are 1) planets conjunct the North Node, or 2) planets in some kind of aspect to the North Node. When a planet or planets conjunct the North Node, a situation exists wherein this planet has directly acted to help the individual evolve out of past conditions in the past few lifetimes, sometimes the lifetime just before this one. The specific nature of the planet or planets describes how this was done. If a planet forms any other kind of aspect to the North Node, that planet has obliquely acted to help the individual evolve out of past conditions in the last few lifetimes, sometimes the very last lifetime before this one. The number of aspects to the North Node relatively determines the reduction of time spent in fulfilling past conditions.

For an example, let's use the same planet of Venus, and put it conjunct the North Node. In this case, then, the Soul's inner relationship and nature of the external relationships that are formed are the central dynamics that have acted to directly evolve the individual out of the conditions of the past reflected in Pluto conjunct the South Node. The Soul will have the awareness that it is our inner relationship that creates our external relationships. Thus, relationships will be experienced in a very positive manner in the context of the actualization of Pluto's polarity point. The house and sign that Venus and the North Node are in will describe the specific nature of the Soul's inner relationship and external relationships, and how the evolution out of past conditions has, and will, be achieved.

Let's use the example of Venus forming an inconjunct to the North Node. In this case, the dynamics symbolized by Venus have acted obliquely, or indirectly, to evolve the individual out of past conditions. Relative to the inconjunction the individual has experienced crisis in the context of his or her inner relationship and the external relationships. The specific nature of the crisis and the Soul's inner and outer relationship patterns is indicated by the house and sign position of Venus. Crisis is meant to induce the awareness of the behavioral patterns associated with Venus that must be changed in order for evolution to occur. The Soul will have used crisis in a positive manner in this context. This is unlike the previous example of Venus inconjunction to the South Node because that aspect indicated an evolutionary state of re-living, or repeating these core dynamics. In this case where Venus is inconjunct the North Node, it indicates the areas symbolized by Venus have been used to indirectly evolve the Soul out of past conditions relative to the house and sign position of the North Node, and Pluto's polarity point.

If other planets are conjunct the South Node with Pluto, then those functions (planets) are not only directly linked to the past, but are subject to the same three possible evolutionary/karmic conditions described in the section Pluto conjunct the South Node. Apply these same principles to these planets to help determine their condition. If the planetary ruler of the North Node is conjunct Pluto and the South Node, conditions pertaining to the past are intensified two-fold.

Check aspects of the North Node to itself to determine the amount of time necessary for fulfilling these past conditions. If a planet is square the nodal axis and Pluto, that planetary function (by house and sign locality) is interwoven between the issues of the past and future. The most common behavioral manifestation is a situation wherein the individual attempted to evade or escape the issues pertaining to the past. The evasion or escape was linked to the intense degree of conflict or tension that the individual experienced relative to the issues implied by the house and sign position of Pluto conjunct the South Node, and the house and sign of the squaring planet. While avoiding the South Node problems, the individual attempted to solve the problems related to the issues described by house and sign position of the North Node. In so doing the individual skipped steps. The individual did not succeed in resolving the issues pertaining to the South Node and Pluto within the context of their house and sign positions.

In this life, the individual must recover or relive those skipped steps. Only then will the full promise of the North Node be allowed full actualization. Until then the individual is torn in two simultaneous directions, at one time expressing behavior associated with the South Node and Pluto, and at other times manifesting behavior associated with the North Node. The solution is to fulfill the issues pertaining to the past within the context of Pluto and the South Node. The North Node can then be fully actualized.

In general, the number of aspects to the North Node will indicate the time necessary for fulfilling or reliving prior karmic conditions. In some cases this need is completed at the first Saturn return. This time factor is significantly decreased when the aspects are nonstressful in nature, because they tend to indicate a general understanding and partial resolution of these issues in prior lives. A preponderance of stressful aspects tends to imply a lack of understanding or resolution of these karmic issues coming into the life. However, no hard and fast rules can be applied because the evolutionary and karmic analysis must include the individual's evolutionary and karmic condition, or state. In general, however, an individual's progression along the evolutionary path will correlate to a decrease in the amount of time necessary for fulfilling prior karmic issues.

To illustrate the principles of Pluto conjunct the South Node, let's use the same example of Pluto in Leo in the 8th house, but now conjunct the South Node. The planetary ruler is the Sun in Virgo in the 9th house. Pluto's polarity point is Aquarius in the 2nd house, and the North Node is also in Aquarius in the 2nd house. The planetary ruler of the North Node is Uranus in Gemini in the 6th house. We will first analyze the core evolutionary intentions and meaning of Pluto in Leo in the 8th house conjunct the South Node, and then discuss the different evolutionary and karmic conditions that could exist (three possible manifestations of Pluto conjunct the South Node). Again, the specific condition of the individual with Pluto conjunct the South Node can only be determined by observing and asking questions about the individual's life.

What are the karmic and evolutionary lessons or conditions of the past in this case? Pluto in Leo in the 8th house correlates with the past desires and intentions of the Soul to transmute all internal limitations to create a metamorphosis beyond such limitations. The individual will desire to penetrate to the core of his or her psychology, motivations, intentions, and desire nature. The Soul will penetrate others in this same manner. This psychological metamorphosis and penetration became a part of the creative actualization process. Transmutation and personal evolution is linked with the Soul's special destiny, and the creative actualization process.

Pluto is conjunct the South Node. What are the limitations of the past that must now be resolved, and are most likely being re-lived in some manner? Simply stated, the Soul is looking outward for an external source of metamorphosis, a sense of personal power, and emotional security. The individual is dependent on an external source for metamorphosis to occur. It is this very orientation that is creating blocks to further growth. There is, most commonly, a deep insecurity within the Soul that creates a compulsive need for constant positive external feedback, and a need to be considered or acknowledged as special or important. The need for constant positive feedback will be a block in the context of full creative self-actualization. Delusions of grandeur are inhibiting further growth as well. A pyramid reality structure has been created wherein all other aspects of life revolve round the individual's own needs. Thus, narcissism must be purged from the Soul. This dynamic will be mirrored, or reflected, in the creative actualization process. There has been an over-identification with the Soul's creative energy, and special purpose from an egocentric point of view. Again, the degree that these core dynamics block evolution is dependent on the evolutionary condition of Pluto/South Node conjunction, which has been previously described.

The planetary ruler of the South Node by house and sign position will graphically describe additional areas of blockage relative to Pluto conjunct the South Node. The Sun in Virgo in the 9th house reflects that actualization of the desires and intentions symbolized by Pluto and the South Node occurred through the belief system and the form of service to society that the Soul performed. The individual has, and will, desire to understand him- or herself in a cosmological, philosophical, or metaphysical context. This leads to the formation of a specific belief structure. The beliefs to which the Soul orients will be based on the need to improve and perfect itself. The type of service that is performed will reflect the individual's philosophical and metaphysical understanding and orientation to life. In the Consensus state, the Soul will conform to mainstream religion, in order to creatively actualize, and affect personal metamorphosis. The Soul's psychological understanding and interpretation of life will reflect whichever mainstream religion it has gravitated toward from a conditioned standpoint. In another case, the Soul may be attempting to individuate, yet is compensating for this by the act of conformity. This would occur in the beginning stage, or 1st stage, of the Individuated state. In all cases, the Soul will be intensely inwardly critical, and this criticism will be projected into the external environment in some manner. If the Soul is in the Individuated state, for example, criticism will revolve around others who are not attempting to liberate, and conforming to the mainstream of society.

In addition, conditioned guilt will be a very crucial factor to overcome relative to beliefs. Most often, the individual will attempt to convince and convert others to his or her own beliefs, claiming that these beliefs should be true for all. Relative to the correlation of sado/masochistic behavior to the Virgo archetype, the individual will make him- or herself feel guilty, inferior, and worthless (masochism). This will be reflected in the specific beliefs that have been absorbed by the individual. The other potential is to feel guilty, and angry because of this guilt, and project this inner orientation onto others in such a way as to make others feel inferior (sadism). Victimization must be eliminated from the psyche. In all cases, the intention is to align with natural law. Natural law could then be used to create self-improvement and self-purification. The form of service will then be in alignment with natural law, and be in harmony with the Soul's evolutionary/karmic intentions. With this natal signature, a natural ability to teach others as a form of service, and creative actualization are indicated (planetary ruler of the South Node is the Sun in Virgo in the 9th house). Teaching could then be a way in which personal metamorphosis is achieved whenever the need presents itself. The need to relive these specific dynamics until they are resolved is symbolized by Pluto's conjunction to the South Node. This evolutionary intention will create an intense need to confront and purge (transmute) negative patterns of behavior that are preventing growth.

Pluto's polarity point and the North Node are in Aquarius in the 2nd house. What are the evolutionary intentions for this life, and the way to resolve the past conditions described by Pluto conjunct the South Node? The need to become self-reliant and self-sufficient are the primary lessons that must be learned in order for evolution to proceed. The individual must identify his or her own inherent capacities and talents in order to effect self-sufficiency on both a monetary and emotional level. Any dependency upon an external source for personal metamorphosis will be purged as self-reliance manifests. The individual will learn to look inward and use him- or herself as the symbol for transformation. The generalized need for detachment, self-objectification, and liberation from past patterns of excessive self-focus is reflected by the Aquarian polarity point. These lessons will be learned through the dynamics indicated by the 2nd house. In essence, the Soul must now link the special purpose to a socially relevant need in the context of the inherent capacities and abilities that have been identified. The need to be recognized as special by the external environment will be totally purged as these lessons are acted upon. This type of acknowledgment and validation will form within the individual. Delusions of grandeur will be purged from the Soul as this evolution takes hold as well. The need for self-empowerment, and to re-empower others, is critical in this evolutionary scenario. The North Node is in the same house and sign as Pluto's polarity point. Thus, the evolutionary intentions symbolized by Pluto's polarity point will be actualized through the same core dynamics discussed as we analyzed the polarity point. These core evolutionary needs and intentions are re-emphasized and intensified relative to Pluto's polarity point being in the same house and sign as the North Node.

The planetary ruler of the North Node is Uranus in Gemini in the 6th house. Uranus in Gemini in the 6th house correlates with the evolutionary lessons and intentions of the North Node being actualized through service to society, self-purification, and learning humility. The Soul will have a very intense self-analytical focus because of the need for self-improvement. The focus upon self-improvement leads to a natural humility. The form of service that is performed must allow the evolutionary intentions of the North Node to be developed. In other words, the individual must discern the proper work function that is in alignment with his or her evolutionary intentions. The issue of victimization is re-emphasized. The Soul will take in a diversity of information from the environment revolving around the need to be of service to society, and to affect self-improvement.

Discrimination must be learned in the context of knowing what information to take in, and what information to leave out. Generally speaking, information that reflects consensus conditioning relative to mainstream ideas, opinions, and biases must be disregarded. Discernment relative to what information reflects religious indoctrination versus natural truths, and opinions versus facts, must be developed. The Soul will realize that the paths to truth are relative, and will no longer need to convince or convert others to his or her point of view, or beliefs. The teaching abilities discussed earlier could manifest through written form, or through verbal communication and dialogues with others (Uranus in Gemini). The information that is taught a person will help others self-improve, self-heal, and will include a diversity of information and facts from society that reflect natural principles.

To determine the evolutionary condition of the individual with Pluto conjunct the South Node we must ask questions revolving around his or her ability to realize the polarity point of Pluto and the North Node. Thus, in this example, we would ask questions revolving around the individual's ability to effect self-reliance, and awareness of his or her inherent capacities. We will also ask the person questions regarding his or her ability to objectify reality, detach from the immediacy of subjective reality and personal problems, and link the special destiny to a socially relevant purpose. If the individual does not seem to have any awareness of these evolutionary needs, and is totally blocked from being able to realize these lessons, then a karmic condition of reliving these past dynamics is being experienced. Again, this is a rare condition.

If the Soul is in some ways able to manifest and develop these evolutionary lessons symbolized by Pluto's polarity point and the North Node, and is to some degree aware of the blockage problems indicated by Pluto conjunct the South Node, but has not fully actualized the evolutionary intentions for this life, then a simultaneous state of karmic fruition and reliving is being experienced. Some of the areas described by Pluto and the South Node will be in a state of karmic fruition, and other areas will be in a state of karmic re-living. This is by far the most common condition when Pluto conjuncts the South Node.

If the individual has a very deep understanding of these issues and is fully working to actualize Pluto's polarity point and the North Node, then the Soul is in a state of karmic fruition. There will be something unique and special about the individual's life relative to the area described by Pluto conjunct the South Node. The person will be able to help others in the context of the lessons that the individual has learned indicated by Pluto conjunct the South Node, because he or she had actualized the evolutionary intentions for this life. This is also a very rare condition when Pluto conjuncts the South Node.

Pluto Conjunct the North Node

When Pluto conjuncts the North Node it always symbolizes that the individual has been working to transform the area described by Pluto conjunct the North Node within the last few lifetimes, and is meant to continue in the direction. The results of the evolutionary transformation and metamorphosis can create tremendous growth in this life. Every other contributing factor in the birth chart will be channeled or focused through the North Node conjunct Pluto. The principle of Pluto's polarity point does not apply in this condition. However, there are other mitigating factors that we need to consider. If a planet conjuncts or forms an aspect to the South Node, than that planet is subject to the same three conditions discussed in Pluto conjunct the South Node. Evaluate the stressful and non-stressful aspects to Pluto to determine the probable condition of the planet. If a planet is in a fruition condition, then the specific nature of that planet, its house and sign location, and aspects it forms to other planets, and their own house and sign locations, will contribute in a positive and integrated way toward the fulfillment of the evolutionary intentions described by Pluto conjunct the North Node.

If a planet conjunct the South Node is in an apparent reliving condition, the specific nature of the planet, and the house and sign locality it is in, will act as a conflicting force that to some degree blocks the individual's ability to fulfill the evolutionary intentions reflected in Pluto's conjunction to the North Node. The key to resolving this condition is for the individual to resist the temptation to avoid this factor and the impact on his or her life. Instead, the individual should face those issues head on, and integrate and resolve them in the context of Pluto's conjunction to the North Node.

If there are planets in both conditions simultaneously, then determine which planets form stressful aspects to the South Node, and which planets form nonstressful aspects. The planets forming nonstressful aspects to the South Node will contribute in a positive and integrated way to the fulfillment of the evolutionary intentions described by Pluto's conjunction to the North Node, and the planets forming nonstressful aspects to the South Node must be faced head on and resolved within the context of Pluto's conjunction to the North Node. (It is interesting to note that politician John Kerry has Pluto conjunct the North Node.)

Let's use the same example of Pluto in Leo in the 8th house, now conjunct the North Node. The planetary ruler of the North Node is the Sun in Virgo in the 9th house. The South Node is in Aquarius in the 2nd house, and its planetary ruler is Uranus in Gemini in the 6th house. Pluto's polarity point does not apply in this condition. What specific areas has the Soul been working to transform in the last few lifetimes, and is meant to continue in the same direction in the present moment? The individual has been working to create a very deep inner metamorphosis of his or her existing limitations, and to evolve to greater levels of development and awareness. The ability to penetrate to the core of the psychological make-up and arrive at the bottom line of any source of stagnation will most likely be a very developed capacity. The individual could then penetrate others in the same way. The Soul will be able to change and grow as necessary, and will be able to motivate others to grow as well. The creative actualization process is based on, or linked with, the inner metamorphosis beyond existing limitations. The creative actualization process will reflect the individual's psychological knowledge. The Soul has worked to purge all sources of external dependencies upon the environment in general in the context of creating continual personal transformation and metamorphosis.

The creative actualization process itself has been a focus of intense metamorphosis. The Soul is learning to be in control of the special destiny and shape it out of the strength of the will. The individual is learning not to overly identify with his or her creative energy and the special purpose from an egocentric point of view. The manner in which the Soul creatively actualizes the special purpose is very important from an evolutionary standpoint. The choices that the Soul makes in the context of actualizing further growth are critical, as well. The Soul has core evolutionary lessons of self-empowerment, and the need to empower others as well. The individual has been working to eliminate the need to be constantly acknowledged as special and important, and narcissism has been purged in this way. The Soul must transmute the need for constant positive feedback from the external environment. The pyramid reality structure that has been created must be purged from the Soul. The individual's special destiny must be linked to a socially relevant purpose. Detachment from the pyramid reality structure and objective awareness is developed in this way. These are the core areas that the Soul has been working to transform in the past, and is meant to continue focusing on these areas in order to actualize evolution. The degree of growth that can now be actualized is tremendous if the individual continues to transform these areas.

The planetary ruler of the North Node is the Sun in Virgo in the 9th house. The evolutionary intentions described by Pluto's conjunction to the North Node will be actualized through the individual's belief structure, and the need to be of service to society. The individual must align with natural law, and purge all old conditioned, man-made beliefs that are blocking evolution. The individual is learning humility, self-improvement, and how to be of service to society. The service that is performed will reflect the Soul's belief system. The individual is also learning lessons of discrimination in the context of eliminating illusions and delusions, and purging all forms of self-doubt and undermining activity. Any pattern of victimization must be eliminated. These lessons have, and will, allow the evolutionary requirements of Pluto's conjunction to the North Node to be actualized, or fulfilled.

The South Node is in Aquarius in the 2nd house, and its planetary ruler is Uranus in Gemini in the 6th house. The South Node is Aquarius in the 2nd house, symbolizing that the individual has worked to develop self-reliance and has identified his or her own inner capacities in order to achieve a self-reliant attitude and orientation to life in general. The Soul has worked to create a positive inner relationship, and has developed the ability to meet its own emotional needs from within. The individual has been learning to provide his or her own positive feedback and validation from within. The necessary objectivity and detachment from a pyramid reality structure, and the need to link the special destiny with a socially relevant need, has already been a focus of evolution in the past in the context of Pluto's conjunction to the North Node. The individual has desired to actualize his or her own unique essence, or individuality, free from the conditioning patterns of the past. The Soul is trying to liberate, or break free, from any conditioning of the mainstream, or consensus society, and integrate into society, based on his or her own unique individuality. The capacities and abilities that the individual has identified revolve around the need to express and actualize inherent individuality, and de-condition from the mainstream society.

The planetary ruler of the South Node is Uranus in Gemini in the 6th house. The individual has an emphasized focus on the need for self-improvement, self-purification, to learn humility, and the need to be of service to society. The issues of discrimination and purging victimization are re-emphasized. The Soul has collected a variety of information and facts from the external environment in order to achieve the lessons of the 6th house Uranus. The left brain will be very developed. Thus, the individual will have the ability to logically organize information together in a linear manner, and communicate this knowledge to others. The dynamic of learning to be of service to society is re-emphasized, and indicates that the form of service must allow evolution to continue. The form of service, of course, must be in alignment with the Soul's evolutionary intentions. The lessons and intentions of the South Node were actualized in this way.

Pluto Square the Nodal Axis

When Pluto squares the nodal axis, the Soul is in a unique evolutionary situation. The individual is equally torn between issues pertaining to the past, and issues pertaining to the future. This division exists each moment in the individual's life. This karmic/evolutionary condition indicates that the individual has neither succeeded in totally resolving nor learning either the issues pertaining to his or her evolutionary past, or the issues reflected through the North Node. Because Pluto is square both nodes, the issues pertaining to each have been acted upon prior to this life. Yet neither has been totally developed, understood, resolved, or integrated. The individual is on an extremely important evolutionary threshold. The choices that the individual makes relative to his or her desires are extremely critical as they concern the evolutionary journey and progression. The individual is simultaneously attracted and repulsed by the issues, orientations, and lessons of both Nodes. The issue of skipping steps described before is magnified two-fold. The need to relive and resolve those skipped steps in order to integrate the issues with respect to the Nodes is magnified two-fold. The skipped steps apply in both areas. Until the individual consciously understands the lessons and how to apply them, his or her behavior alternately expresses the orientations implied by the South and North Nodes. (Note that both former President Richard Nixon, and Vice President Al Gore had Pluto square the Nodal axis.)

The polarity point of Pluto applies in this situation. The polarity point of Pluto must be activated to begin the integration and resolution of this evolutionary condition. The mitigating factors to check for are these:

1. If Pluto applies to the South Node, then the polarity point of Pluto and the North Node, with its planetary ruler, must be integrated through the South Node. The individual will then have a consistent bottom line to which the evolutionary intentions described by Pluto's polarity point and the North Node and its planetary ruler,

can be continually referred. Thus, the South Node and its planetary ruler will transmute into new levels of expression.

2. When Pluto applies to the North Node, the polarity point of Pluto and the South Node with its planetary ruler must be integrated through the North Node, with its planetary ruler facilitating the process. In the same way, the individual will have a bottom line to which the evolutionary intentions described by Pluto's polarity point and the South Node and its planetary ruler, can be continually referred. The North Node, and its planetary ruler, can then transmute into new levels of expression.

If other planets conjunct or form aspects to the nodal axis, apply the same techniques that were demonstrated under the discussion of Pluto conjunct the South Node to determine their evolutionary condition. Determining the Node that Pluto applies to will explain how to integrate and handle those issues. As you determine what Node is applying to Pluto keep in mind that the mean motion of the Nodes is retrograde. Thus, the normal rules to determine what applies to what are reversed. As an example, let's put Pluto in Libra at 28 degrees and the South Node in Cancer, and the North Node at Capricorn at 28 degrees. Due to the retrograde motions of the Nodes, the North Node in Capricorn in this case is moving toward Pluto, and the South Node in Cancer is moving away from Pluto. The Node that Pluto last formed a conjunction with is the Node that Pluto is applying to. Thus, Pluto applies to the South Node in this example, and the integration point of the issues implied in Pluto's square to the nodal axis is the South Node in Cancer in the context of Pluto's polarity point.

Let's use a brief example in order to fully apply the principles that we have just learned when Pluto forms a square the nodal axis. Pluto in Virgo in the 6th house and now it is squaring the nodal axis. The South Node is in Gemini in the 3rd house and the North Node is in Sagittarius in the 9th house. Mercury is in Cancer in the 4th house. The planetary ruler of the North Node is Jupiter in Aquarius in the 11th house. What are the specific skipped steps symbolized in this natal signature that the individual must now relive and recover? Remember the core underlying archetype of Pluto in Virgo, and the nodal axis in the 3rd and 9th house that we already described in previous examples. Pluto applies to the South Node in Gemini in the 3rd house because it is the Node that last formed a conjunction with Pluto. The skipped steps indicated in Pluto's square to the nodal axis will be recovered and integrated through the South Node in the context of actualizing Pluto's polarity point, and integrating the North Node. In other words, integration of Pluto's polarity point and the North Node will manifest through the South Node in Gemini in the 3rd house, with the planetary ruler Mercury in Cancer in the 4th house facilitating this process. In this way, the North Node and its planetary ruler will transmute into higher levels of expression.

In this case, the Soul's bottom-line orientation and desires coming into the life are to learn humility, achieve self-improvement, and learn to be of service to society. Vital lessons of discrimination and purging victimization are reflected in this natal Pluto. There will most typically be a deep inner existential void within the individual that is more than just a basic aloneness that we can all feel at various times in our life. There will be an intense degree of self-critical and negative focus, which then leads to deep feelings of inferiority and lack. The individual will create perpetual crises until these dynamics are resolved. Crisis is intended to induce self-analysis, which then leads to self-knowledge. In other words, crisis is meant to bring these issues to a head. There will be either a masochist or sadist (or both) pathology that must be purged from the Soul.

The South Node in Gemini in the 3rd house correlates with the Soul's mental structure relative to the nature of the information that is collected from the external environment. This mental structure is based on the needs, desires, and intentions described by Pluto in Virgo in the 6th house. The mental structure is an area in which the individual has skipped steps that must now be recovered in the context of negative and destructive intellectual patterns in general (Pluto in Virgo in the 6th house). Relative to the North Node in the 9th house, the individual has been flip-flopping back and forth between developing his or her mental and intellectual capacity, and then attempting to form a specific belief structure in which to interpret and create a holistic understanding of these facts. In so doing, the individual has not developed, resolved, or integrated either of the areas indicated in the North and South Nodes. These skipped steps are now brought into the current life.

The South Node in Gemini in the 3rd house correlates with the individual's intellectual patterns and mental structure, relative to the types of information he or she is collecting from the external environment. The individual has collected a variety of information that revolves around the need to be of service to humanity, and for self-improvement. The inner critical, negative focus, however, has created a situation where the information that the individual took in reflects his or her feelings of inferiority and lack, and is based on self-doubt and self-undermining activity. A negative mental pattern of self-defeat, self-punishment, victimization, and undermining behavior is very likely in this scenario. The Soul has, and will use, intellectual methods to avoid facing the inner existential void. In addition, the individual will attempt denial of this inner chaotic state that is filled with crisis. The individual will create many excuses as to why he or she will not do what must be done when it is the proper time to act. This reflects the need for self-punishment. The individual will rationalize this type of behavior, and these rationalizations will be reflected in the type of information that is collected from the external environment. In other words, the Soul is unconsciously seeking information that validates or supports this inner orientation and psychology. The individual is, most commonly, looking outward in society for information to achieve self-improvement and self-purification. A very common expression of this dynamic is absorbing information based on the prevailing consensus' notion of self-perfection that only reinforces the sense of inferiority and lack. The Soul is hooked by the words that appear to offer self-perfection and self-improvement, but truly only deepen the inner feelings of lack, inferiority, and doubt. The Soul has attempted to fill the deep inner void with intellectual information and excessive mental activity. The individual will argue that his or her own viewpoints are the only legitimate ones, and others who do not agree are considered to be wrong. Any information that does not support the individual's own point of view is considered invalid. The information that the individual has collected is not necessarily wrong or invalid, but it is limited in some manner in the context of Pluto's square to the nodal axis.

The planetary ruler of the South Node is Mercury in Cancer in the 4th house. This symbolizes that the individual's family and early child-hood environment deeply impacted the development of the intellectual structure. Most commonly, the family environment did reinforce the pre-existing feelings of lack and inferiority in some way in the context of the messages and information that was promoted as valid. In addition, the family environment reflected the individual's mental attitudes of victim-ization, self-undermining activity, and doubt. Information and viewpoints of this type are presented by the family and by others in the close and personal environment, as a vehicle for self-improvement and self-purifi-cation. The individual may have been subjected to the projected vibra-tion of not being good enough if he or she did not comply with, and conform to the family's own intellectual viewpoints. In the same way, this vibration will then be projected onto others who do not validate the individual's pre-existing ideas and notions. This symbol reflects a high de-gree of sensitivity to the family environment, and especially to the verbal and spoken communication between family members. The individual is insecure about disagreeing and conforming to others in the family. The Soul has generated dialogues and collected information from the family environment, and will tend to deny or reject the points of views of oth-ers who do not conform to these views. This dynamic is created because of insecurity in the context of embracing change and personal growth in general. In other words, the act of conformity to the family's viewpoints constitutes the Soul's unconscious sense of emotional security.

The North Node in Sagittarius in the 9th house correlates with the in-dividual's belief system, and the need to understand life from a metaphysi-cal, philosophical, and cosmological standpoint. There is an evolutionary need to align with natural law, and to purge all conditioned, man-made beliefs that are preventing further growth. The belief system is a crucial part of the evolutionary skipped steps in the context of the South Node and Pluto's square to the nodal axis. The beliefs that have been developed are not necessary wrong, but they are limited in some way. Again, the in-dividual has flip-flopped back and forth between developing his or her mental and intellectual capacity, and then attempting to solve problems and unresolved issues of the natal Pluto through developing a specific belief structure without resolving the dynamics reflected in the South Node. Unresolved issues in both of the areas symbolized by the Nodes must now be recovered.

In other words, the belief system that has been created also reflects the emotional distortions of the natal Pluto in Virgo in the 6th house (especially in the context of sado-masochistic behavior). The individual absorbed beliefs that, yet again, reinforced his or her sense of inferiority, lack, and self-doubt (conditioned man-made beliefs). Most commonly, there is a dependency upon the external beliefs in the environment. The nature of the individual's beliefs, of course, is determined by the Soul's evolutionary condition. In all cases, the skipped step indicated by Pluto square the Nodal axis will imply that the belief system and intellectual structure are areas that have not been fully developed or resolved in the ways already described. The individual will attempt denial that anything is wrong, and will use these beliefs as rationalizations and excuses for maintaining the negative and destructive behavior of the past (rationalizations not to change). This dynamic is symbolized by Pluto in Virgo/6th house square the nodal axis in Gemini/3rd house, and Sagittarius/9th house. The individual will try to convince and convert others to his or her own belief system, and again, claim that these are the only legitimate or true beliefs. This clearly indicates that the dynamics of constant crisis, deep feelings of inferiority, denial, and facing the deep inner existential void have not been fully resolved.

The planetary ruler of the North Node is Jupiter in Aquarius in the 11th house. This symbolizes that the Soul must liberate, decondition, and transform the conditioning patterns of the past that are preventing further growth. In the context of the North Node in Sagittarius in the 9th house there must be an alignment with beliefs that allow the Soul to liberate, and decondition from the influence of mainstream society in general. The individual is seeking to align with a belief system that creates a necessary detachment from subjective reality, and allows true individuality to be expressed within society. The individual can then objectively view any situation and emotional dynamic in general. The individual will feel different inwardly from most others in society, and will desire to bond with like-minded people. The Soul may feel insecure relative to feeling different, especially from those in the family environment (Mercury in Cancer in the 4th house). The individual will desire to express his or her own unique essence, yet may fear rejection and criticism from others if he or she acts in this way (Pluto in Virgo in the 6th house). The Soul must de-condition and liberate from all conditioned, man-made beliefs that are inhibiting further growth, and do not reflect the person's true individuality. The individual will align with natural law through the act of deconditioning and liberation.

However, relative to Pluto's square to the nodal axis, the individual may have suppressed his or her individuality and conformed to the peer group. The peer group mirrored the individual's pre-existing belief structure, which, again, is an extension of the family's viewpoints and beliefs. In this case, the Soul will interpret (North Node 9th house, Jupiter in Aquarius in the 11th house) the feeling of being different in a critical, negative manner (Pluto in Virgo in the 6th house). The individual may even feel that there is something wrong with him or her because of being different, and the inability to conform to the family, or mainstream society. The Soul cannot fully embrace the emotional body because of these dynamics (Jupiter in Aquarius relative to the planetary ruler of the South Node Mercury in Cancer in the 4th house). The individual must detach and disengage from the mainstream of society, and feel secure within his or her individuality. This includes detachment from beliefs of the peer group, and the individual's family if those people do not support his or her ongoing evolution. This liberation did not occur or was not completed prior to the current life in the context of Pluto' square to the nodal axis.

The Soul created a lifestyle based on this belief structure, and conforming to the prevailing peer group. The individual most likely projected this expectation of conformity onto others in the environment, and also projected the inner vibration of "not being good enough," if conformity did not occur. It is important to understand that this dynamic is created because of the Soul's own feelings of lack, inferiority, and doubt. Even though the individual may have outwardly adopted the lifestyle and beliefs of others in the consensus, the individual did feel isolated and alienated from the peer group, as well as others in society who were simply conforming to mainstream society. Yet, the Soul did not act to de-condition from conditioning patterns of the past that are blocking evolution. This is a critical evolutionary step that must be taken in order to resolve the skipped steps symbolized in Pluto's square to the nodal axis. Detachment and disengaging from the existing reality occurs because the individual now desires to liberate from past conditioning patterns in the context of the pre-existing belief structure. This dynamic is symbolized by the North Node in Sagittarius in the 9th house, and its planetary ruler Jupiter in Aquarius in the 11th house. At some point in time, the Soul will desire to rebel against man-made, conditioned beliefs, which will then lead to liberation, and deconditioning from past conditioning patterns that are inhibiting further growth. The Soul will have the ability to quickly change and transform his or her existing belief system and decondition from the current conditioning patterns of the past if these lessons are put into motion.

The polarity point of Pluto is Pisces in the 12th house. The Node that last formed a conjunction with Pluto is the South Node in Gemini in the 3rd house, and its planetary ruler is Mercury in Cancer in the 4th house. The resolution of the skipped steps that have been described will occur through the South Node with its planetary ruler facilitating the process. This will become the bottom line upon which the skipped steps can be resolved, and consistent integration can occur. The polarity point of Pluto and the North Node will be integrated through the South Node. The polarity point of Pluto must be activated before any evolution can manifest.

The general evolutionary lessons and intentions of Pluto's polarity point in Pisces in the 12th house are the need to dissolve all barriers that are preventing a direct and conscious merging with the Creator, learning faith in the Divine, purging delusions from the Soul, learning self-forgiveness for all the Soul's faults and imperfections, and unconditional love of oneself and others. Remember that Pisces symbolizes that an entire cycle of evolution is now coming to culmination. The Soul must dissolve all old mental/physical/spiritual patterns that are creating blocks to evolution, and from establishing a direct and conscious merging with the Source. The individual will learn self-forgiveness for all his or her imperfections, faults, and mistakes. In this way, unconditional love of oneself and others will manifest.

Karma Yoga is an Eastern term that refers to the actualization of the proper work function of the individual, which can then further expand the horizons of personal awareness. By developing an awareness of the Divine, the Soul can achieve an inner purification that allows the Divine to operate through the individual as a channel through the work function, and performing service to society. The awareness of proper priorities and the awareness of the Soul's correct work function occur as the individual cultivates a relationship with the Divine, or the Source. The individual must learn to have faith in the Creator, and realize that no matter what problems are currently being experienced, there will always be a solution. The Soul will then realize that only a relationship with the Divine can fill the deep inner void, and why the experience of aloneness was so intense.

The South Node in Gemini in the 3rd house symbolizes that these evolutionary intentions will be actualized and integrated through collecting a diversity of information and facts that will serve to purge all self-doubt, feelings of inferiority and lack, and self-undermining activity. In this way, the previous sado-masochistic pathology will be brought to culmination (polarity point in Pisces in the 12th house). The individual must open up to information of a truly transcendent and universal nature that promotes continual spiritual development. Embracing universal, timeless laws serves to undermine the existing psychological dynamics of inferiority, lack, and the need for self-punishment. The individual will be able to generate dialogues with others of this nature, and learn to communicate with others in a nondefensive manner. The Soul can receive and communicate very positive and beneficial information.

Mercury in Cancer in the 4th house symbolizes that the lessons reflected in the South Node in Gemini in the 3rd house will be actualized through the family environment, and with others who are in a close personal relationship with the individual. The individual's self-image must be positive. A negative self-image will be transformed by the nature of the information that is absorbed from the external environment in the ways that have just been described. Confrontations of an intellectual and philosophical nature may take place in order to enforce these necessary lessons. This is symbolized in the South Node in Gemini in the 3rd house, and the North Node in Sagittarius in the 9th house. The individual must learn to provide his or her own emotional security and nurturing from within, and thus be inwardly secure, no matter what the nature of the family environment, or external environment in general. The Soul must learn to be secure within its mental and intellectual ideas, viewpoints, and orientation. Generally speaking, the individual must be secure enough to generate and express ideas and information that do not conform to the mainstream of society. Communication of this knowledge to others is also critical from an evolutionary standpoint. The individual will then feel secure about expressing his or her own unique individuality through his or her belief system that is in alignment with natural law. The Soul will understand that truth, and the path to truth, is relative. There will be no need to defend any viewpoints as right, or convince or convert others to a specific belief system.

This illustration is meant to clearly apply the principles of Pluto square the Nodal Axis. Again, we must determine the node that Pluto is applying to in order to analyze how the resolution of the skipped steps will be actualized and integrated. In order for evolution to occur, Pluto's polarity point must be activated. The planetary ruler of the Node that Pluto is applying to will act as a facilitator for the actualization of the evolutionary intentions for the life, and the resolution of the skipped steps. In this case, the resolution occurred through the dynamics indicated by the South Node. The South Node, by house and sign position and aspects to other planets, then serves as a bottom line upon which Pluto's polarity point and the North Node is continually refereed and actualized. The integration of Pluto's polarity point and the North Node manifests in this way. The South Node and its planetary ruler can now transmute into higher levels of expression.

Other Planets in Aspect to the Nodal Axis

As described in *Pluto, Volume I*, when planets aspect the nodal axis and Pluto has no direct aspect to the Nodes, then those planets have played a major role (by house, sign, and aspect to other planetary functions) in shaping the kinds of experiences that the person has had for evolutionary and karmic reasons. The type of aspect (generally described as stressful and nonstressful, but for a full understanding we must look at the specific aspect the planet is forming) determines how the individual has responded to those experiences and will supply clues as to the probable evolutionary condition of those planets. Of course, the dynamics symbolized by the aspect(s) must be put in the context of the main evolutionary/karmic dynamic in the birth chart.

Let's use a brief example to illustrate this point: For the sake of a simple example, let's put Mars conjunct the South Node. Generally speaking, Mars correlates with our subjective desire nature, and the way in which we consciously act out the desires emanating from Pluto, or the Soul. Mars is the lower octave of Pluto (a lower octave is a denser expression of a higher vibration). Mars correlates with the need for freedom and independence, in order to fulfill a sense of special destiny linked with perpetual self-discovery, and a continual state of becoming. Experience is a vehicle through which self-discovery can be realized. Mars correlates with the need to initiate, or generate, whatever experiences are necessary in order for self-discovery to occur. Experience is a vehicle through which personal self-discovery and, thus, growth can manifest. Mars correlates with the psychological dynamics of anger, fear, and the development of the intrinsic identity or individuality.

When Mars conjuncts the South Node, it will correlate with a Soul that has unresolved anger and fear. The person will have an intense and emphasized need for freedom and independence in order to develop his or her own identity. The individual must learn to act upon desires that allow growth to continue and are in alignment with the evolutionary intentions for the current life. The specific dynamics that have been unresolved are symbolized by the house and sign position of Mars and the South Node. These dynamics have been experienced in the past and are most likely being relived or re-experienced relative to the conjunction to the South Node. In other words, it is very likely that the person is reliving certain life conditions that are indicated by the house and sign position of the South Node and Mars in order to resolve old dynamics specifically correlated with Mars. A conjunction is a stressful aspect, and it will always symbolize that the planetary functions that are conjunct are uniting to operate as one unit, or one function. We can correctly interpret the meaning of any planet that is in aspect to the nodal axis by synthesizing the archetype of the planet, and the meaning of the specific aspect that the planet forms to the nodal axis. This is to be put in the context of the meaning of the house and sign position of the planet and the node that forms an aspect to the planet.

3

The Four Natural Evolutionary Conditions of the Soul

A core principle on which evolutionary astrology is founded is the evolutionary states, or conditions of the Soul. As Jeffrey Wolf Green writes, there exist four natural evolutionary conditions, or states, of human evolution. There are three substages within each evolutionary state. These evolutionary states are the *dimly evolved state*, the *consensus state*, the *individuated state*, and the *spiritual state*. These states reflect the Soul's natural evolutionary journey as it reunites and merges with the Creator. Evolution proceeds as separating desires within the Soul become exhausted, and the desire to know the Source becomes increasingly more dominant. In the final substage of the Spiritual condition, the Creation-realized masters of our time like Jesus, Yoganada, and Sri-Yuketswar, manifest to help other Souls merge with the Source.

We can all validate this natural truth, or natural law, by validating the experiences we have had in our own lives as we interacted with others. Again, we do not need any cosmology or belief system to validate the truth of these principles. There is an observed evolutionary difference in a person who is focused on buying a new car or other new possessions, gaining material wealth, and who conforms to the majority in the society, than to a person who values individuality, and thinking and acting independently outside the confines of mainstream society. We must factor in this evolutionary state for an accurate interpretation of any birth chart—one size does not fit all. Evolution occurs in each state as the Soul exhausts all desires that are intrinsic to the specific state, and substate (purging separating desires from the Soul). As mentioned before, the center of gravity within consciousness, shifts from the ego to the Soul itself as evolution takes place. This shift from the center of gravity within consciousness, from the ego to the Soul, occurs permanently in the third stage of the spiritual evolutionary condition.

It should be clear, then, that we cannot determine the evolutionary state of a person by looking at the birth chart. We must interact with the client by asking simple questions, and from the answers of the individual we can determine their evolutionary state. The birth chart now has the proper context for an accurate interpretation. A good technique to quickly determine a person's evolutionary state is to ask the client the purpose of the chart interpretation. We can determine the evolutionary state of the individual by the nature of his or her answers and description of their own life events, or experiences. This is why it is critical to thoroughly understand these evolutionary states, and how to adjust a birth chart to an individual's specific evolutionary condition. Another critical point to address is that there is movement within these states, which is called a transition or "on the cusp" of one substage of evolution into the next. The Soul is transiting, or on the cusp, of one evolutionary state into the next when the individual expresses qualities of both evolutionary substages, and has not fully integrated, or evolved into, the higher of the two evolutionary conditions. For example, an individual could be transitioning from the first stage individuated evolutionary condition into the second stage individuated condition. In this case, the Soul will express the behavior of both these evolutionary substages, and fluctuate between the behaviors associated with them until the transition into the higher evolutionary substage is made. This condition can occur within any evolutionary state and substate. Again, we can only determine if this evolutionary condition is operative in any Soul by asking the proper questions, and by observation and correlation.

These descriptions of the evolutionary states are taken directly from the material taught by Jeffery Wolf Green.

The Dimly Evolved State

Roughly two to three percent of all Souls are in this evolutionary condition. These are Souls that are evolving from other forms of life, plants and animals, into human consciousness. Thus, the Soul's self-awareness is very, very limited to the time and space the individual personally occupies. These people will have a very low IQ because of their limited self-awareness, and common terms used to describe these people are *mentally retarded* and *cretinism*. These types are very joyous and innocent. The root desire within this condition is to be like everybody else, or like those in the consensus state.

Conversely, there are Souls that are forced back into this state of evolution because of karmic causes in the past. These Souls are de-evolving. The terminology used to describe the first category of people in this state is used to describe those that have de-evolved as well. However, the Souls that are de-evolving are very, very angry at the humiliating limitations of this state, and remember experiencing higher evolutionary states. The intense anger of these Souls creates a real problem as the person commonly tries to hurt him- or herself, or others around them. There will be a piercing white light manifesting from the pupil, and an inward experience of a very deep anger in the person's auric field.

The Consensus State

Roughly 75 percent of all Souls are in this evolutionary condition. Here, these individuals will simply be vicarious extensions of the majority of society's expectations, norms, customs, regulations, beliefs, morality, and so on, because of the need to conform to society, and thus, belong to it. The Soul's reality is the reality of the mainstream, or consensus—reality itself. There is no way for these individuals to think for themselves. This state, astrologically, correlates with Saturn because of the underlying dynamic of conformity. For example, if a scientist told a person in this state that astrology was a bogus science, the individual would believe this opinion without question. The root desire that will propel the Soul forward in this state, from the first substage to the third substage, is the desire to get ahead, to get ahead of the system—the consensus society they belong to.

In the first substage of this evolutionary state, these individuals will have a very limited self-awareness, essentially limited to the time and space they occupy, a limited awareness of the surrounding community, and even more limited awareness of the country of origin. Yet, these individuals can be incredibly self-righteous relative to beliefs, the judgments based on those beliefs, and how life is interpreted; what is right and wrong and so forth. It is as if these people are social automatons, and an apt analogy to describe this state is worker bees in a hive. These people are the lowest social strata of the society of birth.

In the second substage of the consensus, the desire to get ahead of the system leads to the need to learn, on a progressive basis, how society works, or is put together. The person now perceives that others in a higher social strata have more from a materialist point of view, and careers or social positions that the individual does not have. They do want to remain in the lower social strata, and so must learn the laws, regulations, norms, and traditions that govern consensus society. The individual becomes progressively more aware of the community, the country of birth, and others around them because of this need to learn how society works. In addition, the Soul becomes aware, on a preliminary basis, of other countries. However, the person's identity is still simply a vicarious extension of the consensus moralities, judgments, beliefs, and so on. The self-righteous attitude is most commonly maintained and other countries that do not operate under the known society's conditioning are not seen as equal. The motto is "we are right and they are wrong." Nationalism manifests in this stage as a result, and this state typically correlates with those individuals in the middle strata of society. The awareness of political leaders and those in positions of social power who have a grand abundance of material wealth leads the Soul into the next substage because of the desire to maintain those social positions. This creates the need to become even more aware of how the system works: the community, country of birth, and other countries.

In the third substage of the consensus state, the Soul now desires to get on top of the system, or society. This leads to positions of social power and prestige from that viewpoint. The CEOs of companies, political leaders, mainstream religious leaders, and others who are in positions of social prominence are in this substage of the consensus. The person knows how the system works, and can use this knowledge to lead others in the consensus. The person will, at some point within this substage, exhaust all desires that exist within the state in total. The meaning of life will be progressively lost as the desires and lifestyle created no longer hold any meaning. The person will now ask the question: "Isn't there more to life than this?" This very question leads to a growing alienation from the consensus reality, and normal way of life defined by the consensus. This is the transition from the consensus state to the Individuated state. The desire that propels the Soul into this state is the desire to liberate from all external conditioning patterns that previously defined the Soul's sense of reality in general, and its sense of personal identity, or individuality.

The Individuated State

Roughly 20 percent of all Souls are in this evolutionary condition. Astrologically speaking, this state correlates with Uranus because the individual now desires to liberate from and rebel against the consensus state from which it is evolving away. Instead of the Soul being defined by the consensus society relative to its sense of reality and personal identity, the Soul now desires to discover who it is outside of such conditioning. In other words, these Souls want to discover their own unique identity from within themselves, and liberate from all conditioning patterns of the consensus. This allows the Soul to objectify itself, or divest itself of emotion and view itself impersonally. This leads to objectivity, and the ability to view ourselves outside the actual time and space we are living in. In this state of evolution, to use the same example describing the consensus state, if the scientist were to say astrology is a bogus science, the person would respond by saying "No, thank you, I will think for myself." Souls in this evolutionary condition feel inwardly different: different than a majority in the consensus society. Because of the need to liberate from the consensus awareness, Souls in this state progressively expand their awareness to include ever larger wholes, or frames of reference. The Soul can no longer relate to the country of birth. As a result, the Soul now feels a progressive detachment from society, as though the

person is on the outside looking in. Again, this allows the Soul to objectify itself relative to personal awareness and self-perception. Rebelling
against the consensus beliefs, moralities, values, what constitutes meaning in life itself, and so on, the Soul now begins to question the assump-
tions of the consensus that define what reality is and is not. Such Souls
now begin to experiment by investigating other ways of looking at and
understanding life itself. This includes beliefs and philosophies from
other countries and areas that will allow an ever-increasing expansion in
their own consciousness, and thus, their sense of personal awareness.

In the first substage, the Soul will typically try to compensate for the
feeling of being different, of not belonging to the consensus, and coun-
tering a sense of alienation by trying to appear normal. This compensation will then cause the Soul to structure its outer reality to conform
to those in the consensus state: normal work, normal kinds of friends,
normal appearance, and so on. This inner compensation is based upon
inner insecurity, a reaction to the feelings of alienation, and inwardly
knowing that the Soul is different. The Soul has not been in this evolutionary state before the current moment in time, and self-consistency is
rooted in past behavior. This compensation will lead to a very intense
feeling of living a lie. Even though compensation may be operative,
such Souls will still be inwardly questioning the consensus viewpoints,
and inwardly establishing their own individuality through independent
thinking and investigation. This will occur through reading books or
taking classes that go way beyond the norm in the context of consensus society. Some will seek out others of like mind, and who also feel
inwardly different and alienated from the majority of society. Through
bonding with those of like mind, compensatory behavior will give way,
and the Soul will further distance itself from the consensus. These Souls
will either do any kind of work just to get by, or actualize a work that is
symbolic of their individuality.

In the second substage, the individuated state, the archetype of Uranus is at its highest point of expression relative to its correlation with
rebellion. The rebellion is so extreme that the Soul has now thrown
off any idea or philosophy that has come before at any level of reality.
Such Souls will seek out other alienated Souls in a kind of inner existen-

tial void, related to such intense rebellion and alienation from society. There is a deep fear of integrating into society in any way, because they fear that society will absorb their hard-won individuality, which is defined through the act of rebellion. In the context of evolution, one day these Souls will realize that this fear is a fear only, and society can never absorb the person's unique individuality. With this realization, the Soul will integrate back into society, but with the individuality intact, and can move into the third and final substage of the individuated state.

In the third substage of this state, the Soul now has a true and unique gift that is meant to be used to help the consensus evolve. This gift now has to be integrated into the consensus society. Yet, the Soul in this stage is not inwardly identified with the consensus in any way, and it's standing very, very distant from it. The person has evolved through the individuated state in such a way that his or her consciousness is aware of the entire world, and the relativity of beliefs, values, morality, and so on. As such, the Soul will have the feeling of being a citizen of the world, versus a singular country or nation. Pondering the very essence of the nature of creation, existence, and who the individual really is begins to take place. This is what allows for the transition into a spiritual state of evolution as the Soul progressively opens its consciousness to embrace the timeless, the universal, and God, or the Source. A good example of a person in this evolutionary stage is Albert Einstein. Einstein is quoted as saying, "When mediocre minds encounter Genius, expect violent opposition." This psychology allows the Soul to make the effort of helping the mainstream evolve for the effort's sake, and not necessarily attached to the outcome. At some point in time, the Genius capacities and revolutionary inventions that manifest through Souls in this evolutionary state will be accepted and incorporated into society.

The Spiritual State

Two to three percent of all Souls are in this state of evolution. Astrologically speaking, this evolutionary state correlates with Neptune, because the root desire now becomes to know and unite with God, or the Creator. The Soul now needs direct contact with the Source. Mere faith and belief is not enough—the Soul now needs proof of the Creator's existence through actual contact, or communion. It is important to understand that in this state of evolution, God will be experienced in his natural form, not defined by consensus religion. Because of this root desire, consciousness progressively expands into the universal and the timeless in such a way that the Soul becomes aware of this living universe within—the wave within the ocean, and the ocean within the wave. Progressively, in this state of evolution, the Soul shifts the center of its consciousness from the ego to the Soul, and the person can simultaneously experience his or her own identity reflected in the ego while being centered in the Soul—the ocean that is aware of the waves it is manifesting.

The Soul contains the memories of all the prior lives it has ever lived, and from this standpoint the Soul can now progressively center in its cosmic identity versus its egocentric identity, as the person aligns with God and his or her own Soul nature. The Soul is aware of its cosmic, eternal identity reflected by the Creator, yet is also aware of the current life and egocentric structure it has created to continue its ongoing evolution. Evolution proceeds, then, in this state as the person shifts the center of their consciousness from the ego to the Soul. Progressively as the Soul evolves through this stage, it becomes consciously aware of God, or the Creator. The consciousness of the person becomes truly universal—the inner experience of the entire universe within one's own consciousness. This awareness allows perception of the very point of creation to manifest within consciousness, or the interface of the unmanifested and the manifested. As this occurs the Soul becomes aware of all the natural laws that govern the existence of Creation itself. In very high degrees of evolution within this state, the Soul is utterly identified with these natural laws in such a way that it can merge with them, and use them in conjunction with God's will, or the will of the Creator.

In the first substage of the Spiritual evolutionary condition, the Soul will progressively realize just how small it is from an egocentric point of view. A good analogy to use to describe this awareness is the grain of sand on the entire beach. Of itself, this awareness has a naturally humbling effect on the Soul, and the current ego (symbolized by the Moon) it has created. This humbling effect promotes the shift of consciousness from the ego to the Soul, and ultimately to a conscious merging with God. The Soul will naturally desire to commit itself to the desire to consciously merge with the Creator, and will devote itself to spiritual practices and forms of work. The work function, itself, will be based upon serving others as a reflection of serving God. In this way, the Creator can be consciously experienced through the person's work. In Eastern terminology this is called Karma Yoga. As a result, many people in this substage will open healing centers, or include healing arts of some nature. The Soul now becomes aware of all its imperfections, faults, and knows what it needs to improve within itself. The danger here is to create an excessively self-critical focus, where the individual feels never ready or good enough to do the work that he or she is being directed to do. In essence, the Soul does not feel worthy of the Creator's love and blessings. This psychology will manifest as excuses or rationalizations that appear like logical arguments in the context of implementing the proper steps to actualize the intended work. The way out of this trap is to realize that the path to perfection is accomplished one step at a time. In this state, the Soul will have an increasing perception of the spiritual or third eye, and will merge with it. In this way, various degrees of cosmic consciousness or realization will be experienced. This is what leads the Soul into the second substage of this evolutionary condition.

The second substage is the most problematic in this state because the center of gravity shifts back and forth from the ego to the Soul like a rubber band. The intention of this is to completely destroy any egocentric attachments and identifications that the Soul has, in the context of the ego identifying with itself as a separate entity. This commonly manifests as spiritual delusions of grandeur, and the individual points to him- or herself as the way to know God, while at the same time denying this behavior. In varying degrees of intensity, the person will manifest the delusion that he or she has some unique toehold on the truth, and is on some special spiritual mission for the salvation of humankind. It is important to add here that, as the Soul desires to know and merge with God, all the impurities and distortions within it will be exposed by the light of the

Creator in order to be purged once and for all. These distortions are always held within the subjective ego that has still identified itself as somehow separate from God. The egocentric identifications of this nature will always lead to the behavior described above, where the individual points to him- or herself, instead of God or the Creator. In the worst forms, this will manifest as types like Rasputin, Bagawan Rajneesh, Claire Prophet, and the like. There will always be some secret egocentric agenda in these types, and they will peddle themselves as the only way to know God. As the Soul evolves through this phase, it learns the nature of this core impurity, and experiences natural guilt. The Soul then uses this guilt to program its own spiritual downfall, or "fall from grace." The downfall, or fall from grace, is created because of the natural guilt, and the need to atone for the guilt. The act of atonement, and purging of this guilt leads the Soul into the third and final spiritual substage.

In the third and final substage of the spiritual state, the center of consciousness is finally and permanently shifted from the ego to the Soul. These individuals have an emphasized desire to purge all separating desires through active service to God. They will experience their individuality as a reflection of the Source, as well as the rest of Creation. These types will have no need for acclaim to their ego, and will emit a very pure, innocent light. The structure of consciousness is totally founded upon giving to others, and there is no ulterior motive or agenda behind it. The Soul knows that it is here on behalf of the Source, and will experience and interpret life in this manner. Others can be drawn to these types like a magnet because of the tremendous wisdom, compassion, and healing energy of the Soul. Conversely, they may attract others who project all kinds of ulterior motives and agendas, and wholesale persecution because the purity of the Soul exposes the distortions and delusions of others. These people will then feel threatened by the individual, because they are invested in others believing in the persona, or false mask, they have created relative to trying to conceal their own darkness, and impurities. The feeling of being threatened causes these types to react in such a way toward the Soul in this substage. In the beginnings of this substage, the work that Soul creates will reach, or the person will be involved with, the local or immediate area of the individual. As the Soul evolves through this phase, the work will progressively expand outward to include the whole world, and these types will be remembered long after their physical passing. This final substage of the spiritual state culminates in the avatar condition. Souls in this evolutionary state are sought by others as gurus. Examples of such Souls include Jesus, Yogananda, Yuketswar, Babaji, and Buddha.

Applying the Evolutionary Conditions in Chart Analysis
Pluto in Different Evolutionary Conditions

Now that we have thoroughly described the evolutionary states, we will apply these principles in brief examples. First, let's take Pluto in Libra/6th house and put it in different evolutionary states. How would Pluto in Libra/6th house operate in the consensus state? Again, we must first understand the core correlations of these archetypes and evolutionary intentions and desires of the past before we can adjust, or incorporate, the evolutionary condition of the Soul. Remember what we have said about the archetype of the 6th house and its correlation with learning humility, self-improvement, and service to society via an inverted pyramid effect. Remember that the Libra archetype correlates with initiating a diversity of relationships with others in order to establish a sense of its own individuality through comparison and contrast. Personal and social balance and equality are learned in this way. Pluto in Libra in the 6th house, then, correlates with a Soul who desires to effect humility, self-purification, and service to whole in the context of relationships. The types of relationships the person forms and the resulting sense of individuality that is generated is based upon this core need to be of service to society, and to effect self-improvement. The need to learn balance and equality has, and will be, approached in this way. These core correlations of Pluto in Libra in the 6th house can now be adjusted to reflect the evolutionary condition of the Soul.

Simply stated, Pluto in Libra in the 6th house operating in the Consensus state will manifest as the person's service to society being mundane work (an example of this is a veterinarian who desires to serve through helping animals, or a doctor, or social worker who helps others).

The individual will identify with this form of work in such a way that he or she could not separate their sense of identity from the work itself. In addition, there will be an intense degree of criticism emanating from this person toward others who do not conform to the consensus in general. The need for self-improvement and an intense degree of inner criticism within the Soul is projected outward onto others in this manner.

There will be an inner existential void within the person, and the Soul will attempt to fill that void with excessive work, and a variety of other avoidance and denial types of activities. This creates the "busy bee" syndrome, and a variety of other avoidance-associated behavior. The relationships that the person forms will then be a reflection of this inner orientation. The need to be needed will be dominant within consciousness, and the individual will attempt to use relationships as yet another way to fill the existential void. Codependencies, imbalances, and extremes of all sorts are created in this way. The person will relate to others primarily through the prism of the outer work function, and social status that is associated with a career or job.

The relationships that the person forms will conform to the consensus viewpoint of what relationships should be like, and what constitutes a good, or healthy relationship. This, of course, does not mean the person is truly happy within the existing relationship. It would not be uncommon, for example, for a person with this natal Pluto to attract a very critical partner, or to be a very critical partner. The person would feel victimized by life, especially in the context of the current relationship. Evolution will proceed as the Soul learns to value the equality of all people, the unique individuality of itself and of others, and perform service to society that truly benefits others, based on this awareness (this is the transition or evolution into the individuated state).

The core desire that propels the Soul in this stage, as described in the beginning of the chapter, is the need to get ahead or on top of society in the context of material possessions and social status. The individual must learn how society works on that bias. In this example, then, the work function and type of relationships that are formed must allow such an evolution to take place. We can adjust these bottom-line associations to reflect any specific substage of the consensus. In all cases, the Soul's relationships and orientation to work and service will simply conform to the consensus model within society.

Pluto in Libra in the 6th house, operating in the lowest substage of the consensus, symbolizes that the form of service will be very mundane in nature, and in the lowest strata of social status. The person does not have the ability to understand issues that pertain outside of his or her immediate environment, and subjective reality.

In the second substage of this condition, the person would desire a work position of higher social status than in the previous state, because of the desire to learn how the system works and to get ahead of the system from that point of view. The need for self-improvement is relative to securing a more socially prominent and higher paying job in order for material wealth to be accumulated.

In the third stage of the consensus, the individual will desire to, and most commonly secure, a job that is at the of the top of the social strata. The service to society will manifest in this way as the person now needs to know what inner improvements he or she needs to make to secure a job of the highest social prominence and keep it.

The person will now be aware of the totality of society, the community, and other countries. The awareness must be developed in order to secure a job of social prominence and to get ahead of, or on top of, the system. The job will most commonly be based upon improving society and the community. A job in which the person helps others secure a job of social prominence would be very likely in this example. The person, progressively, cannot relate to the very career or job function that he or she has actualized, or the relationships that he or she created based on these desires, needs, and orientation. This leads into the individuated state, because the individual can no longer relate to the values, norms, customs, or taboos of the consensus society in general.

Now, let's look at Pluto in Libra in the 6th house in the Individuated state. Generally speaking, in this evolutionary state the work function must reflect the Soul's individuality in some way. The Soul now desires to liberate from past cultural conditioning patterns of the mainstream (Consensus) society. With Pluto in Libra in the 6th house, liberation will occur through the work function, and the relationships that are formed on a personal and social level.

The partner whom the Soul attracts will have to have the same need for liberation and individuation. The partner must support the development and actualization of a unique form of service, free from cultural conditioning. If psychological compensation exists relative to feeling different than the majority, this distortion will manifest as a perpetually undermining activity. The relationships that are formed with others will reflect this inner compensation and undermining activity.

For example, the person could attract a partner who is very critical toward his or her need to develop a unique form of service, and undermine the person's intrinsic individuality. Again, the core dynamic that creates imbalances, extremities, and codependent relationships is the need to be needed, and trying to effect emotional security through attracting a partner who will provide validation for the individual. An identity crisis or confusion will be experienced because of an attempt to define him- or herself through the work function, and the relationships that are established. Victimization must be purged with the realization that inner life reflects outer life. The person must feel secure to express his or her own unique essence and individuality. This individual will most likely criticize him- or herself for feeling and being different, and because he or she cannot conform to the majority of others in society. Again, we can clearly understand what types of partners the person will attract if this self-critical, self-undermining activity is in place.

The need to experiment within relationships, and experience different ways of being in relationships that go outside the mainstream is vital. Experimenting with different forms of service, and unique methods of self-improvement that are symbolic of the Soul's individuality will occur as well. Negatively expressed, the person will use relationships and the work function to fill an existential void. Until the person realizes that only a relationship with the divine can fill this void, all the emotional distortions that have been described will continue. The key in this scenario is to form a relationship with another person of like mind, who is also trying to express his or her own individuality through liberation from the mainstream of society. This type of partner will support the actualization of an individualized form of service to society, and unique methods of self-improvement.

In a negative application of this natal Pluto, the person may be very critical toward others in relationships, and in the consensus who are not developing their own individuality. Positively expressed, the individual will desire to be in relationships based upon mutual coequality and independence rather than codependent partnerships. The desire to be of service to society will allow a truly unique and individualistic expression of service to manifest through the work function (examples of this are those who teach in alternative schools, provide alterative forms of medicine, and psychologists who promote the essential unique identity of all people). These Souls will understand and highly value the equality of all Souls, and their right to express their own unique individuality. The person will be developing the ability to objectify him- or herself through relationships, and the form of service that is performed.

In the first stage of the individuated condition, compensation will most commonly manifest due to insecurities in expressing unique individuality. However, experimentation on how to serve society in the context of expressing individuality, and how to be in a relationship that reflects this same need, will manifest in some manner. The person may inwardly criticize him- or herself for this need, and simply for feeling different than the majority. This will lead to the feeling of "what is wrong with me, why can't I fix myself to conform?" Relationship types that do not support the evolutionary need and intention to liberate from the consensus and express unique individuality will need to be eliminated.

There will be a need to form bonds with like-minded people so security within actualizing individuality can manifest, and compensation can give way. Self-improvement will revolve around purging compensation issues. The person will need to be in an environment where the work function is based upon service to society in the context of helping others express, or allow others to express, their own individuality. Self-objectification, liberation, and deconditioning from the consensus society can take place through the work function and relationships if the individual acts upon the impulse of individuation.

In the second stage of the individuated condition, the Soul's need to express and actualize its unique individuality is at its highest point, or most intense stage. The person's sense of alienation from the consensus has peaked, and the person needs to bond with others of like mind who also feel alienated. Most commonly, however, Souls in this state are on the fringes of society. There is a fear to integrate into society, and anger at those who attempted to act as an authority figure in a negative context, because the individual fears losing his or her individuality.

In this case, these dynamics will be expressed through rebelling or rejecting mundane forms of service, and the traditional ways of being in relationships. The individual's relationships must reflect the intense need to liberate from the mainstream society, and to actualize the unique individuality of the Soul. The person must realize that the fear of loosing his or her individuality through integrating in society is a fear only. The anger at outer authority, deep sense of alienation, and negative rebellion (rebelling just to rebel) will be purged as this realization is integrated. Positively expressed, the person will help others who feel just as alienated themselves, and are working through the same emotional dynamics. The work function will be based upon service to these types.

Pluto in Libra suggests the capacity for counseling work, whatever form that counseling may take. In this evolutionary condition, the counseling would reflect the awareness of individual psychology, and individuality. The Soul could potentially help others who are stuck in compensatory behavior, and fear integrating into society through counseling work of some nature.

In the third stage of the individuated condition, the person now has truly developed a gifted form of service to be used on behalf of others in the consensus society. The person's form of service to society will be founded on the need to help and serve others in the context of helping the consensus evolve. The person has genius capacity, and must use that capacity to benefit others. The individual will express this genius ability through his or her work function, and the knowledge of relationships that the person has attained.

A totally new form of service may be invented, or the person will transform an existing form of work that already exists. The person can objectively understand what needs to be improved within the existing society. The consensus's notion of relationships will be transformed through this individual's insight, and the person has the potential to help others in crisis-oriented relationships. The person now has developed the capacity to objectify him- or herself in a dispassionate and detached manner in order to analyze what must be improved and adjusted. The person can objectively view others in the same way, and help them actualize their own gifts of a unique nature.

In a negative expression, the individual will still attempt to fill the inner void with a unique form of service, or work function, and the relationships that are formed. The person may still be very critical of those in mainstream society, as a reflection of the inner critical focus that has not been resolved. The individual is overly identified with his or her genius capacity, from an egocentric point of view.

Pluto in Libra/6th house operating in the spiritual state will manifest as Soul who has the awareness, or knowledge, that inner life reflects outer life. The Soul will learn that the partner is a reflection of Its own inner reality. However, this knowledge may be resisted. This knowledge will need to be acted upon in the context of finally purging victimization, and creating relationships of mutual co-equality and independence.

In this stage of evolution, the imbalances and extremes will resolve around one partner attempting to play the "spiritual teacher" to the other, and dominating the relationship in this way. The partner being dominated is unconsciously looking for a spiritual teacher type to "save" him or her. In addition, the Soul may be excessively critical of the partner's spiritual development or techniques, and undermine the partner through such criticism (Pluto in the 6th house). Of course, these roles can fluctuate, or change, within the same relationship, or in different relationships. The reason that relationships of this nature will be created is because the need to be needed has not been purged from the Soul. The inner existential void will dissolve as the person merges with God, and learns to have faith in the Divine. The form of service will have to reflect the individual's evolutionary capacity and the desire to be of service to God, or the Creator.

The work function will allow evolution to occur, and self-purification in such a way that the Divine expresses itself through the Soul in the context of the work function. In Eastern spiritual terminology, this is called Karma Yoga. Continual self-purification, and humility will manifest through service of this nature. Relationships will be a vehicle for healing and self-purification. All imbalances, extremes, or inequalities will be purged, and an identity crisis will be eliminated. The individual is now looking inward, not outward, for a personal sense of identity as he or she aligns and merges with the Creator. In this way, the individual has learned to identify and meet his or her own inner needs, and is not dependent on an external partner to satisfy these needs.

An essential point of discrimination that must be learned in this evolutionary stage is whom to serve and whom not to serve. In the context of Pluto in Libra, this will always involve situations where another is unconsciously trying to create a codependent relationship with the individual, and does not truly apply what was given before, yet is still asking for more giving. If the person learns to withhold giving in these situations, true service will be performed. The person must learn to balance the time spent serving others, and time alone to meet his or her own legitimate needs.

The individual must not overly identify with his or her specific work function or spiritual capacities from an egocentric point of view. The Soul will realize that it is just a channel for the divine to flow, and that all capacities come from the Creator. In a negative expression, the Soul will undermine its inherent spiritual capacities, and not fully develop these abilities because of the need for self-punishment. In addition, the Soul needs to discern the proper work function that promotes the actualization of the individual's innate spiritual capacities, and allows personal growth to manifest.

Inner and outer crises will be used to promote, or signify, the awareness of what inner adjustments must be made from within the Soul. As the Soul learns to respond to crisis in a positive way, and to have faith in the Divine, the experience of inner and outer crises will dissolve. Inner peace and tranquility will replace constant anxiety. An excessively negative or critical focus will be eliminated. The person will have tolerance for the mistakes, imperfections, and faults of others. The individual will not project a negative and critical inner attitude onto others, or into the external environment. The relationships that the Soul forms will be based upon equality and balance, and will reflect the natural law of giving, sharing, and inclusion (Pluto in Libra).

In the first stage of the spiritual evolutionary condition Pluto in Libra/ 6th house will manifest as an emphasized desire to purify, improve, serve others, and purge the Soul of all egocentric delusions of grandeur. The work function and form of service will be very devotional in nature. The potential trap is to overly identify with some "spiritual" capacity or talent from an egocentric point of view. This dynamic creates obvious evolutionary blocks. The form of service should be in harmony with the individual's evolutionary and karmic requirements, and natural abilities. Clearly, discrimination is a critical issue relative to the form of service to others and the Creator should take from an evolutionary standpoint.

A potential trap, mentioned previously, is to become so consumed or fixated on the Soul's faults, imperfections, and shortcomings that the individual becomes paralyzed, and is unable to act. The solution to this problem is to create motion in the context of continual action, and to realize that the path to perfection occurs one step at a time. In other words, whatever is being analyzed must be integrated through motion or action. Most commonly, the Soul will undermine his or her own spiritual capacities and gifts. Crises would then be experienced in order for this dynamic to be brought to the full light of day, and the individual could then adjust his or her behavior accordingly. The intense degree of self-analysis symbolized in Pluto in the 6th house will be used positively to create the necessary inner improvements and self-purification as the person learns these evolutionary lessons.

In the second-stage spiritual condition, the need to finally purge all egocentric delusions of grandeur, and any over-identification with the Soul's spiritual capacity and abilities, from an egocentric point of view, is intensified. For example, a dynamic could be created where the individual associates only with others who are perceived as spiritual teachers—fulfilling his or her need to be perceived in this light as well. The Soul will have the distorted need to be seen as a spiritual teacher, and a desire to play the role of the savior, or who can help another heal and fix their faults, shortcomings, and lacks.

The individual could also manifest the opposite extreme; being dominated by someone who represents him- or herself as a spiritual teacher, and a savior, attempting to hook the other person into a codependent relationship. Again, the need to be needed has not fully been purged from the Soul, and manifests in a second stage spiritual state in the ways we have just described. It is important to understand that, in the majority of cases, both extremes manifest as a compensation for deep insecurities that have not been resolved.

These dynamics are most often unconscious, and the individual may truly desire to help, serve, and give to others. We must understand these dynamics in the proper perspective in the context of evolution. As mentioned earlier, all egocentric impurities of this nature can lead to a situation where the individual is pointing to him- or herself as the way to know the Source. There is a distorted need for egocentric acclaim or recognition in some way. The ego will finally be destroyed in the sense of identifying with itself in the context of the individual's work function and spiritual capacities from an egocentric standpoint, if the proper actions are taken to resolve these issues. The natural guilt from acting in this manner will fuel the Soul to serve God and others in a sincere, humble, and selfless manner.

In the third stage spiritual condition the Soul has now completely purged all egocentric identifications with the work and service that it is meant to do on behalf of the Source. The Soul will desire to improve its own capacity in the context of serving God. The potential trap in this evolutionary condition is to never feel that the Soul has a deep-enough capacity to serve God, or the Creator. These types of Souls can never do enough for the Source in the context of service. The Soul will be the essence of humility, and will attract others who may need help in some way. Specifically, this service will revolve around helping others align with their natural work function which will allow these people to be of service to others and the Creator, and to self-improve and self-purify through spiritual development. Helping others practice Karma Yoga will be a deep theme of service in this example. The relationships that are formed on an intimate level will reflect very, very deep healing and giving to one another. Total mutual independence and coequality will manifest, and others will be drawn to the Soul to learn these very same lessons.

Adjusting the Main Evolutionary Karmic Dynamic to Different Evolutionary Conditions

Now that we have looked at the natal Pluto in all the different evolutionary conditions and substages, or stages, of each condition, we can put the main evolutionary/karmic dynamic in different evolutionary conditions and substages. This illustration is intended to aid the student to gain a deep, comprehensive understanding of how to adjust the main evolutionary/karmic dynamic in the birth chart to any evolutionary condition.

Let's use the same example that appeared in the previous chapter to demonstrate the nodal axis and its relationship to Pluto. In that example, Pluto is in the 8th house in Leo, and the South Node is in Pisces in the 3rd house, and the North Node is in Virgo in the 10th house. The planetary ruler of the South Node is Neptune in Libra in the 10th house. The planetary ruler of the North Node is Mercury in Cancer in the 7th house. Pluto's polarity point is Aquarius in the 2nd house. How would this natal signature be expressed by a Soul in the first stage individuated evolutionary state?

The basic underlying dynamics and desires of the 8th house Pluto are, again, the desire to penetrate to the core of the Soul itself, and the Soul's desire nature, motivations, intentions, and the reasons for those motivations and desires. In this way, the 8th house Pluto is penetrating to the core of its own psychology, and the reasons why the Soul is psychologically structured in a specific manner. The Soul desires to transmute and purge all sources of internal points of stagnation and limitations in order to create a metamorphosis beyond such limitations. This is why the 8th house Pluto desires to penetrate to the core of its own psychology, and to the core of the Soul itself.

Relative to Pluto in Leo, this psychological penetration and the inner metamorphosis that it creates has become a part of the creative actualization process. The psychological knowledge that the Soul has attained has been used to creatively actualize the special purpose or destiny that is deeply felt within the Soul. Creative actualization of Soul's special purpose will be linked with Its psychological knowledge and abilities in some way coming into the life. Delusions of grandeur are most often associated with this signature in the context of feeling that the individual's personal psychological orientation and knowledge is better than others who do not share the same psychological orientation. Clearly, there is an overidentification with the Soul's psychological understanding from an egocentric point of view. The delusions of grandeur are, most commonly, due to very deep insecurities within the Soul.

In the first stage of the individuated condition, the psychological knowledge of the Soul will reflect the wisdom that we are all constructed in our own unique and different ways, for different reasons. The individual will realize that no one size fits all in the context of existing psychological explanations and theories of the mainstream, or consensus, society. The Soul will highly value unique and intrinsic individuality, and will naturally desire to align with a psychology that is founded upon this orientation and knowledge. This knowledge will be used to creatively actualize the Soul's special purpose, or destiny. The special purpose will be linked with the psychological understanding of the unique and individualized psychology of the Soul itself.

It was stated earlier, that this phase of evolution correlates with the dynamic of compensation for the Soul's unique individuality, because of feeling different and alienated from the consensus. The individual experiences insecurity because of feeling different from the vast majority in society, and an increasing sense of alienation from society. In this case, if psychological compensation is operative within consciousness, the individual's psychological knowledge of the innate unique individuality of every Soul will not be openly expressed.

The individual will compensate in the context of expressing his or her own individuality by conforming to the socially accepted psychological explanations and orientations of mainstream society. The person will externally conform to explanations and psychological theories of the mainstream, even though he or she cannot truly relate to this psychology. The Soul will secretly investigate and explore psychology and areas of life that are considered taboo (Pluto in the 8th house), and go far beyond the consensus understanding of life in general. The Soul will also desire to bond with others of like mind who are liberating and deconditioning from the conditioning patterns of the consensus society. Thus, the Soul is creating a "living lie" until compensation is purged from the psyche. The evolutionary blocks and limitations that must be overcome are evident.

Creative actualization of the person's special purpose and destiny will manifest in a similar way, and will not truly reflect the individual's true capacity or evolutionary state until compensation gives way. In other words, the Soul will still creatively actualize in a way that is socially acceptable. The Soul's deep insecurities create a distorted need for constant external recognition and validation. This need will reflect itself in the creative actualization process. This, of course, will lead to a situation of inner implosion and frustration as the individual cannot relate to him- or herself through the mainstream psychological explanations, and the way in which the individual is creatively actualizing him- or herself. The true special purpose of the Soul would, thus, not be actualized due to the act of compensation. However, the need to individuate will create tremendous internal and external confrontations as the Soul encounters the limitations that compensation creates, and desires to grow past these limitations in order for evolution to take place (Pluto in Leo in the 8th house).

The South Node in Pisces in the 3rd house correlates with a diversity of facts and information that has and will be collected in order to generate the necessary psychological knowledge symbolized by the 8th house Pluto in Leo. However, typically the individual will only absorb facts and information that supports his or her pre-existing psychological orientation and understanding. The Soul is in the process of culminating an entire cycle of evolution symbolized in the South Node in Pisces. The person must dissolve all mental patterns that are creating stagnation, limitations, and preventing further growth.

The information that is collected will be of a spiritual and transcendent nature (South Node in Pisces). Delusions will be purged from the Soul by aligning with universal laws and truths. In this context, the individual will be aware of information and facts that support the knowledge that everybody has a unique individuality, and is constructed in their own way for their own reasons. No one psychological theory or explanation can be applied to all people. The individual will not be able to relate to any information based on the notion that one size fits all in any way, even if compensation and conformity to such ideas is in place. In other words, the person may not openly take in the information that supports the truth that we are all unique individuals because of insecurities relative to expressing his or her intrinsic individuality. With South Node in Pisces, this information may be taken in on an unconscious, or subconscious, level. At some point in time, the person will desire to take information of this nature, and liberate from conditioning patterns of the mainstream society through collecting information of a transcendent nature.

The individual may be confused as to why he or she cannot relate to the information, facts, and ideas of the mainstream consensus society. Confusion occurs because the Soul is not conscious of the dynamic of compensation for feeling different. Confusion of this nature is symbolized in the South Node in Pisces. The individual will consciously be aware that he or she does feel different, but will not understand why this feeling exists. Again, compensation creates the situation of living a double life, or a living lie, in which the individual will try to appear normal, or like the majority in order to feel secure. The individual will mimic, or try to act like, the majority in society in the context of the type of lifestyle that the Soul creates. However, the individual cannot truly relate to the mainstream reality, and will investigate and explore areas that go way beyond the norms of consensus society.

In this example, the Soul could very easily unconsciously duplicate the mental attitudes and behavior of those in the consensus through osmosis, even if such behavior does not truly reflect the person's actual individuality. The person will not be able to relate to him- or herself inwardly through such mental attitudes, and the sense of confusion and inner meaningless and dissatisfaction will be intense (South Node in Pisces/3rd house). Again, this behavior is not conscious. Thus, the insecurities, conformity, compensation, and repression of the person's true individuality are not conscious (these patterns of behavior become conscious as the individual experiences stagnation, frustration, depression, and wants to change these patterns).

The planetary ruler of the South Node is Neptune in Libra in the 10th house. What type of external reality and career will the person create relative to the psychology of compensation? How is Soul establishing its voice of authority in society in the context of the career? What type of inner conditioning patterns are creating stagnation, frustration, and futility? What extremities are being created in this way? What types of relationships is the person forming, and what its the person's approach to those relationships?

Simply stated, in this evolutionary condition the planetary ruler in the 10th house correlates with conformity to the consensus in the context of establishing the person's voice of authority in society, and the type of career he or she desires to actualize. The career and actualization of authority will be based upon the prevailing mental opinions and attitudes of the consensus, and will lead to the creation of delusions based on susceptibility to such information (south node in Pisces/3rd house, Planetary ruler Neptune in Libra/10th house). Repression and suppression of the intrinsic individuality of the Soul will lead to inner frustration, depression, and futility. The need to purge such conditioning patterns is essential, as well as is the need to take full responsibility for the individual's own actions.

In most cases, the individual will be judging him- or herself for being different, and for not being able to conform to the majority (South Node in the 10th house). This will lead to a state of feeling guilty, simply for being different. Inner judgment will lead to intense patterns of outer judgment of others who do not fit into the majority. Yet, underneath this conditioning, the Soul will feel different, and will desire to be with others who are also different, and who value individuality (Neptune in Libra). The individual will desire to experiment with a variety of ways of being in relationships in order to develop and express his or her own individuality.

Compensation and conformity will lead to extremities, imbalances, and codependent relationships. The core issue or dynamic that creates these problems is the need to be needed. The individual will alternate between attempting to express his or her individuality within the context of a relationship, and then conforming to the dictates of the partner. These dictates will revolve around a partner who demands conformity to his or her expectation of who the individual should be, or who the partner wants the individual to be in order to fulfill some projected needs of the partner.

In this way, authority issues are created in the relationship as the person experiences being dominated by the partner, and then attempts to express his or her own needs and authority within the relationship. This dynamic is based on displaced needs of the individual and the partner which create projected expectations (Neptune in Libra). If such emotional patterns are in place, the person is attracting a partner who is mirror of his or her father in early childhood, or the person who acted as the key authority figure in the individual's early life (Neptune in Libra in the 10th house relative to Pluto in Leo in the 8th house). Such a partner will attempt to control the formation of the person's intellectual and mental development. In the worse case scenarios, the partner will completely dominate the individual, and tell the individual what to think, what not to think, and how to behave in all areas of life. These expectations of the partner will always be founded upon the prevailing consensus notions of what relationships should be like, and the roles of men and women within relationships (Neptune in Libra / 10th house).

The other extreme that could potentially manifest is the person dominating another in the ways described above, and expecting the other to conform to his or her own expectations and displaced needs. The person will attempt to control and shape the development of the other individual's mental orientation, and suffocate the individual in this way (south node in Pisces / 3rd house relative to the planetary ruler Neptune in Libra / 10th house). Again, this behavior will duplicate, or mirror, the behavior of the key authority figure of the individual's early environment. In the first stage individuated condition, this suffocation will be experienced in the context of attracting a partner who demands conformity to the consensus, and does not allow the expression of unique individuality. Another manifestation of this dynamic is attracting a partner who is also compensating for his or her true individuality. Positively expressed, both individuals will become aware of this dynamic and desire to help each other purge the psychological act of compensation from the Soul. Both partners will desire to create a relationship based on mutual giving, sharing, inclusion, and coequality. This occurs as the individual desires to purge the distorted dynamics described above, and grow to greater heights (Pluto in the 8th house).

Pluto's polarity point is Aquarius in the 2nd house. The North node is in Virgo in the 9th house. The planetary ruler of the North Node is Mercury in Cancer in the 7th house. How will evolution proceed in this evolutionary condition? Remember the bottom line, core evolutionary intentions of the polarity point in the 2nd house Pluto in Aquarius. The generalized need to establish self-reliance and self-sufficiency will now be put in the context of being inwardly secure within the person's own unique individuality. The Soul will necessarily have to withdraw from the outer environment in order to internalize consciousness. The individual will learn to identify his or her inner resources—the capacities that can be utilized in order to effect survival on an emotional and physical level. The Soul must identify its own intrinsic resources that reflect some inherent unique capacity that will continue to be developed. Compensation can give way as self-reliance, and actualization of a unique capacity that expresses the Soul's individuality. In addition, the individual will identify his or her own essential needs, and be able to meet those needs totally from within. The individual will identify and experience his or her own inherent essence, or individuality, through a deep internalization process symbolized by the 2nd house polarity point.

These evolutionary intentions of the 2nd house polarity point are the core dynamics that trigger, or induce, the realization of the evolutionary intentions symbolized by the Aquarius polarity point. In other words, the evolutionary requirements of the Aquarian polarity point are learned through 2nd house types of experiences. The generalized needs of the Aquarius polarity point are the need to link the person's special purpose to a socially relevant need, detach from a pyramid reality structure, and develop an objective awareness of the Soul and life in general. In this case, these evolutionary requirements demand that the Soul's unique natural capacities and talents must be linked with a relevant societal need. In other words, these capacities must reflect the Soul's true individuality, and be able to meet a key need of the majority in society in some way. The necessary liberation from past patterns of narcissism, and an objective awareness of the Soul and of others will emerge into consciousness through the process of linking a capacity with a societal need. Detachment from personal problems, and from the immediacy of subjective reality (the pyramid reality structure) will manifest. Egocentric delusions of grandeur could then be objectified and purged from the Soul. The Soul must not overly identify with its unique creative capacities from an egocentric point of view. The individual must realize that his or her inner resources and creativity come from God, or the Creator, and that he or she is just a channel for the Divine.

The North Node in Virgo in the 9th house symbolizes that the lessons of the polarity point of Pluto in Aquarius/2nd house will be learned, or actualized, through the Soul's belief structure. In this case, the individual's specific belief system must allow the expression of his or her own unique individuality, and not conform to mainstream consensus religion in any way. The person will experience a progressive and continual expansion within consciousness as he or she embraces natural laws, and philosophies that are based upon the acceptance and actualization of people's inherent individuality. The beliefs that the Soul aligns with must teach unity in diversity, and that there are many paths that led to the same goal (God). The North Node in Virgo correlates with the beliefs supporting active service to society, learning humility based upon service to others, and the need for self-improvement. Humility is learned through becoming aware of all the areas in which the Soul must improve and adjust, in order for service to take place, and evolution to manifest. Specifically, elimination of all beliefs within the Soul that are not in alignment with natural law must occur. A healthy discrimination will emerge into consciousness as the individual now knows what information to take in, and what information to leave out. This discernment will always be based upon facts and beliefs that reflect natural law, and those that do not. In this way delusions carried over from the past can be eliminated (South Node in Pisces in the 3rd house relative to North Node in Virgo in the 9th house). Victimization must also be eliminated from the Soul. This will occur as the individual accepts the responsibility for compensation, and the life circumstances that were created because of compensatory behavior.

The planetary ruler of the North Node is Mercury in Cancer in the 7th house. This symbolizes that the lessons of the North Node will be actualized through initiating relationships with others who can support mutual independence, and coequality within relationships. The partner will value the person's true individual nature, and both can mutually help the other overcome insecurities relative to expressing their true individuality. Relationships of this nature will serve to purge the extremities, identity confusion, and imbalances of the past. Mercury in Cancer correlates to relationships being formed in the individual's family environment, and with others who are very close to the individual. The individual must develop a positive self-image, and be secure within his or her ideas and thoughts that are unique in nature. These lessons can then be passed down to the individual's children. Internal security will be realized, and reflected through attracting a supportive partner who promotes balance, equality, and mutual independence. True emotional giving and receiving will take place as the individual learns to nurture him- or herself from within in this way. Emotional balance will then manifest through such a relationship, and inner nurturing. In addition, the individual will develop discernment when initiating relationships. This is a critical lesson described in the North Node in Virgo. The dynamics of codependency, imbalances, extremes, and the need to be needed will be eliminated from the Soul as the individual creates relationships of mutual independence, coequality, and true emotional nurturing and giving (Mercury in Cancer in the 7th house).

We can imagine how the natal Pluto, South Node, and its planetary ruler will automatically be reborn to higher levels of expression as the person embraces these evolutionary intentions. The Pluto in Leo/8th house position will now not be psychologically bound by, or dependent upon, constant positive acclaim by others, and the need to be externally acknowledged as special in any way will be purged from the Soul. The individual will not compensate for his or her unique individuality, and will encourage and motivate others to actualize their own unique essence. The Soul will not be dependent on any external source to create transmutation and metamorphosis beyond current limitations. The knowledge of a psychological nature that has been attained can be used to help others creatively actualize in an individualistic and unique manner. The individual will validate him- or herself from within. In this way self-reliance will be developed from within the Soul. The individual will acknowledge the creativity and special nature of others without feeling threatened or insecure. The Soul's special purpose will reflect its true individuality, and will be linked with a relevant societal need. All delusions of grandeur will be purged. Objectivity and detachment from the subjective reality, and a pyramid reality structure will manifest. The individual will be secure within his or her own unique identity. Thus, the Soul will not conform or compensate because of the need for acclaim or acceptance by others in the mainstream society (Pluto's polarity point in Aquarius in the 2nd house). Imagine the transmutation of the Soul's intellectual structure and types of information that will now be absorbed into the psyche. The past cycle of evolution can now be brought to full culmination, and the past cycle of evolution can now take place automatically, as old delusions and psychological limitations of the past are purged, and evolution occurs. Information of a transcendent, spiritual nature that reflects universal truths are the basis of the individual's psychological orientation and creative actualization process (South Node in Pisces in the 3rd house).

The individual's career and relationships will reflect this inner evolution and orientation as compensation and conformity to the consensus society is eliminated (planetary ruler of the South Node Neptune in Libra in the 10th house). Again, the critical factor in this example for the Soul to evolve relative to the evolutionary state is to purge all compensation and conformity patterns from within the Soul, and to feel inwardly secure in order to express unique individuality. This metamorphosis is reached by cooperating with the evolutionary intentions symbolized in the Aquarius in the 2nd house polarity point, the North Node in Virgo in the 9th house, and planetary ruler Mercury in Cancer in the 7th house, in the ways that have just been described in this example. This illustration is meant to demonstrate how to take any birth chart and adjust it to reflect the individual's evolutionary karmic condition, or state.

4

Analyzing the Same Chart in Different Evolutionary Conditions

Now that we have demonstrated how to adjust the main evolution-ary karmic dynamic in the birth chart to reflect the Soul's evolution-ary state, we will analyze the same chart under different evolutionary conditions. These illustrations should help to further clarify and apply the principles of how to interpret any birth chart in any evolutionary condition. These illustrations will reveal how dramatically the Soul's evolutionary condition will alter the interpretation of the same chart. The key to successful chart interpretation is to grasp the core arche-types that are symbolized in the main evolutionary karmic/dynamic, and then adjust these archetypes to the evolutionary state of the Soul.

   In this chapter, we will use the well-known, beloved Master Yoga-nanda to graphically illustrate how the evolutionary condition of the Soul will dramatically alter the interpretation and manifestation of the same natal chart.

   In Yogananda's natal chart, Pluto is in Gemini in the 10th house retro-grade, conjunct Neptune in Gemini in the 10th house retrograde. Pluto is opposing Venus and Mercury in Sagittarius in the 4th house. Yogananda has the South Node in Scorpio in the 3rd house conjunct Uranus, also in Scorpio in the 3rd house. The planetary ruler, then, of the South Node is Pluto, making the aspects already described. Pluto's polarity point is

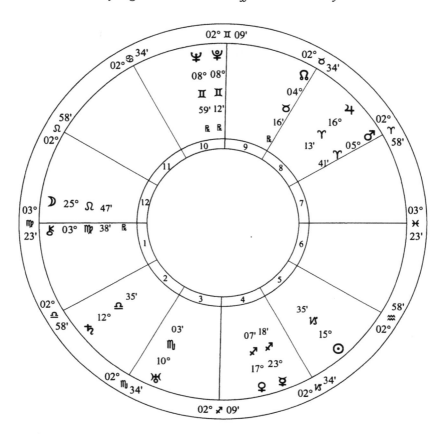

Yogananda—January 5, 1893, 8:46 pm, Gorakhpur, India

in Sagittarius in the 4th house. The North Node is in Taurus in the 9th house. The planetary ruler of the North Node is Venus in Sagittarius in the 4th house, making the aspects already described. He has a grand trine in his natal chart, which is symbolized in Mercury conjunct Venus trine the Moon in Leo in the 12th house, and trine to Jupiter in Aries in the 8th house. A grand trine is a powerful aspect, and will always symbolize that there is an incredible evolutionary growth potential related to the conscious integration and understanding of the evolutionary intentions for the life. The individual has the awareness of the past that lead to the moment, and the potential to further actualize the evolutionary intentions for the future relative to this awareness. The dynamics that will contribute to the birth chart in this way are specific to the areas symbolized by the planets that are forming the grand trine by house and sign locality. Yogananda is a truly God-inspired avatar who helped countless Souls reach the light of God, or the Creator, as he himself had done through his own personal evolution. Many, many people benefited from his presence in this way, and are familiar with his spiritual teachings and writings.

His natal Pluto in Gemini in the 10th house retrograde is conjunct Neptune in Gemini in the 10th house retrograde. The 10th house Pluto correlates with the past desires and intentions of the Soul to establish a voice of authority in society, and purge outdated, crystallized conditioning patterns that are preventing further evolutionary growth. The desire to establish a career or outer work function that reflects this voice of authority demands that the Soul become aware of its intrinsic capacities and abilities, and adhere to the socially required rules, regulations, and laws that will allow that career to manifest positively.

In this case, relative to Yogananda's highly evolved state, Pluto in the 10th house correlates with the position of authority in society that he had in the past, and will continue to have coming into this life. He was, and is, accepted as a voice of authority in the context of spiritual development, and on how to directly know the creator. The center of gravity within his consciousness has permanently shifted from the ego to the Soul, and he has direct communication with the Source. He has a penetrating insight into the nature of cultural/religious conditioning, and how consciousness operates when it has become conditioned in the context of man-made law. Yogananda perceived very clearly the impact that man-made laws and religious doctrines had on any Soul, and how to help any individual realign with natural laws in order to recover his or her natural consciousness. The retrograde placement of Pluto symbolizes that he is repeating this role, or position of authority, from the past into the present moment in time.

Pluto in Gemini correlates with the types of information Yogananda has collected and communicated with others that is based upon his own inner understanding of the timeless, natural, universal laws (Neptune conjunct Pluto) on which his intellectual structure is founded. Again, he was, and still is, accepted as a spiritual authority because he did not desire to have a position of authority for the sake of personal power or authority itself. He was dedicated to helping others to find their own inner voice of authority by aligning with God, or the Creator. Yogananda emphatically taught that only direct perception and experience of the Divine, or the Creator, can promote evolution and spiritual development.

He spent many years in an ashram, a spiritual community, training under his own master, Swami Sri Yuketswar. He also spent many years training other younger disciples in the ashram. Later on he started a school for younger children (Ranchi School) who wanted to start on the spiritual path, and he personally taught those who enrolled (Venus conjunct Mercury in Sagittarius in the 4th house forming the grand trine to the Moon and Jupiter).

This was a school started for young children that was devoted to teaching spiritual as well as educational principles. He started the widely known organization called SRF, or Self-Realization Fellowship. All of these accomplishments demonstrate Yogananda's natural gift of using his voice of authority to inspire others to find their own voice of authority through direct contact with God. *New Frontier* magazine wrote a touching description of Yogananda's impact on those in the West in the book, *Where There Is Light* (Self-Realization Fellowship, 1989): "Unlike any other purveyor of transformative thinking before or since, Yogananda was one of the most respected and accepted Eastern mystics in this country. Perhaps best known for his *Autobiography of a Yogi* (New York: The Philosophical Library, 1946), which has inspired countless millions around the world, Paramahansa Yogananda, like Gandhi, brought spirituality into the mainstream of society."

The spiritual aspect of his voice of authority, or the fact that he is accepted specifically as a spiritual authority, is symbolized by Neptune retrograde conjunct Pluto in Gemini in the 10th house. Both planets are retrograde, which illustrates that he has had this role as a spiritual authority before, and that he is continuing his mission to spread the teachings of the masters to the masses, and help those who are in true need. The placement of Neptune signifies that he very easily saw through the delusions of others, because he had completely purged all delusions of his own in the past. In addition, he has been persecuted in the past by others who were threatened by his purity (Neptune) as well. These types did not want to face their own impurities, and were threatened by the nature of the work Yogananda was dedicated to establishing. He relived this experience in this life (retrograde). One very significant example of this is when he encountered an individual who attempted to turn his followers against him by calling him a "charlatan." Yogananda always pointed the way home, or to God, not himself. This is the easiest way to know who is a true spiritual teacher, and who is not.

The South Node in Scorpio in the 3rd house correlates with his ability to penetrate to the bottom line, or core, of his own intellectual framework, and transmute any limitations within his intellectual structure. He could easily penetrate to the core of how any Soul's intellect was constructed, and the limitations that the person was creating because of his or her intellectual structure. He always taught that God can only be truly known through direct experience and perception (South Node Scorpio). Any information that is absorbed should be directly tested to prove its validity. He warned against mere book learning and memorizing intellectual facts, because it does not teach the important principle of direct inner experience and perception. The point in this is not to rely solely on the words of saints and Masters, but to use books and teachings as helpful aids in spiritual development.

Clearly, he has natural psychological abilities. He was able to detect any Soul's weakest possible psychological dynamic, and suggest the means of metamorphosis beyond those weaknesses. All limitations within his own Soul were purged in the same way (South Node conjunct Uranus in Scorpio in the 3rd house). He had an incredible ability to motivate and inspire others through the sheer power and intensity of his words. Yogananda wrote many books helping others to spiritualize and merge with the Creator, such as *Autobiography of a Yogi*, *The Second Coming of Christ* (Self-Realization Fellowship, current ed. 2008), and *The Divine Romance* (Self-Realization Fellowship, current ed. 2000). His capacity to capture the essence of the human experience and condition with his words, and to empathize with the suffering that is being experienced on this planet, has touched millions of people. Yogananda interviewed many saints and holy people in order to generate the knowledge that he needed, and to write these books. The diversity of facts, information, and viewpoints he collected by interviewing holy people of a diverse nature were used to reflect that the same core spiritual principles of a timeless, universal nature were being expressed by these individuals despite the diversity of their natures. This is symbolized by the South Node in Scorpio in the 3rd house relative to the natal Pluto conjunct Neptune.

Uranus is conjunct the South Node—this correlates with the issue of liberation and deconditioning through the information Yogananda collected, and then communicated to others. It symbolizes that he was spiritually liberated from birth, which means liberated from all delusions, any egocentric identification, and the karmic need to be on Earth. He incarnated only to help humanity on behalf of the Creator. In addition, Uranus conjunct the South Node in Scorpio symbolizes that sudden, traumatic loss through death could have very likely occurred. The death of Yogananda's mother at his young age was a deep source of pain and trauma that he did overcome (Pluto opposing Venus in Sagittarius in the 4th house reiterates this theme as well).

The information that Yogananda shares is meant to help others liberate from their own delusions, and from past limitations that are preventing further growth. In addition, this symbolizes the trauma that he suffered relative to others who did not want to face their own inner delusions and impurities. He received many wounding projections (Uranus) in his lifetime. The persecution and trauma that he suffered will be understood in the perspective that whoever holds a light to dispel the darkness will encounter many, many challenges, but will always emerge victorious. In other words, he was able to remain essentially detached from those who persecuted him and the trauma that he suffered because of his ability to objectively see such behavior for what it is, despite the personal pain to himself (Uranus conjunct the South Node). The planetary ruler of the South Node is Pluto conjunct Neptune in Gemini in the 10th house. This reemphasizes the need to establish his personal voice of authority in society, and the role of spiritual authority that he played through being a guru during his lifetime. He still has this voice of authority today. Yogananda's adamant teachings of direct perception of the validity of any information, and of the Creator is reflected in this planetary ruler as well.

There is a grand trine in Yogananda's natal birth chart. This is a powerful aspect that symbolizes the potential for a totally conscious understanding and integration of the dynamics that are represented by the planets that form this aspect by house and sign locality. The functions within consciousness symbolized by the planets, and how these functions are operating within consciousness reflected by the house and sign position of the planets can then work in a positive manner toward the integration and actualization of the evolutionary intentions for this life.

The grand trine in Yogananda's chart is formed by Venus and Mercury in Sagittarius in the 4th house, his Moon in Leo in the 12th house, and Jupiter in Aries in the 8th house. Simply stated, this correlates to all the trauma and persecution he suffered being used to further motivate himself to continue his spiritual teachings and helping others reach the light of God. He understood the reasons for the trauma and persecution, and the ways to counteract it. Specifically, damage and wounds to his self-image needed to be healed because of the projections from others (Uranus conjunct the south node). This is symbolized by his Venus and Mercury in Sagittarius in the 4th house opposing (throwing off these projections) his Pluto, and forming the trine to the natal Moon (self-image) in Leo in the 12th house. In addition, his relationship with his guru, Swami Sri Yukestwar, and a few others in his personal life that could fully see him and embrace him in the context of Yogananda's evolution served as a way to help heal these wounds. Yogananda writes a loving description of his guru in *Autobiography of a Yogi*, "How lovingly and tirelessly had he labored, that this boy Mukunda someday be transformed into the monk Yogananda" (SRF, 218).

Teaching was another way that Yogananda healed his wounds and created a positive self-image because he was striving to help others do the same. This provided a clear reflection point of his true nature (Venus in Sagittarius in the 4th house). His family environment was very loving and supportive of who he was as a Soul, and what he needed to do in order to fulfill his special destiny. This is reflected in Venus and Mercury in Sagittarius in the 4th house trine his Moon in Leo in the 12th house. He used God, or the Source (Moon in the 12th house) as the primary reflecting point of his true nature (trine Venus in Sagittarius in the 4th house), the way to dissolve the pain of the past, and to heal from the wounds of projections. In this way, he could continue to creatively actualize himself in a way that was in alignment with his true nature, and in alignment with God's will (Moon in Leo in the 12th house).

The trine to Jupiter in Aries in the 8th house correlates with the belief structure that he used to motivate himself to continue the work, and to purge the negative influence and impact of persecution from his psyche. He had the proper interpretation of these events (Jupiter). This positive interpretation of negative events allowed him to overcome any of his own fears that he may have had relative to persecution of the past, and to continue his work, no matter what outer obstacles he encountered (Jupiter in Aries in the 8th house in the context of the grand trine). He stated many times during his life that the only way to overcome fear is to look it in the face, and it will cease to trouble you. Yogananda also spoke against violence, and the negative influence of anger.

These dynamics all correlate with Jupiter in Aries in the 8th house. His belief system did contribute in a positive manner toward the actualization of his evolutionary intentions for this life. This dynamic is symbolized, or reflected, in Jupiter's formation in the grand trine. The main issues Yogananda needed to focus on in his lifetime were specific to his inner relationship with himself (Venus in Sagittarius in the 4th house), the types of inner messages he was giving himself to counteract negative outer messages (Mercury in Sagittarius in the 4th house), and healing his self-image (Moon in Leo in the 12th house, and Venus and Mercury in the 4th house). His belief system and how he interprets the events of his life is a critical dynamic in the context of evolution. Clearly, his belief system created positive evolutionary results. The grand trine, again, symbolizes that he understood these dynamics and was able to overcome them. All these issues described above contributed in a positive manner toward the actualization of his evolutionary intentions.

Pluto's polarity point is Sagittarius in the 4th house. The North Node is in Taurus in the 9th house. The planetary ruler of the South Node is Venus in Sagittarius, making the aspects already described. The generalized evolutionary requirements of the polarity point in the 4th house are learning internal security, and minimizing and thus purging all sources of external emotional dependencies and expectations. In this way emotional conduct and the self-image will be transmuted to higher levels of expression relative to the natal 10th house Pluto. Yogananda had certainly purged all his emotional dependencies and expectations prior to his life, and had learned the lessons of internal emotional security to the deepest possible level. In this case, then, the 4th house polarity point symbolizes the ongoing metamorphosis of his self-image in the context of healing from the persecution, trauma, and wounding projections of the past. In this way, he could continue to be inwardly secure, no matter what outer opposition he encountered. He could continue to give to others the emotional nurturing and warmth they needed.

Yogananda taught others how to nurture themselves first in the ways that they needed, instead of being dependent on others or any external source to provide emotional security. He taught that true inner emotional security can only come from aligning with God, or the Creator, and nurturing ourselves through that relationship. He lived in the United States as his teachings grew in popularity, and he founded Self-Realization Fellowship. He had to leave his family, guru, and his familiar and beloved India to live in the United States. This, obviously, required tremendous internal emotional security. He taught equally the principles and importance of both the Divine Mother and the Divine Father (Pluto's polarity point in the 4th house). Yogananda had reached a state of total integration of both genders within his Soul, or a totally integrated and balanced state of the anima/animus dynamic.

The Sagittarius polarity point reflects his traveling to the West, to the United States, to teach the spiritual principles that India is founded upon. The transmigration of ideas across cultures occurred in this way. Yogananda was directly exposed to the philosophical belief system of the West, and used this knowledge of Western culture and its core belief structure to inspire others along the spiritual path. He incorporated these beliefs in his own teachings and writings, and thus effected an expansion in his own consciousness in the context of including these beliefs in a way that he had not done previously. He had the amazing ability to take a diversity of facts, information, and data, and synthesize this knowledge in such a way as to illustrate a central point or principle of his own teachings, which were always based on natural law. He could create a holistic and comprehensive understanding of many facts and information of a diverse nature by interpreting the information based on natural laws reflected in the teaching of the Masters. Yogananda himself stated that the primary mission of his life was to teach others the divine principles imparted by Jesus, and other spiritual Masters. He encouraged those in the East and the West to combine the wisdom of spirituality, technology, and science into a cohesive body of knowledge.

The North Node in Taurus in the 9th house correlates with his gift of teaching natural laws to others in a very simplified manner. The wisdom that he had was taught through simplifying the main principles of Christ's natural teachings. Of course, these teachings are fully founded upon natural laws. Yogananda helped others become self-reliant, and he motivated others to be their own natural teacher. He advocated that all individuals experience for themselves the truth and wisdom spoken by the Masters, and not to be dependent on the Masters or a "teacher type." The values, and meaning that these core principles are based on became a way for others to effect self-reliance, and to create a positive inner relationship.

Yogananda had already learned the evolutionary lessons of aligning with natural law, and effecting self-reliance, and was now teaching these lessons to others. The symbol of the North Node in this case reflects that he had identified his own natural intrinsic capacity to be a teacher, and to provide simple, yet profound, teachings based upon natural laws and truths. Teaching allowed him to expand his own consciousness (9th house North Node) because he had to identify the core, essential needs of others and incorporate these needs in his teachings. The act of teaching served as a vehicle through which he could expand upon his existing material, because he had direct contact with many individuals who attended his lectures, read his books, and so forth.

Yogananda advocated combining the technological and scientific wisdom of the West with the spiritual wisdom of the East. He was able to take a diversity of facts and discoveries of a scientific nature that validated the spiritual principles of the East. This is another aspect of self-reliance, because it promotes identifying inherent capacities of individual's on a personal and collective level. He cited many scientific professors, spiritual masters, and saints, and research conducted in universities across the globe that supported the central, core principles of his teachings—all founded on natural law.

The planetary ruler of the North Node is Venus in Sagittarius in the 4th house, making the aspects previously described. The 4th house Venus reflects that healing his self-image and those in his personal environment whom he considered family will be the way in which he develops the lessons of the North Node in Taurus in the 9th house. His relationship with his guru provided deep healing for him early in life (he met his guru when he was seventeen years old). Yuketswar had, clearly, reached Yogananda's state of God-realization and evolution. Yuketswar devoted many years to helping Yogananda reach his full potential and evolution through the act of being his guru. This relationship created emotional nurturing on the level that Yogananda needed. His self-image transmuted to higher levels of expression in this way in the context of healing through such a relationship. His loving family environment also provided a deep source of nurturing and emotional healing. His family validated Yogananda's natural ability to teach others, and supported his life direction as he grew in years.

The opposition that Venus and Mercury form to Pluto, again, correlates with his ability to throw off the projections, persecution, and negative messages of the past in the context of his inner relationship and self-image. The opposition also symbolizes the opposition he received from some people in society who were threatened by his purity, and the work he was committed to spreading to the masses. Another aspect of this opposition is when his mother died early in his life. He loved his mother as his dearest friend on earth, and she was totally devoted to nurturing Yogananda's every spiritual inclination. When she died, he was faced with filling the void that his mother's death caused through direct contact with the Divine Mother. He lovingly tried to console others in his family after this event, and his family acted in the same manner. However, the event triggered a divine thirst so intense that he attempted to run away from his home to the Himalayan mountains, in order to become a Christ Yogi. This plot failed, and his family captured him in mid-flight. The members of his family tried to quench Yogananda's spiritual thirst in a variety of ways, such as taking him to meet numerous saints, and permitting him to go on sacred expeditions to other cities in India. Later on, he met his guru, which eliminated the need to escape to the Himalayas. His spiritual needs were met through his relationship with his guru, his direct contact with the Divine Mother, and his relationship with his family. The traumatic event of his mother's death was intended to further motivate and propel Yogananda in his quest for contact with the Divine Mother, for the Creator in general, and to help others merge with God.

We have now interpreted the main evolutionary/karmic dynamic of Yogananda's birth chart relative to his evolutionary state. Again, the intention of this chapter is to illustrate how to adjust the core evolutionary/karmic dynamics in a birth chart to any evolutionary condition of the Soul. A good method to fully illustrate and apply the evolutionary conditions of the Soul is to interpret the same chart in different evolutionary conditions. Now, let's cast Yogananda's natal chart in a lower spiritual evolutionary state, specifically the first-stage spiritual evolutionary condition. How will the evolutionary condition of the Soul alter the expression of the same natal birth chart?

The theme, or underlying desire, in all the substages of the spiritual state is the desire to know, merge, and serve the Creator, or God. In the first stage spiritual evolutionary condition, then, this desire has just begun to be acted upon, or actualized from an evolutionary point of view. The Soul's innate spiritual capacities and talents are being developed and applied on behalf of serving the Source and others. The Soul's form of service to the Creator is devotional in nature. In this case, the core desire to know and merge with the Source will be actualized through the Soul's career, and aligned with timeless, universal principles that allow mental expansion to occur (Pluto in Gemini in the 10th house conjunct Neptune). The Soul will express a personal voice of authority in society by actualizing a career devoted to service to the Source and to others.

In this evolutionary condition, the natal Pluto in Gemini in the 10th house retrograde conjunct Neptune retrograde will correlate with previous cultural/religious conditioning patterns that have not yet been resolved. The person may have unconscious resistance toward submitting to a higher voice of authority relative to integrating into society (Pluto in 10th house retrograde). However, the individual will have a sincere desire to serve others and God through establishing his or her voice of authority in society. Ultimately, this resistance is based on submitting to the Creator's will, which is a higher priority. The dynamic now reflected in resistance to adhering to consistent spiritual development, and the often strict discipline that is required in order for spiritual growth to occur. In addition, the Soul most commonly will have unresolved problems relative to authority figures in both personal and external environments. The critical point here is that the source of this problem is being projected into society, and onto others who are perceived as authority figures.

There is a need and desire to learn emotional maturity by accepting the responsibility for the Soul's own actions, and experiencing the consequences of these actions. Emotional maturity manifests naturally as the Soul accepts responsibility for its own actions. The key to evolution in this case is to find a voice of authority from within, through a relationship and connection with the Source (Pluto conjunct Neptune, both planets retrograde). A natural expression of personal authority will occur through such actions, and active spiritual development.

The individual cannot look outward to society or to a career to provide a voice of authority, as was done in the past. The sense of dissatisfaction relative to overidentification with the career, from an egocentric point of view, and gravitating to past cultural conditioning patterns, is quite intense in this evolutionary state. These dynamics are symbolized by Pluto's retrograde position conjunct Neptune also retrograde in the 10th house. The person could be experiencing a form of divine discontent because of the emphasized need to align with the Source, and transmute these past limitations. The main cause of stagnations and limitations in this case is overidentification with a career or social position, from an egocentric point of view. This dynamic is created because emotional security is linked with the social career, social status, and past conditioning patterns of the nature. These dynamics create blocks toward achieving further evolution.

Positively expressed, the career will be a vehicle through which the Soul can spiritually develop, and can resolve the dynamics that are being relived in the current moment in time. The individual may be repressing or suppressing his or her own true individuality and spiritual capacities because of the need to be accepted by mainstream society. Self-judgment relative to not being able to conform to the majority of society may be blocking evolution. In the context of first-stage spiritual evolutionary condition, judgments will also revolve around not being good enough or pure enough, because of the distorted system of judgment created by man-made religions that demand perfection. This internalized idea then creates judgmental patterns toward others in general.

The dynamic of conditioned guilt, or of learned guilt, is a potential source of stagnation for the Soul, because it has blocked further growth related to the need to purge outdated and crystallized conditioning patterns of the past. In some cases the career that the Soul desires to create is blocked from being actualized because of conditioned guilt. Another type of guilt that is also associated with the 10th house is called acquired guilt. Acquired guilt is based on wrong actions, and the need to take responsibility for those actions in order for change to occur. In all cases, the intention in this evolutionary condition is to dissolve egocentric overidentification with any career, and the social status of that career. The Soul must align with a standard that reflects a natural system of judgment founded on natural law—what is intrinsically right and wrong from an ultimate point of view. Emotional security must come internally, and cannot be linked with any external source.

There is a need to eliminate outdated, crystallized conditioning patterns of the past. Any behavior that is linked with past cultural conditioning patterns that dictate how the Soul must behave from a socially acceptable standpoint must be transmuted. The Soul will certainly have acted to spiritually develop prior to the current life, and this will continue to be the theme of the life. Purging delusions from the Soul, aligning with God, or the Source, and dissolving or culminating an entire cycle of past evolution have been desires and intentions in the past.

The individual must dissolve all barriers that are preventing a direct connection to the Creator. Soul's career or societal role will be a vehicle through which this connection to the Creator can manifest.

The career will be founded upon the theme of service to God, and to others, by helping others establish their own voice of authority. This is symbolized by Pluto's conjunction to Neptune. Pluto and Neptune in Gemini reflect that the career and voice of authority within society will be based upon the Soul's intellectual capacities and knowledge. The information that is collected and applied will reflect around time-less, universal laws, and the need to actualize and establish a personal voice of authority in society. Examples of how this could manifest are through spiritual counseling or therapeutic work of some nature. Past life regression would be a possible career for a person with this natal signature (Pluto conjunct Neptune in the 10th house, South Node in Scorpio in the 3rd house conjunct Uranus).

The career will be linked with the Soul's mental and intellectual capacities and knowledge in this way (Pluto conjunct Neptune in Gemini in the 10th house). Biases, opinions, viewpoints, and any information that is based on past cultural conditioning must be eliminated. Emotional security is linked with the ideas, information, and facts that have already been collected in the past, and the Soul's previous mental organization or structure. The need to defend these viewpoints and facts as right and others as wrong can still be areas of weakness and stagnation in this evolutionary state. Again, the information that the Soul has collected is not necessarily wrong, but it is limited in some manner.

However, the individual will be looking for information of a timeless, universal nature that promotes identification and merging with the Creator. Cultural norms, traditions, laws, and taboos will not provide any lasting meaning at this stage in evolution. The Soul will have a penetrating insight into the nature of cultural conditioning, and how all human beings are impacted by such conditioning. The awareness of how societies and cultures are structured, or organized, is inherent.

The South Node in Scorpio in the 3rd house correlates with an intake of a variety of facts and data from the external environment. This information is collected in order to create a penetration and transmutation of the psychological limitations of the Soul's intellectual organization, and mental structure. Any information, facts, or viewpoints that are based on cultural conditioning must be purged. The individual is looking for information of a psychological nature, which is used to penetrate to the core of any behavioral dynamic. Psychological knowledge then creates the ability to transmute limitations of an intellectual nature. At this stage of evolution, the information that the person absorbs must be founded upon the need to spiritually develop, and merge with the Creator.

There is an absolute need for psychological and intellectual depth that must be fulfilled. In other words, the Soul will perceive information, viewpoints, and facts presented at the consensus level of understanding as superficial and lacking in depth. The information that is collected will naturally be based on the need to actualize a personal voice of authority within society, and to purge all old, outdated, and crystallized behavior, or conditioning patterns of the past. The need to take in information of a timeless, universal nature that promotes natural spiritually versus man-made or patriarchal spirituality is essential. The actualization of the desires and intentions symbolized in the natal position of Pluto will occur through the metamorphosis and transmutation of all the Soul's limitations of an intellectual nature. True service to others and to the Source can manifest as an inner voice of authority is established from within the Soul. The individual's voice of authority can then be integrated into the existing society in a positive manner. The person will have natural psychological abilities, and the capacity to communicate this psychological knowledge to others. This dynamic is reflected in the natal position of Pluto in Gemini conjunct Neptune, relative to the South Node in Scorpio in the 3rd house.

Uranus is conjunct the South Node. This correlates with a need and intention to collect information of a transformative nature that allows deconditioning and liberation from past conditioning patterns to occur. Information of this nature will be founded on the psychology of liberation from cultural conditioning, and the need to decondition from the impact of society in order to express the Soul's true spiritual individuality. Uranus correlates to paradoxes. In this case, the Soul will experience a paradox in the context of the spiritual wisdom that is known on an intellectual level, and when it is not applied on a consistent basis in daily life. Such wisdom must be integrated at an emotional level, in order for evolution to occur (Venus/Mercury in Sagittarius in the 4th house opposing Pluto/Neptune conjunction in Gemini, and the South Node in Scorpio in the 3rd house conjunct Uranus).

The fear of loss, abandonment, and betrayal is a core dynamic that is inhibiting further growth, and must be liberated from in order for evolution to continue. A common problem in the first stage spiritual evolutionary state is the need for consistent spiritual development. Typically, Souls in this evolutionary state will not make a consistent effort to develop spiritually. When this dynamic is operative within the psyche, it reflects resistance to submitting to a higher voice of authority. Clearly, in this case, the higher voice of authority is the Creator's authority. This dynamic must be purged in order for the Soul's true potential to be reached, and spiritual development to continue.

The theme of loss through traumatic events, specifically death, is highly emphasized in this signature (Pluto opposing Venus, South Node in Scorpio conjunct Uranus). In addition, being hooked by words that are presented as spiritual truth, and thus falling prey to fictitious spiritual-teacher types, is a distorted dynamic that must now be purged from the Soul. In intimate relationships, the Soul will attract either silver-tongued-devil types or wounded birds who have no true understanding of the Soul's individuality. At some point in time, the Soul will rebel from such partners (South Node conjunct Uranus) and relationships in order to accomplish the necessary evolutionary requirements for this life. In other cases, the Soul, itself, may take on the persona of the devil or teacher. In all cases, the information that must be absorbed will reflect the natural truth that there is no one way to spiritually develop, to motivate others to liberate from any information that reflects cultural conditioning, and is blocking further growth.

A good example of deconditioning and true liberation through external information is reading books written by spiritual Masters who are devoted to helping others merge with the Creator. These books will include timeless, natural laws of a universal nature that facilitate true healing from past traumas, as well as transformative knowledge that can be applied to deconditioning from past conditioning patterns and express true spiritual individuality (Uranus). The need to express true unique individuality through spiritual development in the context of the type of information that is collected is symbolized by Uranus conjunct the South Node in Scorpio in the 3rd house. The individual will seek to bond with others of like mind. The Soul will gain an objective awareness of itself, and of other people through collecting information of this nature.

A necessary detachment from the mainstream or consensus society has been operative within the Soul coming into the current life. With Uranus conjunct the South Node in Scorpio the Soul will have a very highly developed capacity to stay detached from his or her environment, and to objectify reality. However, this ability may not be acted upon because of resistance to the evolutionary intentions. As mentioned earlier, the fear of loss, abandonment, and betrayal will create stagnation in the context of evolution, and will create dependencies upon the group with which the individual is involved until these fears are resolved. In this case, the Soul will need to have others who share the same spiritual psychology and perceptions in order to feel secure. In other words, the Soul will unconsciously seek out a group of like-minded individuals in order to feel secure, and growth cannot occur. The Soul must develop the attitude of "if I need to be a group of one, then so be it." The individual must understand in an objective way that anyone who is different will be projected on, and has experienced persecution to some degree. This understanding will allow the fears and unresolved trauma of the past to be purged from the Soul.

Unresolved trauma must be overcome in order for evolution to continue. Again, with this natal signature, the previous experiences of traumatic and sudden loss, betrayal, and abandonment are quite intense. The Soul could be projecting these traumas on to others who are in the personal environment, and into the current moment in time in general. The individual is not fully engaged in the emotional body because of the trauma that is unresolved. In other words, the Soul is unconsciously projecting that these traumas are going to occur again in the present, and is not embracing the totality of the emotional body because of the impact of trauma that is unresolved. Negatively expressed, this will manifest as rationalizations of why the individual will not change, or manipulation of the information that the Soul takes in, in order to rationalize some negative characteristic. This information will support the Soul's existing psychological orientation, based on conditioning patterns of the past (Pluto in Gemini in the 10th house retrograde). The individual will stay fundamentally detached and aloof from emotional interaction with others. Rationalizations could very likely manifest in the context of manipulating the others and the social system in order to receive the social status and social recognition linked with the career relative to Pluto in Gemini in the 10th house retrograde.

Positively expressed, the Soul will have a very unique method of serving others through his or her intellectual capacities and psychological knowledge. The individual will motivate others to liberate and decondition from the impact of society. The Soul's inner structure of consciousness will be completely transformed if information of a transcendent (Neptune conjunct Pluto) and transformative nature is consciously applied in life. External reality cannot help but reflect this inner transformation. The Soul will have a penetrating insight into the nature of psychology in the context of cultural/religious conditioning, and the ability to powerfully communicate this knowledge to others. The individual will be able to objectively guide others to actualize and express their own individuality through the type of psychological knowledge that is shared. The South Node conjunct Uranus in Scorpio indicates that growth could occur at a very accelerated pace if the Soul seeks to cooperate with the evolutionary intentions for this life.

The planetary ruler of the South Node is Pluto in Gemini in the 10th house conjunct Neptune, and both planets are retrograde. This re-emphasizes the need to create a metamorphosis of past conditioning patterns, and outdated and crystallized behavior linked with past conditioning patterns. The dynamic of defending the previous viewpoints as right and others as wrong is re-emphasized. There is an intensified need to establish a personal voice of authority within society based on the Soul's spiritual capacities. The individual, generally speaking, actualized the South Node by collecting a diversity of information that revolved around the need to establish a voice of authority in society, and merge with the Creator. Again, timeless universal laws must be the foundation upon which spiritual development and a personal voice of authority within society takes place.

All cultural/religious conditioning patterns, and overidentification with the career or social status from an egocentric point of view must be transmuted. There is also an intensified need for transmutation of the pre-existing intellectual structure and mental organization in order to purge information that is based on cultural/religious conditioning patterns. The retrograde position of these planets correlates with the experience of reliving these specific dynamics in order to resolve them. The need to liberate from mainstream methods of expressing authority in society and intellectual patterns of the consensus society is symbolized by the retrograde position of Pluto and Neptune. In this case, the Soul will have an intensified need to stay detached from the mainstream society, and to allow the necessary expression of the spiritual identity to occur through a career. It can be seen though this signature that the Soul will attempt to willfully assert or prove the spiritual viewpoints and truths that are considered right in a forceful manner (South Node in Scorpio in the 3rd house conjunct Uranus). This dynamic is linked with the need to assert personal authority in a distorted manner because, in the majority of cases, the Soul's individuality and voice of authority has been suppressed/repressed by those in society (Pluto in Gemini in the 10th house conjunct Neptune, both planets retrograde).

The grand trine formed by Venus and Mercury in Sagittarius in the 4th house, the Moon in Leo in the 12th house, and Jupiter in Aries in the 8th house reflects the potential for these specific areas within consciousness symbolized by the planets and their house and sign position to operate in a very positive manner toward the actualization of the evolutionary intentions for this life (symbolized by Pluto's polarity point). The Soul will understand why certain life circumstances are being experienced, and the proper changes can then be made, in order to actualize the current evolutionary intentions. In this stage of evolution, the grand trine will most likely be expressed as an ease of integration of the dynamics reflected in planets that form this aspect (there can be an ease of resistance symbolized in nonstressful aspects if resistance is in place). As described before, generally speaking, the Moon correlates with the self-image, and current egocentric structure of the Soul. Venus correlates with our inner relationship with ourselves, and the external relationships that we attract based on our inner relationship. Mercury correlates with our intellectual structure, the type of information we are collecting, and how we organize that information. Jupiter correlates with our belief system, which then determines how we interpret life itself. Jupiter symbolizes the philosophical, cosmological, or metaphysical meaning that we give to life, and how we understand our connection to the universe in this same context.

Simply stated, the Soul will need to overcome insecurities relative to expressing his or her true spiritual individuality by aligning with natural law (Venus in Sagittarius in the 4th house). The Soul must create a positive self-image and inner relationship by internalizing emotional security, and nurturing him- or herself from within. The relationships that are formed will be positive and supportive of the Soul's growth needs. The nature of both internal and external communication will reflect this positive transformation in the context of the Soul's self-image and inner relationship (Venus conjunct Mercury in Sagittarius in the 4th house, South Node in Scorpio in the 3rd house).

The individual must dissolve any overidentification, from an egocentric point of view, with his or her special purpose linked with a social position. This will be accomplished by creating a positive self-image (Moon in Leo in the 12th house) using God, or the Source, as the primary source of internal security. The Source will be used as a clear reflection point of his or her true spiritual identity. The Soul's beliefs must be aligned with natural law, and allow a continual metamorphosis of limitations to the belief system to occur. With Jupiter in the 8th house, there will be an intense psychoanalysis of the beliefs that the Soul absorbs, and any beliefs that are preventing further growth will be eliminated. The Soul must be free enough to initiate whatever experiences are deemed necessary, in order for continual growth and metamorphosis of the belief system to occur. The individual will desire to eliminate any man-made, conditioned beliefs that are based on mainstream religion, and will require direct perception and proof of the validity of these beliefs. Purging old conditioned beliefs of the past from the psyche permits evolution to manifest. These specific functions and areas within consciousness will be acting in a positive manner in order to actualize the evolutionary intentions for this life if the individual cooperates with his or her evolutionary intentions. In other words, the grand trine reflects that the evolution of the Soul's internal and external relationship (Venus), self-image (Moon), belief structure (Jupiter), and intellectual framework (Mercury) will work together in a positive way to actualize the evolutionary intentions for the life.

Pluto's polarity point in Sagittarius in the 4th house correlates with the evolutionary intentions to learn inner emotional security, and eliminate all forms of external emotional dependencies and expectations. The Soul's self-image and emotional conduct will be reformulated in this way. With this natal signature, it would not be uncommon for the individual to be born into a family where there was an evolutionary discrepancy between him or her and the parent(s) (Venus in the 4th house opposing Pluto, South Node in Scorpio conjunct Uranus). This type of life experience generated essential evolutionary lessons that have just been described because the individual had to learn to meet his or her needs from within.

The individual must reflect on the nature of his or her emotional dynamics, and become aware of how he or she is emotionally constructed and for what reasons. The required reflection (10th house Pluto) generates, or creates, such an awareness. The individual will express his or her personal voice of authority within society in a totally transformed manner. The need for social status will be transmuted through the internalization of emotional security. Emotional security will no longer be linked with the career or outer sociological role, but emotional maturity will manifest as the individual accepts the responsibility in his or her own actions and emotional dynamics. In addition, a very deep aspect of the 4th house polarity point is the integration of the anima/animus, or integration of both genders within the Soul. In this example, the integration of the anima/animus is crucial because of the Soul's evolutionary state.

The polarity point of Sagittarius reflects the evolutionary requirement to expand consciousness to include belief systems founded on natural laws. The Soul must create a holistic interpretation and under-standing of all the facts that have been collected. This can be accom-plished by merging with a comprehensive metaphysical, philosophical, or cosmological system that intuitively resonates with the individual. The realization that truth is relative will occur in this way, and there will no longer be a need to defend the pre-existing viewpoints as right and others as wrong. Relative to the first-stage spiritual evolutionary condi-tion, the Soul will then have a very deep knowledge of a metaphysical, cosmological, and philosophical nature. The Soul must learn that there is a limit to what the empirical mind can know in and of itself. This real-ization is intended to propel the individual toward the development of the intuitive faculty symbolized by Pluto's polarity point in Sagittarius. Again, the information that has been collected is not necessarily wrong, or invalid, but it is limited in some manner. This is why the intellectual structure must be reformulated by learning the evolutionary lessons we have just described.

In other words, the meaning of the polarity point of Sagittarius in this case is to further expand consciousness in a metaphysical, cosmo-logical, or philosophical context by aligning with natural law. By acting in this way, the individual will have an amazing capacity to synthesize a diversity of facts and information into a holistic understanding, or com-prehensive system. The ability to demonstrate how a diversity of facts emanate from a single or central spiritual principle will be unsurpassed. This is the teaching potential symbolized in the Sagittarius polarity point when it is positively expressed. The Soul must be totally honest relative to its own emotional needs. Insecurities within the emotional body, and communicating true emotional needs will be eliminated as the Soul seeks to establish internal emotional security. The lessons symbolized by the 4th house polarity point will be the types of experiences that will occur in order to learn the evolutionary intentions of the Sagittarius polarity point. The individual will now feel emotionally secure within his or her own beliefs and viewpoints. Internal emotional security and the develop-ment of a positive self-image, free from the bindings of repressive cultural conditioning, will create an alignment with natural law. It is because a positive self-image has been created that the Soul will be able to nurture others in the ways that they need.

The North Node in Taurus in the 9th house re-emphasizes the need to align with a specific belief system that is based on natural law, in order to create a holistic interpretation and understanding of all the facts, information, and viewpoints that have been collected from the external environment. Development of the intuition is also re-emphasized. The Soul's belief system, and how the individual is interpreting life is a critical issue from an evolutionary standpoint. The Soul is striving for a lifestyle that is self-reliant, or sufficient in nature, and emotionally honest in the context of intimate relationships specifically. In addition, an objective understanding must manifest that anybody who is different will be persecuted and projected upon in some way (Uranus conjunct the South Node).

The Soul must not interpret these events as something negative about him or herself, or in a negative manner in general. The individual must identify his or her own intrinsic resources in order to effect self-reliance and self-sustainment. Aligning with natural law will create a natural self-reliance, and a positive inner relationship. As the individual aligns with natural law, his or her own inherent capacities and resources that can be used to achieve self-reliance on an emotional and physical level will become apparent. The individual's inner orientation and vibration will be founded upon such a merging with natural laws. The Soul's value system must reflect natural law, and the desire to be of service to others and to the Creator. This individual will have the ability to teach natural laws, and the diversity of information that he or she has collected from the environment, in a simplified manner. By aligning with natural laws and identifying his or her natural capacities to effect self-reliance and sustainment, the evolutionary intentions of Pluto's polarity point can be actualized.

The planetary ruler of the South Node is Venus in Sagittarius in the 4th house conjunct Mercury. These planets are forming an opposition to Pluto. This symbolizes that the Soul's inner relationship with him- or herself is a vital factor to work on in order to reach the evolutionary intentions for this life. The individual must overcome insecurities in the context of expressing his or her natural essence, and the natural laws that are the guiding light of the individual's life. The person must learn to provide internal emotional security and not look outward for any external factor or source to provide emotional security. This lesson will manifest through intimate, personal, and family relationships (Venus in the 4th house).

Emotional honesty, aligning with natural laws, and emotional nurturing through embracing natural laws in a relationship will be vehicles through which the individual can integrate this evolutionary requirement. The person must learn to throw off (opposition) any negative inner messages and inner relationship patterns that are based on a negative self-image, and insecurities in the context of his or her true identity and emotional needs. Most commonly there has been a repression of the Soul's true emotional needs and individuality, symbolized by Pluto in Gemini conjunct Neptune in the 10th house, and both planets being retrograde. The individual has built up a tremendous amount of emotional energy because of such repression, which creates distortions (whatever is repressed becomes distorted). The Soul was not being honest with itself or others relative to the emotional needs that were not being meet (Venus in Sagittarius). There is a deep need for emotional honesty, and to be in an intimate relationship with another who is sensitive to Soul's needs, just as the Soul is sensitive to the partner's needs (Venus in the 4th house). The individual must establish, or create, a personal environment where honest emotional processing and vulnerability can be accessed. By learning these lessons, the evolutionary intentions and needs of the North Node can be actualized.

We have just illustrated how the Soul's evolutionary condition will dramatically impact and alter the interpretation of the same birth chart. We will continue this demonstration by putting this same natal birth chart in the individuated evolutionary condition.

In general, in the individuated evolutionary condition, the natal Pluto in Gemini in the 10th house ℞ conjunct Neptune ℞ will be expressed as the need for the Soul to purge all conformity and compensation dynamics in the context of establishing a voice of authority within society. The Soul cannot conform to the consensus, or mainstream society in establishing a voice of authority, because the Soul is seeking to become an individual free from the conditioning patterns of the consensus. The Soul will now question outer society, and those who claim to be a voice of authority within society. The individual realizes that the answers he or she is looking for must be found within, and cannot be dependent upon any external authority to provide information or viewpoints to answer such questions. The need for social status linked with the career to provide emotional security must also be purged in order for the Soul to transmute conditioning patterns of the past. The information, data, and viewpoints of the consensus can no longer be gravitated to for emotional security reasons. Again, the Soul is now looking for information that is an expression of its unique individuality, and does not attempt to claim that one size fits all for any one. A metamorphosis of the mental and intellectual structure will occur by eliminating all information, opinions, and viewpoints that are based on conditioning patterns of the consensus. A possible career that the Soul would gravitate to in this case would be as a teacher who promotes alternative forms of teachings founded upon the idea that every child has his or her own unique way of learning, and unique individuality that needs to be embraced (Pluto in Gemini in the 10th house opposing Venus/Mercury in Sagittarius in the 4th house grand trine with Jupiter and the Moon, and North Node in the 9th house).

The individual will naturally desire to take in information that reflects his or her need to individuate, and embraces the individual needs and nature of all Souls. With Neptune conjunct Pluto, the desire and intentions of the past are to culminate in an entire cycle of evolution, and to dissolve barriers that are preventing a direct and conscious merging with the Creator. In this case, the individual must dissolve all old patterns of compensation for his or her intrinsic individuality, and conform to the status quo. In so doing, the individual will create a metamorphosis of the current structure of consciousness by purging old, outdated conditioning patterns of this nature.

In the higher substages of the individuated condition, the individual will be able to integrate as an authority figure within society, but will have the ability to stay fundamentally detached from mainstream society. In other words, as the Soul progresses in the individuated evolutionary condition security within expressing individuality becomes ever stronger. In the last substage, or the third substage of this evolutionary condition, the individual is then able to help others become secure in the same way by helping the consensus evolve. This is accomplished through new, ingenious ideas, inventions, and innovative capacities of some nature. In this case, the Soul will have the ability to help the consensus evolve through the social position, and new ideas, thoughts, and communicating knowledge that help others decondition and liberate from the impact of social conditioning (Pluto in Gemini in the 10th house). These viewpoints and ideas will question the nature of societal conditioning in general, and will emphasize that true authority comes from within. Authority is based on the Soul's capacities and abilities, and is not dependent on a social career or position.

Let's put this natal chart in the first substage of the individuated condition, in order to gain a more comprehensive understanding of the principles we have just discussed. In the first stage of the individuated condition, the Soul will need to transmute all compensation dynamics relative to insecurity in expressing individuality. The individual cannot relate to the social conditioning patterns of the mainstream society because of the need for individuation. The Soul will feel different from most others, yet will most likely be judging him or herself for being different, and not being able to conform (Pluto in 10th house retrograde). Yet, the need for individuation and liberation from the consensus demands that the individual experiment to discover new ways of being, and of interpreting and understanding reality, or life itself. In other words, the Soul will take in information, facts, and viewpoints that go way beyond consensus understanding, even if the Soul is judging him- or herself for being different, and the need to individuate. The individual may repress or suppress the need to establish his or her own voice of authority within society for a time, and to collect information of an individualist nature, but at some time this need must and will be acted upon. There is a need for the Soul to take responsibility for its own actions, and mature emotionally.

The Soul will also need to deeply challenge or question the nature of societal authority, especially in the context of social position or status

(South Node in Scorpio in the 3rd house conjunct Uranus). The Soul will come to the realization that a career and social status will not provide emotional security, or a true voice of authority. True authority comes from within, based on a Soul's abilities and talents. Pluto is retrograde, which symbolizes that these dynamics are being relived in order to re-solve them. There is a very intense desire and need to purge all outdated, crystallized patterns of behavior that are linked with conformity to the status quo, and compensation relative to expressing individuality. The Soul will need to actualize a career or social role that allows the expres-sion of his or her true individuality to take place. With Neptune retro-grade conjunct Pluto retrograde, there is an intense and deep desire to dissolve all old conditioning patterns of the past in order to align with the Source, or Creator. The Source can potentially express itself through the individual's career if the proper evolutionary steps are taken in the ways just described. Ultimate meaning has been projected into society in the context of establishing a career, and maintaining social status. Disillusion-ment was experienced in this area in order to induce the awareness of this dynamic, and promote a merging with the Creator. This dynamic must be purged so the individual can see clearly his or her true capacities and talents, and to purge delusions from the Soul in general. The realization must surface that only an identification and merging with God can pro-vide true and lasting ultimate meaning.

The South Node is in Scorpio in the 3rd house conjunct Uranus. The individual will desire to collect a variety of information that revolves around the need to liberate and decondition from the consensus, and to create a penetration of the mental or intellectual structure. Elimination of all conditioned viewpoints, ideas, opinions, biases, and information will occur as action is taken on the need to liberate. All limitations of an intellectual nature will be transmuted as such a metamorphosis is achieved. The Soul will be seeking information of a psychological na-ture that incorporates the individual nature and needs of any person, and does not claim that one size fits all. In the context of Uranus and the correlation to paradoxes, the Soul will create a very secretive inner life that is at odds with its external life. In other words, compensation will create a double life, or living lie, in which the Soul will not openly express the need for individuation. The individual's external life will look like those in the consensus state.

Communication skills and psychological capacities are very well developed relative to the evolutionary condition of the individual. The Soul can communicate the need for liberation, individuation, and the feeling of being different to others as compensation gives way. The individual will be intellectually defensive in the context of the need to defend the pre-existing viewpoints and information as right and others wrong. If the individual perceives that another is attempting to control or restrict the development of intellect, rebellion will occur because of the need to individuate. The need to rebel from external authority will be a dynamic that must be overcome if evolution is to continue. In this case, because of the need to liberate from the mainstream, the Soul will most commonly rebel against anybody or any external agent perceived as an authority, who is attempting to control the individual. Clearly, when rebellion manifests in a negative manner, evolution cannot occur until this dynamic is purged from the Soul.

The Soul will need to stay essentially detached from the influence of mainstream society, especially in the context of his or her peer group, if the group is conforming to the status quo. The individual must understand in an objective way that anybody who is not conforming to the status quo will feel different and alienated from the majority. The ability to detach and objectify reality has been developed, but the individual may have resisted the evolutionary need to decondition, and conformed to the peer group relative to compensation issues (South Node in Scorpio conjunct Uranus). The way to overcome and work through compensation and insecurity issues is to bond with others of like mind, and to adopt the attitude of "if I need to be a group of one, then so be it." The fears and insecurities of being different will subside as the Soul bonds with others of like mind, and can develop an objective attitude toward others who judge and project upon the individual for not conforming.

As mentioned earlier in a previous example, unresolved trauma is a critical factor to overcome in the context of evolution, and embracing the emotional body. It is very likely that the Soul attempted to express or assert his or her true individuality at one point in time, and was ostracized, wounded by judgments, and projections by others in the mainstream society (South Node in Scorpio in the 3rd house, conjunct Uranus relative to Pluto in the 10th house, conjunct Neptune in Gemini). Compensation and conformity then manifested. Inner judgments based on being different were projected outward onto others, and the Soul repressed the need to individuate. The intake of information of a transformative type that is founded on the need to liberate and decondition from societal conditioning is a good way to overcome insecurities and fears.

The planetary ruler of the South Node is Pluto conjunct Neptune in Gemini in the 10th house—again, both planets are retrograde. This re-emphasizes the need to transmute and reformulate the Soul's current structure of consciousness relative to past cultural conditioning patterns. The Soul must create a metamorphosis beyond all limitations based on compensation and conformity to the consensus, mainstream society. The mental or intellectual structure must also be reformulated in the same way. Through the process of challenging outer authority, and society's conditioning patterns in general, the individual will be able to establish a voice of authority from within in a manner that reflects his or her true identity and individuality. It re-emphasizes the need to accept responsibility for the individual's own actions, and to emotionally mature. Emotional security must come from within, and not be linked with the social career or position. All biases, opinions, and information that are based on cultural conditioning must be eliminated. In so doing, an entire cycle of evolution can be brought to culmination, and an alignment or merging with the Creator can manifest. Delusions will be purged from the Soul in this way. The individual will no longer look outward to society to provide the answers that he or she is looking for because of the individuation process that is now underway. Ultimate meaning will be found only by merging with the Creator.

The grand trine will express itself positively if the individual cooperates with the evolutionary intentions. If there is resistance to the necessary growth, then the specific dynamics represented by the planets that form the grand trine will operate as areas of ease of resistance to the necessary changes. However, because this aspect is nonstressful in nature, the individual will understand why negative experiences are manifesting if resistance creates the need for difficult situations to manifest. In this evolutionary condition, the grand trine symbolizes the need for internal security within the Soul's individuality, to create a positive self-image based on internal security, and to learn to nurture his or her own individuality instead of looking for another to provide emotional nurturing (Venus in Sagittarius in the 4th house opposing Pluto). The Soul must create a positive inner relationship by nurturing itself in the ways that are needed. The individual must honestly express and communicate his or her emotional needs in the context of actualizing and establishing individuality (Mercury conjunct Venus).

Emotional dishonesty has been a distorted dynamic of the past that must be overcome in relation to compensation and conformity to the consensus society. This was experienced in intimate relationships, and in close personal relationships. With Venus in the 4th house, the individual's family environment may have reflected this dynamic, and thus the Soul has imprinted, or internalized, this dynamic and brought it into his or her adult life. In intimate relationships specifically, the Soul must allow itself to access or open up to the emotional body and be vulnerable. In this way, repression of the emotional body, and dependency upon the external environment in the context of a career or a partner in a relationship to provide emotional security will be transmuted. The need to align with natural law is emphasized, and to throw off conditioned, man-made beliefs of the past that are creating insecurities, a negative self-image, and inner relationship.

The Soul's creative actualization process must be in alignment with a higher purpose as a reflection of the individual's spiritual development. Egocentric over-identification with the special purpose will begin to dissolve in this way. This includes purging delusions of grandeur that are preventing further growth. The special purpose and destiny must be linked with service to the Creator and reflect the Soul's true individuality (Moon in Leo in the 12th house). With Jupiter in Aries in the 8th house, the Soul must purge all conditioned beliefs (Jupiter) that are creating stagnation, limitations, and nongrowth. The individual will desire to create a penetration of the belief structure in order to transmute limitations based on his or her beliefs. There will be a very deep and intense need for freedom and independence in order to discover what specific philosophy or belief system resonates with the Soul, and allows the expression and actualization of the intrinsic individuality to take place. There will be anger at any restriction of the need to explore and embrace beliefs that allow self-discovery and personal metamorphosis to occur.

Pluto's polarity point is in Sagittarius in the 4th house. The North Node is in Taurus in the 9th house. The planetary ruler of the North Node is Venus in Sagittarius in the 4th house conjunct Mercury. The need to internalize emotional security is a vital evolutionary lesson. The individual must purge the distorted need for social status and a career to provide emotional security. Reflection upon the Soul's emotional structure, and of how the individual is emotionally constructed and for what reasons, is necessary. Emotional conduct, expression, and the self-image will transmute to greater heights if these actions are initiated. The individual will accept responsibility for his or her own actions through reflection, and emotional maturity will manifest. The Soul will seek to establish its inner voice of authority and express this authority in society, not solely through social position or career. In this way, dependency upon the external social environment will be transmuted. Compensation and conformity to the mainstream consensus society will be eliminated from the Soul. Internal security will manifest, and the ability to actualize a career that reflects the Soul's true individuality will be developed.

With Pluto's polarity point in Sagittarius, the need to align with natural law is emphasized. The individual must purge all old, conditioned beliefs from the psyche, and align with a belief system that allows the expression of his or her true individuality to take place. In this way, a holistic picture, or interpretation, of all the diversity of information, facts, and viewpoints that have been collected can manifest. The difference between fact and opinion will be learned, and the individual will know what information to take in and what information to leave out. The need to develop the intuition is also symbolized, and the realization must occur that there is a limit to what the empirically oriented mind can know. There will no longer be any need to defend the preexisting viewpoints, ideas, or facts as right and others as wrong. The difference between a reaction and a response is learned in this way.

The North Node in Taurus in the 9th house re-emphasizes the need to align with natural law, and a belief system that allows a holistic interpretation of all the facts and data that has been collected to occur. Again, the individual's specific belief system must reflect his or her true individuality, and not merely conform to consensus, mainstream religion. The need to developed self-reliance and self-sustainment is symbolized in the North Node in Taurus. The Soul must identify individualist inner capacities and resources in order for survival on an emotional and physical level to occur. Self reliance and self-sustainment is achieved by this process. The Soul's inner relationship must be positive, and founded on alignment with natural laws that allow the expression of individuality. By aligning with natural law, and a belief system that reflects individuality, the Soul's natural capacities and resources will be made evident. Natural teaching abilities are symbolized in this natal signature, as stated earlier. In this case, the individual must feel inwardly secure enough to actualize a career or social role in society that is individualistic in nature (4th house polarity point), and the natural teaching capacities of the Soul could then be established.

The planetary ruler of the North Node is Venus in Sagittarius in the 4th house, making the aspects previously described. The Soul must attract a partner who can nurture its unique individuality, and share honest emotions with the other. In other words, the relationship cannot be based on compensation or conformity to the consensus society, or repress the honest emotional needs of the individual or the partner. Internal security must manifest, and embrace natural laws that promote the development and expression of individuality. The family environment is another key issue to resolve if the emotional dynamics that have already been described have not been worked through. The family environment will either act in a positive and integrated manner toward the Soul's evolutionary growth, or it will be unable to support necessary growth. Both situations can exist in varying degrees of magnitude. In all cases, the unresolved emotional issues from childhood and the family environment must be resolved in order for evolution to occur (Planetary ruler of the

North Node Venus in the 4th house opposing Pluto). In this stage of evolution, the emotional dynamics that need to be resolved are learning to internally nurture the Soul's unique individuality, and honestly express true emotional needs in a relationship.

Now, let's put this same natal birth chart in the consensus state. After we make some generalized statements and analysis of how this chart would be expressed in the consensus state we will put in a specific substage of the consensus. We will use the third substage of this evolutionary condition to demonstrate how to adjust the interpretation of a natal birth chart to reflect a Soul's specific evolutionary condition.

Generally speaking, in the consensus state the natal Pluto in Gemini in the 10th house retrograde will correlate with the desire and intention to learn how the system works, or how society is structured and organized. The Soul will have an intense desire to actualize a career that has a high degree of social status (Pluto in the 10th house). Emotional security is dependent on a social position, and the past behavioral dynamics that are linked with conformity to the mainstream, or status quo of society. There will be a dependency upon external information because the individual is not yet able to think independently outside the confines of his or her society. In this stage of evolution, whatever the prevailing consensus opinions, viewpoints, and accepted information are in the external environment will become the individual's viewpoints (Pluto in Gemini). This conditioned information is the only type of information that is absorbed into the psyche. The dynamic of defending those viewpoints and information as right and others as wrong will be quite intense. Again, the intention is to learn very thoroughly how society is organized, in order to actualize a personal voice of authority within society. At this stage in evolution, a voice of authority will manifest solely through a career. Information will be collected based on the desires and intentions of the 10th house Pluto. The individual will be heavily judgmental toward others who are not conforming to consensus society. It is important to remember, or put this dynamic in perspective, that such judgments most commonly are a reflection of the Soul's inner judgments, which are being projected outward onto others. The individual must learn to take responsibility for his or her own actions, and be emotionally mature. These are dynamics that are being relived in order to resolve them (Pluto retrograde).

With Neptune retrograde conjunct Pluto, an entire cycle of evolution is coming to culmination. The past patterns linked with conformity to the status quo and emotional security based on social position and a career are about to dissolve. The individual must learn to find his or her own voice of authority within society in such a way that it is not dependent on the social career or position. Delusions will be purged from the Soul as an alignment with the Creator is established. Ultimate meaning is being projected into the career and social position. In other words, the Soul desires to establish ultimate meaning in life, yet this need is being projected outward in the ways already described in the context of the natal Pluto in the 10th house. There has been a deep desire to spiritually develop, and dissolve all barriers that are preventing a direct and conscious merging with the Creator. The transcendent impulse symbolized in Neptune has been expressed or acted upon through mainstream religion. Susceptibility to the mainstream consensus religious ideas and viewpoints will be very high. This dynamic is symbolized in Pluto in the 10th house in Gemini conjunct Neptune—both are retrograde. However, at some point in time, disillusionment will occur in the context of the mainstream traditional approach to spirituality, and with all the delusive ideas and notions that such consensus religions promote. Disillusionment is meant to induce the awareness that ultimate meaning can only be found from within through a connection to the Creator. In this evolutionary condition, the experience of disillusionment will also serve to promote the realization that mainstream knowledge and information cannot provide the answers that the Soul is seeking (transition into individuated state).

In the third substage of the consensus evolutionary condition, the Soul will have learned how society (or the system) works, and was organized in the past. The Soul will have this knowledge in the current life. The ability to understand the proper steps and adherence to the rules of society in order to actualize a prominent career is developed. However, there may have been resistance to submitting to society's rules to establish a career symbolized by Pluto retrograde in the 10th house. It is very likely that the Soul has desired a career solely for the social status that it held. There was unconscious resistance to submitting to the authority of society relative to following the proper methods and steps to actualize a career. The Soul must learn self-determination and emotional maturity by accepting the responsibility in his or her own actions in this context.

A career of social prominence and a high degree of social status will have most likely been actualized in the past (Pluto and Neptune retrograde). For example, the individual may have been a very well-known political figure who taught others how the political system was organized, in order that others could achieve this position as well.

The Soul will desire to establish his or her voice of authority within society through a career of this nature again, and will have the ability to actualize a career in the highest social strata. Emotional security is based on the societal career, and the information that he or she has collected from the external world. The need to collect a diversity of information has revolved around the need to establish a voice of authority within society through a career, and learning how the system works in order to do so. The individual can communicate this knowledge to others, and base his or her career on the knowledge of how society is structured.

However, the Soul, at some point in time, will no longer be able to relate to the values, lifestyle, and norms of the consensus at this stage in evolution. This awareness leads to the transition into the individuated state. In this stage, the Soul will exhaust the desire for a prominent social career, social recognition, and the need to conform to the mainstream society in general. A growing dissatisfaction and sense of restriction with the career, viewpoints, and superficial information of the consensus reality will manifest as this evolution takes hold. In other words, the increasing dissatisfaction with the mainstream orientation to life creates a growing sense of alienation from the majority of society, and a sense of restriction and frustration because of the patterns of conformity that have not yet been purged.

The South Node in Scorpio in the 3rd house correlates with the intake of a diversity of information of a psychological nature. The information will be used to penetrate to the core of the intellectual structure. This penetration creates a metamorphosis of the current intellectual structure as limitations of a mental nature are purged. The Soul has desired to collect a diversity of information to generate the knowledge of how society is structured or operated in the past, in order to meet the needs and intentions of the natal Pluto. In other words, the Soul has collected a diversity of facts and information that reflect the need to learn how society operates and is structured, and to actualize a career of social prominence. The individual will know what is required to create a career of this nature, and will continue to use this knowledge in his or her career.

The operative psychology that will manifest in this evolutionary state is the consensus psychological understanding of life and reality in general. This type of psychology asserts the gross generalization that one size fits all. The person will conform to this psychology, and psychoanalyze others based on this type of psychological information. However, there is a growing sense of alienation from this type of lifestyle and orientation to reality in general.

The example that was used to illustrate how the consensus state operates in general will suffice to demonstrate how this birth chart will be expressed in the third substage of the consensus. If a psychologist made a statement that was actually an opinion, the individual would accept this opinion as a fact, and then apply it to all people. The individual will not truly question the psychologist or the opinion that is communicated. A simple example of a widely known opinion that those in the consensus view as a fact is that by actualizing a career of high social status and prominence we are, somehow, now in control of our destiny and future. Clearly, the career itself will not provide emotional security, stability, or growth. These qualities can only be developed from within.

By deeply questioning these types of viewpoints and opinions of the mainstream society, the Soul will grow in higher stages of evolution (South Node in Scorpio in the 3rd house conjunct Uranus). At this stage of evolution, growth occurs as the Soul exhausts the desire for social status, gains acceptance from others by conforming to the mainstream society, and begins to embrace individuality and independent thinking (transition into the individuated state).

With Uranus conjunct the South Node, the need to liberate and de-condition from the status quo will be emerging, and becoming more dominant within the psyche. However, the individual will be suppressing or repressing this need relative to the evolutionary stage (Pluto in the 10th house ℞). There will be a deep fear of being different from the majority, and of communicating and absorbing information that goes beyond the consensus mainstream understanding of life. The sense of alienation and detachment from the consensus is developing within the Soul, yet this creates deep insecurities and fears. The projected attitude of "I am right and others are wrong," relative to the viewpoints, ideas, and information of the mainstream society that the Soul is identified with will be quite intense. The fear of being different could manifest as a compulsive attempt to restrict any departure from the social norms and conditioning patterns of the present moment in time (South Node in Scorpio in the 3rd house). The individual will conform to the existing peer group who are also conforming to the mainstream, consensus society.

The need for metamorphosis will be externalized through the information and viewpoints of society. In other words, the individual will be looking outward for an external source to create the desired transmutation of intellectual limitations. True evolution cannot occur in this way because it must come from within, and cannot be based on conditioned information in the external world. Growth will occur in this stage by guiding others to learn how the system works in a nonmanipulative way. Positively expressed, the Soul will have a penetrating insight into the psychology of the consensus, and how to guide others in the consensus state. Those who have been in this state for a very long time develop the capacity to lead it. The individual will have the capacity to communicate this knowledge in a very direct, bottom-line manner to others. For example, motivation of others to learn and adhere to the proper social steps to actualize a meaningful career, and to establish a voice of authority within society in a nonmanipulative way, could be a positive expression of the South Node and Pluto.

The grand trine of Venus conjunct Mercury in the 4th house in Sagittarius, Jupiter in Aries in the 8th house, and the Moon in Leo in the 12th house will create the potential for a positive integration of the issues described by these planets by house and sign locality, in the context of actualizing the evolutionary intention for this life. The individual must internalize emotional security, and not defend his or her beliefs as right and others as wrong. A negative self-image and inner relationship must be thrown off (Venus opposing Pluto, Venus the planetary ruler of the North Node in Taurus).

Emotional nurturing and emotional honesty can then manifest as the person learns to honestly communicate what his or her needs are within relationships, and give to others in this same way. The individual will no longer feel insecure because he or she cannot relate to the values, beliefs, or norms of the consensus. This will allow the Soul to evolve into the individuated state. Emotional security will not be met through career or any external source in society, and must be established through internal emotional security. Internalization of emotional security, then, will revolve around the need to embrace the growing sense of alienation from the consensus society.

The Moon in Leo in the 12th house correlates with the need to dissolve patterns of overidentification with the special purpose or destiny from an egocentric point of view. The Soul must purge the conditioning patterns that promote the idea one must have a high social title or official degree, such as a doctor, an attorney, a teacher, and so forth, in order to creatively actualize a meaningful purpose in life, and to be emotionally secure. The individual is able to actualize such a career, but must not identify with or define the identity through that career from an egocentric point of view. Again, in the final substage of the consensus state, the individual will experience dissatisfaction and restriction with the career as the desire for social recognition and high social status are exhausted. Delusions of grandeur must be purged (Moon in Leo), and an alignment with the Creator can take place as the Soul seeks to make these necessary changes (Moon in the 12th house). The self-image must be positive, and reflect a connection with the Creator in some manner.

Jupiter in Aries in the 8th house correlates with the need to transmute limitations through the belief system. With Jupiter in Aries, a continual state of becoming will be experienced as a metamorphosis of the belief structure, which is where creating points of stagnation and limitations occurs. At this point in evolution, the beliefs that have been taken in will be based on mainstream religions. When such beliefs create blocks or limitations to growth, they must be purged from the psyche. The individual will desire to evolve through his or her beliefs, and must have freedom to discover beliefs that will create growth in an unrestricted way. The growing sense of alienation from the consensus conditioning patterns creates feelings of inner anger, frustration, and restriction at the beliefs of a conditioned nature that are preventing further growth.

Yet, this dynamic is unconscious, and the individual does not understand why these feelings exist. This leads to a situation of projecting this attitude and anger onto others, perhaps people of a different religious background, who are then incorrectly perceived (projection) as the source of the limitations or blocks. In this case, the religious beliefs must be used positively in the context of metamorphosis and sustaining a commitment to guide others to learn how the system works in a nonmanipulative manner. Individuality and independent voice will be developed through the beliefs, as the transition into the individuated state is made. The individual will understand how to use religious beliefs to grow and motivate him- or herself and others to evolve past current limitations. If the Soul desires to understand these dynamics, then the grand trine will be experienced positively. If these dynamics are resisted relative to the nonstressful nature of the grand trine, then these dynamics will represent areas of stagnation that the Soul must consciously resolve in order to actualize the evolutionary intention for this life.

Pluto's polarity point in Sagittarius in the 4th house symbolizes the evolutionary intentions and lessons to learn internal emotional security, and to eliminate all forms of emotional dependencies and expectations. The Soul must learn why it is emotionally structured, or operates in a specific manner. The need for social status, and emotional security linked with a career must be purged. The Soul will then learn how to integrate into society through a career in a nonmanipulative manner. The growing sense of alienation from the consensus must be embraced and understood in a self-secure context.

For example, in this scenario it is very likely that the individual will have actualized a career of high social status and prominence (Pluto in the 10th house retrograde). Yet, alienation, dissatisfaction, and restriction with the career was experienced because that career was given a tremendous amount of meaning that was ultimately not warranted. When ultimate meaning was not found through the career (Neptune ℞ conjunct Pluto in the 10th house), the resulting sense of alienation, dissatisfaction, and restriction was very intense. The Soul simply tired of this type of orientation to life.

With Pluto's polarity point in Sagittarius, there is a need to embrace a religious belief system that allows all the facts, information, and data that have been collected to be given a holistic interpretation and foundation. This can only occur by aligning with natural law, in whatever form this alignment takes. The intention to merge with a comprehensive metaphysical system, in this case a religious system, that creates a holistic picture and interpretation of all the information and facts guides the Soul into an awareness that the paths to truth are relative. This is the transition into the individuated state. The difference between fact and opinion, and truth versus indoctrination, must be learned.

The North Node in Taurus in the 9th house re-emphasizes the need to align with a religious system that creates a holistic interpretation and understanding of all the facts. The alignment with a religious system of this nature must, again, reflect natural law in some way in order for growth to occur. The issue of interpretation, of how the individual is interpreting his or her life and for what reasons, is a critical point in the context of evolution. If the Soul is interpreting life in such a way that he or she feels that conformity must take place, that anybody who does not conform will be harshly judged and ostracized, than growth cannot continue.

Religious conditioning patterns are a very important issue to address relative to beliefs and the resulting interpretation any of us give to life. If the Soul conforms to man-made religious doctrine, then how is that Soul going to actually experience, or directly perceive, the Source? In this stage of evolution, the belief system must allow proper interpretation of the growing sense of alienation from the consensus. The

North Node in Taurus symbolizes the need to become self-reliant, self-sufficient, and identify the Soul's own inherent resources to effect self-sufficiency. By aligning with beliefs that reflect natural law, a positive inner relationship and self-reliance will manifest. The need to defend beliefs and viewpoints as right and others as wrong will be eliminated if these types of changes are made. The Soul will be able to interpret the increasing sense of alienation and restriction felt by conformity to the consensus society in a positive manner. This positive interpretation will create a naturally self-reliant orientation to life, especially in the context of the approach to actualizing a career and voice of authority in society. The intentions of Pluto's polarity point will be actualized by implementing these necessary lessons symbolized by the North Node.

The planetary ruler is Venus conjunct Mercury in Sagittarius in the 4th house, and opposing Pluto. This re-emphasizes the need to internalize emotional security, and to eliminate all forms of emotional dependencies and expectations. The self-image must be positive, and the Soul's inner relationship must also reflect an inwardly secure, positive self-image. The need to align with natural law in the context of the belief structure is vital. Again, a holistic interpretation of all the facts can manifest as this occurs. All viewpoints, facts, and opinions that are preventing growth can be transmuted (South Node in Scorpio in the 3rd house relative to the evolution of the North Node and its Planetary ruler). The issue of interpretation, of how to interpret the feelings of increasing alienation from the consensus is another critical issue in the context of evolution. The individual must honestly acknowledge these feelings, and attract an intimate partner who is at this evolutionary juncture as well. Honest communication of each other's needs can then manifest. The approach and orientation to relationships will be fundamentally transformed as inner security and a positive self-image are created. The individual will bond with those of like mind (Uranus conjunct the South Node re-expressed through the evolution of the North Node and its planetary ruler).

5

Pluto Aspects from an Evolutionary Point of View

What Do Pluto Aspects Symbolize?

This chapter will demonstrate the main principles and evolutionary intentions of Pluto aspects. This material is taken directly from *Pluto, Volume 1,* and is provided in this book because in-depth case studies of famous individuals will be used to apply the principles of Pluto aspects. When Pluto is in aspect to any planet in the natal chart, it will always symbolize that the Soul is confronting pre-existing patterns of behavior that are creating limitations and blocks, and thus causing points of stagnation in the context of further evolution of the Soul. Planets in aspect to Pluto symbolize that these limitations and blocks caused by such pre-existing patterns of behavior have now come under the evolutionary metamorphic process associated with Pluto. The specific planet(s) that form an aspect to Pluto will correlate with the specific behavior, or area within consciousness, that needs to be transmuted in order for a metamorphosis of the expression of the planetary function is realized. For example, there is a core evolutionary intention for all Souls who have Pluto in aspect to Venus. This transmutation will occur throughout the individual's lifetime.

The specific type of aspect (stressful or nonstressful) will determine how the evolutionary process symbolized by the Pluto aspect will be experienced by the individual. The two types of evolution that have previously been described as cataclysmic and noncataclysmic (uniform) are applied to the nature of the evolutionary processes reflected in Pluto aspects. Cataclysmic evolution correlates to sudden and total transformation, or metamorphosis, of past patterns of compulsive behavior that are preventing growth. This is why cataclysmic evolution is associated with stressful, emotionally intense life events. In some cases, traumatic events will occur in order to enforce necessary evolutionary changes. Uniform, or noncataclysmic, evolution manifests as smooth and gradual, yet constantly changing. Pluto aspects that are stressful will manifest as cataclysmic evolution, and the nonstressful Pluto aspects will manifest as uniform, or noncataclysmic evolution. Another important point to remember as we discuss Pluto aspects, is that the Soul's evolution is a commonly unconscious process in most people. As such, the process described in Pluto aspects will not be conscious in most individuals. As counselors we can help clients understand the causes of their blocks, limitations, and sources of stagnation through our knowledge of pre-existing patterns of compulsive behavior that are inhibiting further growth, symbolized by the natal position of Pluto, and aspects that Pluto is making to other planets.

The number of Pluto aspects in any chart will determine the individual's evolutionary pace (the type of aspect does not matter). People who have a high number of Pluto aspects in their natal chart typically have more metamorphic events in their lives than those who have few or no aspects to Pluto. The reason why these unique life circumstances occur is this: Those individuals who have numerous aspects to Pluto desire to confront, transmute, and evolve past current pre-existing limitations within the Soul in an accelerated way. As a result, a metamorphosis of old patterns of behavior into new patterns free from the limitations of the past occurs in an accelerated manner. These people desire to get on with it, so to speak. This, commonly, is a reflection of the individual's desire to return to the Source, even though many individuals will not understand metamorphic events in this light. Those people who have only a few aspects to Pluto are taking a break from the evolutionary pressures symbolized by Pluto.

In addition, we must remember that we cannot analyze a birth chart by isolating one factor alone, and must look at the total birth chart and other mitigating factors to correctly understand the birth chart. Such mitigating factors are a person's natural evolutionary condition, and cultural/religious conditioning. In addition, we must interpret Pluto aspects in the context of the main evolutionary/karmic dynamic described in the birth chart (Pluto, SN, planetary ruler, Pluto's polarity point, NN, and its planetary ruler). The general statements we can make regarding the number of aspects to Pluto are helpful, as they give us a starting point to understand the individual's total birth chart in the context of determining the evolutionary pace, and his or her probable life experiences relative to the evolutionary pace. The specific areas within consciousness that have come under the evolutionary process of Pluto are symbolized by Pluto's natal position in the birth chart (house and sign locality), and the planet(s) by house and sign position that are in aspect to Pluto.

A vital point to include in our understanding of Pluto aspects is that it is our own response to our evolutionary growth requirements that will determine how we experience any Pluto aspect. Our response is based upon our own attitude and orientation to life itself, which is a reflection of our beliefs and values. For example, an individual who interprets change as positive and necessary would not interpret a stressful aspect as stress at all. The experiences that correlate with a stressful aspect would be no less difficult or intense. However, because of the individual's attitude and approach to life in general, the events would be experienced and applied positively. An individual who interprets change in a threatening and negative manner will tend to resist the necessary changes that must be made in the context of evolution. Pluto aspects will then be experienced in a negative manner because of such resistance. This principle is reflected in the two antithetical desires within the Soul relative to the dynamics of cooperation and resistance with the evolutionary intentions for the life.

As such, the four main ways Pluto affects the Soul's evolution, and the three main responses to evolutionary growth are directly related to the manifestation of the evolution symbolized by Pluto aspects. The three main responses to our evolutionary growth requirements described previously are: 1) to totally resist the evolutionary intentions for the life; 2) to change in some ways, and not in others; 3) to totally embrace and cooperate with the evolutionary intentions in a nonresistant manner. The first response reflects a desire to remain separate from the Source, and is not a common response. The second response reflects the desire to return to the Source, and unfortunately is not a common response. The third response is the most common response, and is a reflection of both desires (we change a little each lifetime).

The specific type of aspect that is described as stressful or nonstressful will determine the nature of the evolutionary process symbolized by Pluto aspects. Stressful aspects correlate with an intensified evolutionary desire, or pressure, to transmute and reformulate past patterns of compulsive behavior that are blocking further growth into new patterns of behavior that promote evolution. There commonly is a lack of understanding of the nature of the specific pre-existing patterns of behavior symbolized by the Pluto aspect. The old patterns of behavior that are creating blocks toward further evolution are often forcibly removed, or reformulated, with or without the individual's cooperation. The inner emotional state of stressful aspects can be compared to lava beneath a volcano because of the intense evolutionary pressure, or force at work to transmute old patterns of behavior into new ones. In some cases, these aspects can correlate with areas where individuals have negative karma that must be resolved in this life. Many of these individuals will not understand the causes of cataclysmic events in their life in this way, and so the potential for further manipulation (Pluto) and resistance to accepting responsibility for their own actions is great.

The cyclic metamorphosis of old behavioral patterns is experienced as periodic restful states and cataclysmic states. Cataclysmic states can manifest internally as intense degrees of emotional stagnation, frustration, and compression as the limitations of the pre-existing patterns of behavior are reached, and the individual does not know why these feelings are being experienced. The individual now desires to create a metamorphosis of those patterns so new ones can be born, or emerge within consciousness. These states can also manifest as cataclysmic, or traumatic, events. The individual does not know why the cataclysmic event or change is occurring until after the event itself. Restful states occur either after a cataclysmic event, or when the source of stagnation and limitations has been uncovered through intense concentration and reflection. The Soul can now instigate the proper behavioral changes in order to facilitate evolution. When a cataclysmic event has occurred, the restful state manifests as the individual reflects upon the event itself and the changes that he or she has made. The reasons why, or the behavioral patterns that necessitated the event, will then be understood.

The conflict within the stressful aspects is the evolutionary intention to confront and transmute pre-existing patterns of behavior that are preventing further growth, and the desire to maintain the past, or the old patterns of behavior that are relied upon because they constitute unconscious emotional security. The degree of stress, or difficulty, that an individual experiences is in direct proportion to the degree of resistance toward his or her evolutionary and karmic requirements to evolve past the compulsive patterns of behavior symbolized by the Pluto aspect. When any of us approach life in the same way over and over again it leads into compulsions (Pluto). The evolutionary need is to purge and evolve beyond these emotional/psychological limitations, and the creation of compulsions based on unconscious emotional security factors. Stressful aspects to Pluto, again, correlate to an intensified evolutionary desire and intention to purge compulsive patterns of behavior that are preventing further growth.

The nonstressful aspects to Pluto correlate with a general understanding, and an ease of integration of the required metamorphosis described by Pluto aspects. Typically, there has been partial resolution of the evolutionary need to transmute compulsive behavioral patterns, and an understanding of the metamorphic process itself. There will be a smooth, progressive, yet constant evolution of the planetary function that is in aspect to Pluto (nonstressful, or uniform, evolution). However, these generalized rules cannot be applied in all cases. Nonstressful aspects can manifest negatively as an *ease of resistance* to the necessary changes relative to the two coexisting desires in the Soul. In contrast to the stressful aspects there is a decreased feeling of pressure (desire), or a lack of stress, to change and evolve. If an individual resists the necessary evolution and metamorphosis of Pluto aspects then the nonstressful aspect will be experienced in a negative way, and potentially as very stressful life events. In fact, if resistance is maintained, a cataclysmic event may occur at some point in order to enforce the necessary changes (these aspects can turn stressful in this life through transit and progression, or in a life to come). The key difference in the nonstressful aspects in comparison to stressful aspects is that even as the individual is resisting the growth, he or she will understand why certain life circumstances, or events, are occurring, and why a traumatic event or inner stressful state is experienced. The individual may not like that understanding, but it will be in place. Positively expressed, these types of aspects can manifest as a smooth and continual evolution of the pre-existing patterns of behavior that are blocking growth. The proper changes will be made as they are needed, and the individual will understand why those changes must be made.

Another factor to incorporate to arrive at a total understanding of how Pluto aspects operate, and are experienced by an individual, is the relative age (old or new) of the aspect. To determine the age of the aspect we start from Pluto itself and move in a counterclockwise motion. The only exception to this is the Sun. Generally speaking, we use a 10-degree orb for Pluto aspects. Thus, a Pluto aspect can occur 5 degrees before the exact aspect, and 5 degrees after an exact aspect. If the aspect has not yet reached an exact aspect (or degree), then it is relatively new (the farther away from the exact aspect the newer it is). A new aspect symbolizes that a brand-new evolutionary cycle has just begun, and that the evolutionary impulse of the Pluto aspect is relatively new. If the aspect has progressed beyond an exact aspect, then it is relatively old (the farther away from the exact aspect, the older it is). An older aspect symbolizes that the evolutionary cycle and evolutionary impulse of the Pluto aspect is in a culminating phase. The specific area of metamorphosis has been acted on prior to the current life and is now being brought to culmination. We can imagine how this factor will dramatically impact how a Pluto aspect is experienced by an individual. The common analogy to describe how this progression works is buying a pair of pants. At first they are uncomfortable, but over time they become comfortable because we are used to them. If a Pluto aspect is stressful and in its early stages of development (the evolutionary impulse is new), then my ability to understand and integrate the evolutionary impulse is not as developed as an individual who has the same Pluto aspect in its later degrees. This information can be incredibly helpful in counseling work, because it allows us to understand the person's actual inner experience in an objective way, and suggest the proper steps for change.

The Evolutionary Intentions of Pluto's Planetary Aspects

We will now describe the core evolutionary intentions of Pluto in aspect to each planet. We must first understand the planetary archetype, or the meaning of each planet, in order to understand what specific areas within consciousness have come under the metamorphic process of Pluto. Again, we must incorporate the individual's natural evolutionary condition, cultural/religious conditioning, and the main karmic/evolutionary dynamic of the birth chart in order to accurately interpret any Pluto aspect. The core underlying intentions and correlations of Pluto aspects can be adjusted to reflect the necessary mitigating factors.

Mars

This planet correlates with the subjective and conscious desire nature of the Soul. These desires emanate from Pluto, or the Soul, and are transmitted to Mars. This is why Mars is the lower octave of Pluto. (A lower octave is a denser expression of a higher vibration.) Mars is the planetary ruler of Aries. The two coexisting desires of the Soul are now intensely felt because of the aspect to Pluto, and the resulting need to transmute personal limitations reflected in dual desires within the Soul that are transmitted to Mars. The house and sign position of natal Mars and the aspects it makes to other planets symbolize the nature of the

Soul's conscious desires, and how the desires associated with the natal Pluto will be consciously and instinctually acted upon. Mars symbolizes the desire to discover or recover our distinct identity. A brand-new cycle of evolutionary becoming is initiated, and the process of self-discovery demands an essential freedom and independence to become what we must become from an evolutionary/karmic point of view. The Soul will learn on an action/reaction level because the evolutionary impulse is operating instinctually (Mars).

When Pluto aspects Mars, the evolutionary impulse requires a metamorphosis of the process of action upon the Soul's conscious, subjective desires. Unchecked, egocentric expression must be purged from the Soul (of course, there are varying degrees of this type of behavior). All separating desires must be actively transmuted. All individuals with this aspect will have an intensified need to transmute pre-existing inner limitations linked with his or her desire nature. These Souls will typically resent any restrictions (inner or outer) that are placed upon them to grow, and express the identity. Mars correlates to anger relative to this dynamic. Thus, unresolved anger must be purged from the Soul in order for evolution to occur. Anger must be used for a constructive purpose, not destructive. There is a capacity for total self-generation as well as self-destruction. These dynamics most typically operate on a cyclic basis.

The key to channeling the tremendous amount of raw and powerful energy that is inherent within this aspect is to commit to personal goals that are relevant to the individual's growth and development. In a negative application of this aspect, the Soul will act upon, or follow, one desire after the next, with no real conscious awareness of why he or she is acting in this way. A depletion of personal energy and loss of perspective of the identity will occur until the commitment to personal goals and growth is made. Another critical point in achieving a positive expression of Mars/Pluto aspects is that the Soul understands the source of limitations emanating totally from within, and does not project anger at others who are perceived as the source of the limitations. The need to confront and transmute limitations and express personal identity has created an evolutionary situation wherein the Soul has experienced domination, and/or has dominated others. In the case of an individual who has been dominated, a very intense anger at the person who attempted to dominate him or her will build until the proper actions are taken to resolve this condition. In the case of an individual who has been dominating others, egocentric shocks will occur as the other person asserts his or her own will, not allowing such domination to take place. Hopefully, through such shocks, the necessary changes can then be made.

If the Pluto/Mars aspect is stressful in nature, then it tends to indicate that this process will manifest in a cataclysmic nature, and stressful events will most likely occur in order to enforce the necessary lessons. If the aspect is nonstressful in nature, the individual will most likely be able to easily integrate these evolutionary lessons because of the conscious awareness of the necessary changes that he or she must make. Nonstressful aspects can promote an ease of resistance to the necessary changes, even though there is an understanding of what must be changed. Again, we cannot make an analysis based on an isolated factor alone, and must take into consideration the other mitigating factors that have been described previously.

In all cases, Pluto in aspect to Mars symbolizes that the subjective and conscious desires of the Soul must now be brought into harmony or alignment with the Soul's evolutionary requirements. The deepest challenge in this aspect is to conform or harmonize the personal will with a higher will, or the Creator's will. Acting on and sustaining the separating desires of the Soul leads to negative and degenerative experiences. Consistently acting on separating desires creates stagnation, because of the limitations this behavior creates relative to personal development and depletion of personal energy. The need to take responsibility for the Soul's desires and actions is strongly emphasized in this aspect. In a vast majority of cases, this lesson has not been learned in the past. The impulse for self-discovery and independence needs to be acted upon in a new way, in order for a brand-new cycle of evolutionary becoming to take hold. Again, personal development and the use of the will must be in alignment with the Soul's overall evolutionary needs and requirements. This allows a merging of the personal will and a higher will (Creator's will). The desires of the Soul will be acted out in a new way relative to this change, and transmutation of the limitations of the past. Individuality (or the personal identity) can form in a new way, and the need for freedom and independence will be realized positively. Anger will be used constructively—the intense amount of raw energy that is inherent within this Pluto aspect can be used to create a personal reality that is in alignment with the Soul's evolutionary intentions.

Venus

This planet correlates our inner relationship with ourselves, and the nature of the relationships we form with others based on our inner relationship. Venus has a corulership of Taurus and Libra. Libra reflects the outer nature (projected side) of Venus, and Taurus reflects the inner nature of Venus. Thus Pluto/Venus aspects symbolize that pre-existing patterns relative to our inner relationship, and the external relationships that we form have come under evolutionary transmutation, or metamorphosis. Most commonly, these Souls have not learned how to be self-reliant, especially in the context of an existing relationship. Venus correlates to expectations that we have in relationships, which then create projected needs. The evolutionary requirement is to meet these needs from within. These projected needs create a codependent orientation in relationships. As a consequence, many of these individuals are deluded into thinking that the meaning he or she is looking for is embodied in another person, or the existing partner. It should be clear that relationship structures based on mutual codependencies are causing evolutionary limitations and blocks. As a result of projected needs and expectations in relationships, the phenomenon of conditional love and giving occurs.

The core dynamic that creates the extremities in relationships and personal behavior symbolized by Venus is the need to be needed (Libra symbolizes the need to be needed), and expecting that projected needs will be fulfilled by a partner. Being in emotional control, or being controlled in relationships, must be transmuted in order to create relationships of equality, and mutual independence. A critical issue to address with Pluto/Venus aspects is how we can truly love, value, and give to another if we cannot love, value, and give to ourselves? In addition, overt or covert manipulation of the individual or by the individual with the Pluto/Venus aspect typically occurs in order to have these expectations and projected needs fulfilled. In the evolutionary past, and most commonly in current relationships, intense emotional scenes and conflicts have occurred when these expectations have not been fulfilled, including leaving or being left. In the worst extremes, emotional abuse has occurred in varying degrees of magnitude. Emotional abuse may have been experienced by the individual, or the individual may have been the abuser.

It is essential that these Souls learn to identify their own needs in a relationship, and stop looking for another person to supply or meet those needs. In addition, the need to identify one's own internal resources in order to effect survival (Taurus correlates with the survival instinct) on an emotional and physical level is symbolized by Pluto/Venus aspects. The issue of self-reliance is re-emphasized in this need. Our own values and inner orientation to life is a reflection of what we give meaning to in life, in general. As such, a metamorphosis of the Soul's values, and resulting meaning in life must occur. Specifically, any values and inner orientation that promote dependencies upon others, and are materially based, must be purged from the Soul. Typically, individuals have adopted the values of the prevailing consensus, and are with the current partner because of the need to be needed. In other cases, the individual will compensate for his or her values that are not in conformity with the values of the consensus. The worst extreme that can be reached is when the Soul becomes a vicarious extension, or an alter ego, of another. The individual is completely dominated by another. Another extreme is a person who imposes his or her values, meanings, and needs onto his or her partner. The individual expects the partner to be an alter-ego of him- or herself. Total emotional/psychological control and domination from the standpoint of emotional control is the result of this orientation.

In order to change our external relationship patterns, we must first change our own inner vibration and inner relationship. When these inner limitations and pre-existing patterns of behavior are transmuted, new relationship types based on unconditional love and a new inner relationship of this nature can manifest. These people are now free from the limitations of the past, and will be in healthy, positive relationships. The house and sign of Venus and Pluto will describe the specific areas of metamorphosis that must occur relative to the correlations of each planet.

Mercury

This planet correlates with our intellectual structure, or framework, and how we mentally organize the information we take in from the external environment The manner in which we communicate is reflected in this planet as well. Mercury has a corulership of Virgo and Gemini. Gemini reflects the outward process of collecting facts, information, and data, as well as our intellectual/mental structure, itself. The way in which we communicate this knowledge to others correlates with Gemini. Virgo reflects our inward mental processing, analysis, and organization of collected information. The information we take in via the Gemini function is organized, or put into different compartments, via the Virgo function. Both of these mental processes, then, are contained within Mercury relative to its corulership. The essential point is that the mental organization process that is symbolized in Mercury is based on our own pre-existing notions of what we believe is true or false. In other words, our own beliefs create a filter that determines the nature of our intellectual structure. These pre-existing ideas of what is true and not true will influence what information we take in and what information we do not.

When Pluto aspects Mercury, pre-existing opinions and biases that are creating stagnation and blocks to further evolution must be transmuted. Rigid and fixed patterns of intellectual organization, and the resulting mental structure, must undergo a metamorphosis. Emotional security is linked with the intellectual framework and organization within the Soul. It is not that the information and points of view of these individuals are wrong, but they are limited in some manner. Again, this is based on the pre-existing notions, or ideas, of what is true and what is false, relative to our belief system. All Souls who have Pluto in aspect to Mercury have the inherent capacity to penetrate to the bottom line of any intellectual system. These individuals have a highly developed ability to mentally concentrate, or focus.

There are two potentially extreme forms of behavior that can manifest in individuals who have Pluto/Mercury aspects. The first extreme is being open to any intellectual thought, system, or ideas that are in the environment. This is a reflection of the Gemini archetype and its need to collect a diversity of facts, information, and data from the external environment. In this open-type condition, there is an intense desire for the intake of diverse information, yet the information is not truly assimilated. The individual does not have a formed, or developed, intellectual foundation. Thus, these individuals have not learned to discriminate between what information to take in and what to leave out. In many cases, these types will argue the validity of a variety of points of view, even when those viewpoints are contradictory. In other words, the Soul will always argue the validity of the other point of view when challenged. This type of intellectual structure creates a clear limitation from an evolutionary standpoint. These limitations are experienced as the revolving doors of perspectives created by the Soul. There is a need for intellectual grounding and a foundation to form that will allow a cohesion of differing intellectual systems to be achieved. All other ideas and facts in the environment can be referred to this cohesive intellectual system. A healthy discrimination will manifest in knowing what information is based on opinions and biases, and what is based on actual truth and facts. This discrimination is vital for all those with Pluto/Mercury aspects. The individual should adopt the attitude that the specific intellectual system of organization works for him or her without imposing it on another, or claiming it is the only valid system—this would create an intellectually closed type of individual.

The second manifestation of Pluto/Mercury aspects is the intellectually closed type of Soul. This condition describes individuals who have rigid and fixed intellectual structures based on pre-existing opinions and ideas. Any information that does not reflect the Soul's pre-existing beliefs will not penetrate. These types will argue that their own viewpoints are the only legitimate ones, and all others who disagree will be considered wrong. The point in this condition is that this black and white intellectual structure has created obvious evolutionary limitations that now need to be transmuted. The individual's viewpoints are not necessarily wrong, but limited because of the rigidity of the intellectual structure. These individuals need to embrace other points of view and intellectual systems, and merge with them in such a way that the existing intellectual framework is expanded. Internal and external intellectual confrontations commonly ensue to enforce the necessary changes. Once the proper transmutation of the black and white intellectual organization occurs, these types can validate the legitimacy of others' points of view and adapt or incorporate it into their own mental framework as necessary.

There can be, of course, varying degrees of expression between these two extremes. The actual condition of the natal Mercury and its aspect to Pluto (house/sign locality, type of aspect to Pluto) will describe the probable intellectual nature of the individual (open or closed). For example, if Mercury is in a mutable sign, and making a nonstressful aspect to Pluto, it tends to indicate that the individual is an open type. If Mercury is in a fixed sign, and making a stressful aspect to Pluto, it tends to indicate that the individual is a closed type. In addition, stressful aspects to Pluto will most commonly promote intense intellectual/philosophical confrontation with others. The individual will experience the power of other people's intellectual knowledge through such confrontations. Most commonly, the other person will expose the weakest link in the individual's intellectual arguments and organization. As the individual experiences the power and legitimacy of the other's intellectual knowledge, he or she will absorb this information into the psyche. Intellectual expansion and metamorphosis occurs in this way. Nonstressful aspects will tend to promote a perpetual and smooth transition (evolution) from the previous intellectual structure and ideas that were limited into new patterns of mental organization that expands upon this intellectual foundation, or framework.

A continual metamorphosis of the intellectual structure can take place when the necessary changes are instigated in all Souls who have Pluto in aspect to Mercury. In both cases, or in both types of individuals, the need to confront and transmute pre-existing intellectual patterns of organization that were rigid and fixed in nature, and creating limitations toward evolutionary growth, was accomplished. In addition, the relativity of truth itself is learned through the expansion and metamorphosis of the intellectual system. Again, one of the core evolutionary intentions of this aspect is to learn to validate other intellectual systems and points of view that do not agree with the individual's pre-existing intellectual system. The difference between facts and opinions is learned through this metamorphic process.

Moon

The Moon correlates with the current egocentric structure and self-image of the Soul. The egocentric structure of the Soul allows for a conscious integration of the current evolutionary intentions and a distinct self-image to manifest. It was stated earlier that the ego operates just as a lens on a movie projector does in generating a specific self-image for the Soul—without the lens on the projector there would only be diffused images of light. The Moon is the planetary ruler of Cancer which correlates with these same dynamics. The archetype of Cancer also symbolizes our emotional body in general (water sign), and the specific dynamics that constitute emotional security on a subjective level. Thus, Pluto/Moon aspects correlate to the evolutionary intention to create a metamorphosis of the Soul's emotional conduct in general, and self-image specifically. The core evolutionary intentions of this aspect are to learn to eliminate all external dependencies in order to become emotionally self-reliant. In this way, internal emotional security will manifest. The individual must reformulate his or her instinctual emotional responses to any internal or external circumstance.

This evolutionary intention has most commonly created difficult emotional experiences in childhood related to the key female/mother figure. Typically, Souls with Pluto in aspect to the Moon have drawn female/mother types who were emotionally dominating, controlling, and who had very rigid and intense emotional expectations and standards of conduct. When the Pluto/Moon individual did not meet these emotional expectations, or conform to the emotional standards that were projected upon them, the mother figure projected the vibration of emotional hurt, disappointment, and letdown. The mother may have also withheld emotional comfort in an icy silence. As a result of such difficult childhood experiences, most Pluto/Moon individuals have unfulfilled emotional needs and expectations that are projected upon others. In essence, displaced emotions from childhood are carried over and projected on the partner in adult relationships. Most of these individuals will overtly or covertly manipulate others in order to have these emotional needs met. This dynamic can occur in varying degrees of magnitude. Others can approach these individuals in the same light, and have just as many emotional expectations as the Moon/Pluto individual. The core problem that must be resolved is that these individuals expect to be nurtured in the ways they need, and project this need onto other people. Deep insecurities and a negative self-image create these compulsive emotional expectations and displaced emotions. Clearly, if these individuals do not learn to nurture themselves from within, and become dependent on another to meet their emotional needs, then the necessary evolutionary lessons of learning emotional self-reliance and eliminating external dependencies cannot proceed. This is exactly why many individuals who have Pluto aspect the Moon have had difficult experiences in childhood with the key female (mother) figure.

Conversely, other Pluto/Moon individuals will attract a mother figure who encourages and supports emotional self-reliance and encourages emotional growth and independence—not a dependency upon themselves. This reflects that the individual has acted to learn these core evolutionary lessons prior to the current life. These mother types are able to understand the causes of the individual's emotional winds, moods, and difficulties in general, and can help the individual penetrate his or her emotional dynamics in order to arrive at the same knowledge, and become emotionally self-reliant. In turn, the individual can help others unravel the causes of their own emotional difficulties and moods.

In a negative expression of this aspect, these individuals in adult life can attempt to control and reformulate the emotional expression of others just as the mother type behaved. When these emotional expectations are not met, these individuals can become spiteful, mean, jealous, and vindictive. In the worst cases, physical violence will manifest. Most people will not tolerate this type of emotional control and overbearing behavior for too long. Thus, emotional scenes and intense emotional shocks will occur through experiences of confrontation or separation. These difficult and painful experiences are intended to promote the necessary awareness of where the individual was coming from, and why the emotional scene(s) took place. Potentially, the person can then correct the error and a positive relationship can manifest. In a positive expression of this aspect, the person will encourage self-reliance and not a dependency upon him- or herself. Once these individuals actively and consciously seek to achieve emotional self-reliance and internal security, all emotional scenes and experiences of a negative nature will no longer occur.

Emotions can be compulsively expressed when Pluto aspects the Moon. The individual may intellectually and emotionally resolve to change these compulsive emotional patterns, yet, much to his or her own horror, will act out in the same manner. Self-rage, anger, and loathing, in varying degrees of magnitude, results because the individual feels powerless to change these compulsive emotional patterns. In the worst case scenario, it produces a subconsciousness death wish or thoughts of suicide because of intense emotional pain that has not been resolved. The key to resolving this condition, again, is to consciously seek to learn the lessons of emotional self-reliance, and internal security. Once the individual consciously acts to learn these critical evolutionary lessons, negative emotions will progressively turn positive. The individual's emotional conduct with others will be totally transformed in this way. The individual will display tolerance and patience where previously intolerance and impatience manifested.

All those with Pluto/Moon aspects have the inherent ability to penetrate the emotional dynamics and structure of any individual. This reflects the evolutionary intention and lessons to shed light upon their own emotional dynamics—why they operate emotionally in the way that they do, and for what reasons. As a result of this evolutionary intention, these individuals will be intensely focused upon the motivations/intentions of others. Generally speaking, the awareness of the individual's emotional dynamics, and their ability to be emotionally self-reliant and internally secure depend on the relative age of the Pluto/Moon aspect. If the aspect is old, then these individuals will have an innate psychological knowledge that can be used to help others.

There are two distinct cycles that are operative in those with this aspect. One is an animated cycle, and the other is a shutdown cycle. It is important to understand why these cycles are occurring as they are. Both cycles are natural, but when an extremity of either cycle is reached, emotional distortions and loss of emotional perspective can occur. In other words, these individuals must come to an objective understanding of the nature of their emotional cycles and expression. The metamorphosis of emotional conduct, expression, and of the self-image can then take place through such objective awareness. The periodic shutdown cycles occur in order for the emotional batteries to be replenished. In addition, the individual becomes consumed by the unconscious force of the Soul. This occurs in order to induce perspective, or knowledge, or to release a new seed thought, emotion, or feeling from the Soul to the conscious ego at key evolutionary junctures. External cues from the environment will serve to indicate when an extreme of either cycle is being reached. Commonly, a person in the Pluto/Moon individual's close environment (Moon) will attempt to question the cause and basis of either extreme. Such external feedback can then be used to objectify emotional behavior. Emotional balance can then manifest. Another good way for these individuals to reformulate and transmute displaced emotions and expectations is to commit to a specific system or program that allows objectification of emotional expression to occur. This is very important, because these individuals often hold very painful emotional memories in the unconscious that influence their present emotional behavior and reactions. Thus, the need to gain control of the described emotional states is critical in this aspect. The system that the Soul commits to must allow for a penetration of the emotional body to take place in order for a repolarization of instinctive emotional responses to occur, and objective emotional awareness to be developed.

In all cases, the evolutionary need of Pluto/Moon aspects is to eliminate all external dependencies, and to internalize emotional security. In this way, instinctual emotional responses to internal or external circumstances will be reformulated and transformed. A metamorphosis of the self-image will occur as it progressively turns negative to positive. When these individuals have gained control of their emotional states, and developed objective awareness in general, the depth of emotional insight that they can provide to others is unsurpassed. These people will desire to help others unravel their own emotional winds and moods, and encourage self-reliance, as well as a positive self-image. The type of aspect the Moon makes to Pluto will determine how this evolution takes place relative to the correlations of stressful and nonstressful aspects.

Sun

The Sun correlates with the creative actualization process, and our sense of purpose in life itself. The Sun reflects how we integrate our evolutionary intentions and requirements. There is always a strong sense of special destiny felt within the house and sign of the natal Sun, because it correlates with our special purpose and the need to creatively actualize that purpose. The Sun is the planetary ruler of Leo.

Pluto/Sun aspects correlate with the evolutionary need and intention to identify and develop a unique special purpose, and creatively actualize this purpose out of the strength of the will. The need to transmute and reformulate the previous manner of creative actualization is symbolized when Pluto aspects the Sun. The individual must learn to link his or her special purpose to a socially relevant need, or else the potential to stay stuck in an essentially narcissistic vacuum is very likely. The creative purpose and special destiny must be linked to a socially relevant need in order to be meaningfully expressed to others. In this way, past patterns of narcissistic behavior linked with the creative purpose will be transmuted. All delusions of grandeur must be purged as well. Generally speaking, Souls with Pluto/Sun aspects have something very special to accomplish that can lead to fame and a high degree of social recognition.

Pluto/Sun aspects promote the compulsive need to eliminate all conditions or dynamics that prevent the uncovering or realization of the individual's personal core of power and individuality. Typically, the unconscious need to be acknowledged as special, important, or acclaimed by others in society will create blocks and limitations from an evolutionary point of view. The danger is to become hung up on personal glorification. The Soul must not overly identify with the creative purpose or creative energy from an egocentric point of view. In a negative expression, the means used to achieve social/personal power have been underhanded, devious, and sometimes ruthless. Other Pluto/Sun individuals will not tolerate abusive or underhanded means to gain personal and social power, and will expose those that use such methods to acquire power.

The evolutionary intention is to learn the limits of personal power—of what it is possible to do, or not do. In some cases, abuse of power manifests because of a refusal to acknowledge the limitations of personal power. Most commonly, the individual overtly or covertly manipulates others in order to receive special attention and recognition. Depending on the extremity of manipulation and abuse of power, karmic shocks of confrontation and exposure will occur to induce the necessary lessons of objectivity, detachment, and the awareness of the person's motivations and intentions. In some cases, the individual will be forced to live a life of relative obscurity while being exposed to the accomplishments and recognition of others in order to enforce these critical lessons. On a positive note, the individual can use these experiences to understand the reasons they have occurred, and resolve to make the necessary changes. The challenge in these lessons is to acknowledge the limits of personal power in the context of the special purpose that is being actualized, while simultaneously effecting a continual growth of the creative purpose and identity. In other words, these individuals must not allow the limitations of the special purpose to limit their personal growth in life.

People with this aspect will experience a cyclic metamorphosis of creative energy, life purpose, and learn how creative actualization is implemented. Ever-new dimensions of the individual's creative purpose and potential are revealed. The limitations of the past can be overcome by allowing the actualization process to occur naturally, or to unfold moment to moment in the individual's life. Frustration can occur because the individual can be shown glimpses of the totality, or the full potential, of what he or she could actualize. However, in the context of personal evolution, certain stages of development must occur at certain times, and only at those certain times in order for the actualization process to be successful.

This evolutionary intention commonly promotes an active identification with individuals who are larger than life, and symbolize social power, or have transcended society all together. For example, if an individual desires to become an astrologer, he or she would identify with the well-known, famous figures in the astrological field. In essence, the individual will form vicarious relationships with these figures in order to absorb the creative power (Sun/Pluto) into him- or herself. In this way, a metamorphosis or transmutation of the Soul's creative energy occurs as the individual absorbs the power of the famous figure into him- or herself in a unique, creative, and personal way.

Commonly, these individuals have evolved through a father type (or the parent who wielded the most authority) who attempted to mold or shape his or her identity and creative expression. Some degree of intimidation was typically experienced. The person conformed to the dictates of the parent because of the intimidation, and also because of the need for special attention and recognition. However, because of the evolutionary intentions of the Pluto/Sun aspect, a confrontation must occur at some point in time. Either the parent is left behind because of a refusal to acknowledge the person's unique individuality and creative purpose, or the parent changes his or her behavior after the emotional shock of such confrontations. Conversely, other Pluto/Sun individuals have evolved through a father type who supported and encouraged the actualization of his or her identity, which reflects the individual's cooperation with these core evolutionary intentions. Sometimes these individuals have attracted both types of parents (one parent fulfilling the first role, and one parent fulfilling the second role) or experiences that reflect the person's own evolutionary and karmic needs. In a negative expression of this aspect, the individual will attempt to mold and shape the individuality and creative expression of others. This will always lead to intense emotional scenes and shocks as the necessary confrontations take place. Potentially, through these confrontations, the person can change.

In another negative application of this aspect, individuals can attempt to live through another person's power, in order to experience an osmosis of this power into themselves. In other words, the individual attempts to feel powerful by forming vicarious relationships with others who represent the power he or she is seeking from within. Because of the evolutionary need to identify and develop a unique creative purpose, and actualize it out of the strength of the will, relationships of this nature will terminate at some point in time. The individual must learn to creatively actualize his or her own creative purpose via self-determined efforts. Positively expressed, the individual will creatively actualize a special purpose and destiny that is in alignment with his or her evolutionary/karmic requirements, and reflects his or her true potential and capacities. The Soul will encourage the actualization of others in an objective manner, and help others actualize a creative purpose that allows re-empowerment and further evolution to manifest through the elimination of all unnecessary limitations.

Jupiter

Generally speaking, Pluto/Jupiter aspects promote the need to develop the intuitive faculty. The growth principle is reflected in Jupiter, and a continual expansion within consciousness occurs as the individual embraces intuitive development. Jupiter symbolizes the need to understand our connection to the cosmos in a metaphysical, cosmological, or philosophical context. In this context, Jupiter symbolizes the desire to realize truth, and to the dynamic of honesty (of course, in its distorted form, Jupiter manifests as dishonesty). Jupiter correlates to our belief system, or structure, which is the determinate to how any of us will interpret life itself. One of the deepest correlations of Jupiter is natural law, or laws that explain the existence of creation by the sheer fact that creation exists in the first place. Jupiter is the planetary ruler of Sagittarius. Pluto/Jupiter aspects promote the need to emotionally unite with natural laws of the universe. The development of the intuition occurs through merging with natural law. Individuals have the inherent capacity or ability to intuitively tap into the natural laws or principles that are the foundation of creation itself. This occurs through pondering or speculating upon a question, and the answer occurs of itself in consciousness. It is not a product of deductive or linear thinking. Intuitive knowledge manifests as knowing what we know without knowing how we know it.

This aspect symbolizes that fixed and rigid beliefs need to be transmuted in order for further evolution to occur. The pre-existing belief system creates the limitations that need to be evolved past. Any belief that does not reflect natural law and is preventing growth must be purged. These beliefs constitute the Soul's deep sense of unconscious emotional security. It is not that these beliefs are wrong—in fact in most cases they are right—but they are limited in some manner. It is because these beliefs constitute unconscious emotional security that the need to convince and convert others will manifest. The limitations in the belief system are created because the individual has not yet realized that there are other ways to interpret or apply the same natural principle, or other natural laws of which the individual has not yet become aware. The Soul's belief system has become fixed and rigid in this way. Again, the pre-existing patterns of beliefs constitute the Soul's unconscious emotional security.

There will be an intense need to reject any belief system prescribed by society (mainstream religion), family, or by the individual, him- or herself, who does not allow an active realization of truth to occur. In other words, any religious or philosophical system that denies the individual's right to express their own truth, to embrace an expansion of consciousness through the belief system, and denies the legitimacy of other religious/philosophical systems will be rejected at some point by many of those with this aspect. Of course, others can resist the evolutionary intention of this aspect and join a religious or philosophical sect that proclaims "we are right, and they are wrong." The need to convince and convert others is dominant in these types. Again, the need in this aspect is to transmute the limitations of pre-existing belief patterns that are based upon religious indoctrination, and are not in conformity with natural laws. Of course, the evolutionary state will determine the

Soul's specific belief system, and philosophical orientation. The type of aspect that Jupiter makes to Pluto will correlate to how this evolution will manifest.

Another core issue to address when discussing Jupiter/Pluto aspects is the dynamic of communication. Again, Pluto/Jupiter individuals most commonly have a highly developed intuition. Thus, these individuals typically have trouble expressing or communicating what they know to others in a language that is understood by the majority. The evolutionary need is to learn to communicate the wisdom that is intuited in a language system that is universally understood. A common frustration for those with this aspect is that others do not comprehend what the individual is trying to teach. There are two potential responses to this experience. One response is to adopt an attitude of inferiority, and to try to learn more thoroughly what is being intuited. The other response is to adopt an attitude of superiority, and resist the evolutionary intention to learn to communicate in a language system that is universally understood. All those with Jupiter/Pluto aspects have innate teaching abilities. However, until the individual learns to communicate in a language system that is understood by the majority, he or she will be blocked from being able to teach others in a meaningful manner.

Once Pluto/Jupiter individuals become emotionally secure in the context of their beliefs, the need to defend those beliefs as right, and the need to convince or convert others will be eliminated. All outdated, rigid beliefs that are preventing growth and do not reflect natural law, will be purged from the Soul. The individual will teach and accept valid teaching from others, instead of falling prey to indoctrination and preaching to others. As this metamorphosis occurs the true teaching ability of these individuals can emerge. The natural wisdom of Pluto/Jupiter individuals can then be embraced by others, and trigger intuitive development in those whom they teach.

Saturn

Saturn correlates with the structure of consciousness, and the boundaries or borders of our conscious awareness at any moment in time. Saturn correlates with the culture or society we are born into, and the conditioning patterns of that society. As such, this planet describes the nature of our own cultural/societal conditioning patterns. There is also a correlation with time and space reality. Saturn is the planetary ruler of the Capricorn. This archetype makes each of us aware of our own mortality from an egocentric point of view. This awareness leads to natural maturity. In other words, we are aware via this archetype that we have a certain amount of time to establish our life successfully, and it is this awareness that triggers maturity. The need to accept responsibility in our own actions is reflected in this archetype. Saturn correlates with the external authority we encounter in the society we are born into, and the parent who holds the most authority in the family, who acted to discipline the children (as an authority figure). Typically, this is the father, or key male figure. In addition, there is a need to establish and actualize our own authority in society, or our personal voice of authority within an existing external authority (society). Thus, Saturn correlates to the career, or sociological role we will assume in society.

Pluto/Saturn aspects correlate with the evolutionary intent to purge and transmute all outdated and fixed cultural conditioning patterns that are blocking evolution. Most commonly, these patterns are based on conforming to society's customs and norms, or the mainstream of society. A core dynamic that must be transmuted in Pluto/Saturn individuals is overly identifying with a career or social position from an egocentric point of view. This aspect has promoted deep inner contemplation and reflection in order to guide the person to the awareness of his or her natural capacities and abilities. Pluto correlates with the largest sociological role any of us can play. Saturn correlates to the need to assume that role. The specific aspect between Saturn and Pluto describes how the establishment and actualization of authority has and will take place. The type of aspect describes the Soul's response to the need to establish a personal voice of authority within society. A socialized consciousness will be developed that understands how the system works as the Soul actualizes a voice of authority within society. Any past cultural conditioning patterns that have not been transmuted and are creating a nongrowth situation in the context of evolution must be purged from the Soul. Depression, stagnation, and futility are experienced as the individual desires to grow past the limitations of his or her past conditioning patterns. Any dynamic, or combination of dynamics, relative to the consciousness structure of the Soul that have become crystallized, outdated, and are preventing further growth must be eliminated.

Stressful aspects to Pluto tend to reflect situations wherein the individual has resisted conforming to the socially required methods to actualize the specific career he or she desired. In addition, the duties and responsibilities of that career may have not been taken seriously. Issues of self-determination, emotional maturity, and conforming/submitting to a higher authority are all being learned in this way. Those with stressful aspects to Pluto have tended to need social status to feel emotionally secure. As a result, the career that the individual attempted to actualize was either blocked from being actualized, or he or she was removed from a specific social position. In some cases, self-determination was highly developed prior to the current life, yet underhanded means were used to establish the role. An abuse of personal and social power occurred. The Soul will come into the life with deep feelings of futility, frustration, and depression because the career was blocked from being actualized, and the lesson of accepting responsibility for the individual's action was not learned. The causative factor that creates these negative dynamics is resistance to conforming or submitting to a higher voice of authority, and a fear of being consumed or controlled by powers (authority) perceived as larger than the individual. This fear is then projected upon society. From an ultimate point of view, the resistance to merging with the Source can be seen through the resistance to conforming/submitting to a higher voice of authority (God's authority).

Nonstressful aspects tend to correlate with those individuals who have implemented the proper steps to establish and actualize a career that will allow their voice of authority in society to manifest. They have learned to establish their own authority from within, independent from any career or social position. In addition, they have taken the responsibilities of that career seriously, and are not preoccupied with the actual position, itself. Individuals with nonstressful aspects to Pluto understand that a career must be established based upon qualification and inner capacity. This awareness promotes an understanding of the natural limits of the career or role itself. However, no hard and fast rules can be made because we must factor in the Soul's evolutionary/karmic condition, the totality of the birth chart in general, and the individual's cultural/religious conditioning.

Everyone with Saturn/Pluto aspects has leadership abilities and capacities. Pluto/Saturn individuals can become aware of internal conditioning patterns that are outdated or crystallized, and are preventing further growth. This awareness is reflected externally in the outer changes that are made when a dynamic, or combination of dynamics, within consciousness that are preventing further growth are purged from the Soul. In this way, an ongoing metamorphosis of the Soul's consciousness structure occurs, and past cultural conditioning patterns are purged from the psyche. This metamorphosis will also reflect itself externally through the individual's expression of his or her own voice of authority in society, and the type of career he or she actualizes. Positively expressed, this aspect will produce individuals who naturally desire to help others actualize their own voice of authority in society, and a career or role in society that will allow such authority to manifest.

Uranus

Uranus correlates with the individualizing impulse, or the need to individuate from a psychological standpoint. Uranus is the planetary ruler of Aquarius. There is a need to liberate from all the conditioning patterns of the past in order to individuate. Liberation naturally leads to, or creates, the severing of all attachments that are preventing further growth. The need for liberation triggers the need to rebel from the norms, customs, and taboos of society. This archetype makes us aware that we are all different and unique. This awareness gives rise to the need to liberate from all old conditioning patterns that repress or suppress (Saturn) the expression of unique individuality, objectifying it in order for liberation to occur. Uranus correlates to the psychology of objectification and detachment. This psychology must be in place in order for any liberation from past conditioning patterns to manifest.

In essence, we must impersonally view or see ourselves first before any true liberation can occur. The structure of consciousness (Saturn) will then be transformed based on liberation from past conditioning patterns (Uranus). Genius abilities that we all potentially have are symbolized in this planet as well.

Uranus correlates with the individuated unconscious which holds three types of information: 1) All past memories in detail, 2) that which we have repressed via the Saturn function, and 3) a blueprint of what we can become relative to individuation (our unique individuality unconditioned by anything), and a blueprint of the future from that standpoint. In addition, memories of trauma are held in the unconscious, because traumatic events often ensue in order to enforce the necessary liberation. These traumatic memories will condition our behavior in the present moment if we have not objectified and liberated from the impact of such events.

The evolutionary impulse of Pluto/Uranus aspects is to break free from all internal and external conditioning patterns that bind an individual to the past. All attachments that are preventing further evolution must be purged. An acceleration of the evolutionary pace is symbolized by Pluto/Uranus aspects. Most commonly, these individuals have conformed to the socially accepted norms of their environment, and simply followed the peer group in expressing individuality. These individuals most commonly have looked to the external environment, and to the peer group, in order to achieve liberation. However, true liberation can only come from within through the severing of the past conditioning patterns that have become outdated and crystallized. Thus, a delusive sense of liberation is experienced when this pattern is in place within consciousness. These individuals will have a heightened awareness of their own unique essence, yet may fear expressing this essence because it goes against the socially accepted customs and norms. The fear of being ostracized leads to the emotional/psychological dynamic of conformity and repressing the impulse to transform inner and outer reality. The expression of unique individuality is repressed, and at some point in time this repression leads to a variety of emotional distortions. Detachment and disengagement from the personal environment and the emotional body are examples of such distortions. Unresolved trauma creates detachment from the emotional body, and emotional/spiritual/mental fracturing within the psyche. The individual is not able to fully integrate into his or her current reality. Frustration, inner and outer implosion, and a loss of perspective relative to individuality will occur in varying degrees of magnitude as the individual desires to transmute the pre-existing patterns of conditioning that are binding him or her to the past.

The three types of information that are stored in the individuated unconscious will be released into conscious awareness at key points in the Soul's evolutionary journey. This occurs because of the evolutionary intent of Pluto/Uranus aspects to liberate from and transmute all limitations based on past conditioning patterns, and sever all dynamics that are preventing further growth. As mentioned before, past conditioning patterns dictate how we respond to the present moment in time if liberation from those past patterns has not occurred. This same principle applies to past-life memories, especially when those memories are traumatic in nature. As these memories are released into conscious awareness, the individual can then liberate from the negative influence that those memories may have, and actualize his or her unique essence. Stressful aspects to Pluto indicate that the release of unconscious content into conscious awareness is cyclic. Those with a nonstressful Pluto/Uranus aspect will experience a perpetual or continual release of unconscious content.

Once these individuals have embraced the evolutionary impulse to decondition and liberate from all past conditioning patterns, their evolutionary pace can be quite amazing. They will embrace their own unique individuality and encourage others to do the same. The Soul will not be bound by the repressive conditioning and conformity patterns of society. A truly unique brilliance and genius capacity can be realized by individuals with this aspect. These Souls can then help others in society transform themselves and the world in which we live. Thus, personal and collective evolution is accomplished.

Neptune

Neptune correlates with the transcendent impulse within the Soul. The transcendent impulse is a reflection of the need to dissolve all barriers within consciousness that are preventing a conscious and direct connection to the Source, or God. Transcendence describes transcending the confines of time and space itself. This planet symbolizes how we understand our life's purpose from a spiritual point of view, or our spiritual purpose. Neptune is the planetary ruler of Pisces. The culmination of an entire cycle of evolution is symbolized by this planetary archetype. The need to spiritually develop is triggered by the transcendent impulse. The need is to merge the individual ego with the Source, or the Creator. In this way, a personal identification with the Creator will occur. The analogy of the wave upon the ocean that was used earlier to illustrate the principle of the center of gravity within consciousness, and the metamorphosis of the egocentric structure as it no longer identifies itself as a separate identity as the Soul merges with the Creator, will serve to demonstrate this evolutionary intention as well. In other words, the Soul must center its consciousness within the cosmic ocean, not the wave.

In general, Pluto/Neptune aspects correlate with the evolutionary intention to become aware of the nature of dreams, illusions, and delusions. A direct and conscious merging with the Source must be realized. Neptune correlates with timeless universal laws, and to the infinite. Neptune symbolizes where we are naturally meant to spiritually develop, and also where we are most susceptible to delusions. Neptune symbolizes the need to establish ultimate meaning as well. Illusions and delusions are based upon separating desires which are linked with ultimate meaning in life. The key point within this is that ultimate meaning must be found from within through a direct and conscious connection to the Source.

In essence, Souls with this Pluto in aspect to Neptune have attempted to seek ultimate meaning in the external environment through actualizing illusions and delusions. This has commonly created an evolutionary scenario of chasing dreams. These dreams and illusions become the ultimate meaning that the individual is seeking to establish. However, because of the evolutionary intent of Pluto/Neptune aspects to create a direct and conscious merging with the Creator, these illusions and dreams will be seen for what they are at some point in the Soul's evolutionary journey. The dream may be interesting for a certain period of time, but will not provide true or lasting meaning. These illusions and delusions will lose meaning as the Soul purges the separating desires that created this situation of chasing dreams. All illusions, or delusions are based upon separating desires linked with ultimate meaning. Disillusionment (Neptune) occurs as the delusion or dream is experienced as something less than the individual had hoped or desired. It is through this process of disillusionment, and the resulting feelings of dissatisfaction via the Neptune archetype, that we learn we are cocreator with the Divine, or the Source. Meaninglessness, disassociation, and a sense of emptiness is experienced when ultimate meaning is not found through actualizing illusions and delusions. The intention of this type of evolutionary experience is to promote the awareness that ultimate meaning can only be found within through a direct and conscious merging with the Divine. Seventy-five percent of all Souls living today have Neptune in aspect to Pluto. Thus, the realization that we are cocreators with the Divine is extremely important from an evolutionary standpoint.

Again, when Pluto aspects Neptune, the evolutionary impulse is to become aware of the nature of personal illusions, delusions, and dreams in order to purge them from the Soul. The need to dissolve all barriers and old patterns of behavior that are preventing a direct and conscious merging with the Source is emphasized in all individuals with a Pluto/Neptune aspect. Any area with which the individual is overidentified from an egocentric point of view must be dissolved. A personal identification with the Creator must be established. This process in total allows a necessary culmination to be accomplished relative to the past evolutionary cycle. Divine illumination and inspiration can take hold as the Soul's true identity, as reflected by the Source, or cosmic identity, is revealed to the individual. Divine inspiration and response to the collective need at any moment in time (Neptune) will manifest through the house and sign positions of Pluto and Neptune in the natal chart.

Phases and Aspects

We will now discuss the specific phases and the aspects that occur within these phases in the zodiac from zero to 360 degrees. We can then apply this knowledge to correctly interpret Pluto aspects in an individualized context. There are eight primary phases of evolution and development: the new phase, crescent phase, first quarter phase, gibbous phase, full phase, disseminating phase, last quarter phase, and balsamic (culminating) phase. Aspects occur within these phases that correlate with specific stages of development within human consciousness. Phases and aspects are determined by degrees of separation from two planets. The slower moving of the two planets that are being analyzed is the starting point for such calculations. Count counterclockwise, using the slower moving planet as the starting point, to determine the phase and any aspect that exists between two planets. The only exception to this rule is the Sun, because the Sun is the center of our solar system. The Sun will always be used as the starting point when calculating a phase or aspect to another planet.

As mentioned earlier, aspects are either stressful or nonstressful in nature. Aspects that occur from 0–180 degrees are called waxing, and aspects that occur from 180 to 360 degrees are called waning. The degree in which an aspect occurs correlates to the phase it is in (i.e., a new-phase conjunction occurs at zero to 10 degrees, versus a balsamic conjunction, which occurs at 350 to -360 degrees). The classification of stressful or nonstressful determines the relationship between the two planetary functions within consciousness that are forming an aspect to each other. If an aspect is stressful in nature, then it will typically correlate with stressful, emotionally intense experiences relative to the areas represented by the planets forming the stressful aspect. The stress occurs because, most commonly, the individual does not understand the dynamics that must be resolved in order to eliminate the stress. Let's say that Venus is square Mars. A square always symbolizes creative tension of some nature. We can then take the core evolutionary intention of Venus square Mars, and put it in a specific phase. A first-quarter square will operate very differently from a last-quarter square. The first-quarter phase correlates with crisis in action, and the last-quarter phase correlates with a crisis in consciousness. Thus, the creative tension symbolized by the square will manifest in very different ways, relative to its specific phase. Until the necessary dynamics implied in the square are resolved, there will be tension and stress between the two functions in consciousness symbolized by Venus and Mars. These principles can be applied to any two planets in the birth chart, not just to Pluto aspects.

Returning to the theme of Pluto aspects, the specific phase and type of aspect of a planet in aspect to Pluto describes how the evolutionary impulse and requirements reflected by the Pluto aspect will be internally experienced, and manifest within consciousness. Again, the core evolutionary impulse and requirements of Pluto aspect to Mars, or Venus, or Jupiter will be the same in all cases. The specific type of aspect (stressful or nonstressful) and phase of the Pluto aspect (i.e., new phase or balsamic) symbolizes how that aspect will manifest within consciousness. In other words, the planetary archetypes previously described correlate to the area, or function, within consciousness that has come under the metamorphic process of Pluto. The aspects and phases of Pluto aspects reflect how the required metamorphosis indicated in Pluto aspects will manifest, and are internally experienced by the individual. We can then adjust our interpretation to incorporate the other mitigating factors of the birth chart.

Eight Primary Phases of Development and Aspects Therein

New Phase: 0–45 degrees

The New phase itself correlates with a brand-new cycle of evolutionary becoming relative to the evolutionary intent/purpose. Instinctual, random action is initiated in order for self-discovery to take place. Action/reaction learning is how this phase operates. As such, freedom and independence is required within the new phase in order for self-discovery of the evolutionary intention to manifest. New patterns of behavior must emerge through the initiation of a new direction so the new evolutionary intention can take hold. The formation of individuality is symbolized in this phase.

0 degrees—Conjunction (stressful)

The planets unite in function and operate simultaneously within consciousness. Instinctual action/expression occurs in order for discovery of the evolutionary intention, relative to the planet that aspects Pluto.

Pure, unchecked expression without any egocentric awareness manifests. A brand-new evolutionary purpose/intent is initiated in this way.

30 degrees—Semi-sextile (nonstressful)

The formation of a conscious and egocentric awareness/identification of the new evolutionary intention now manifests in the context of the Pluto aspect. Random action narrows as the specific form the new evolutionary intention will take is sensed. In this way, self-discovery of what the new evolutionary intention is about can take place.

40 degrees—Novil (nonstressful)

The formation of a conscious awareness and identification of the evolutionary intentions of the Pluto aspect now triggers a gestation process where further personal growth (subjective growth/awareness) relative to the intentions of the Pluto aspect can manifest. We become aware that we are moving in a new direction, and that the new direction is very personal in nature. The sense of self-discovery is intensified as we give the evolutionary intention of the Pluto aspect a personal and individual meaning.

45 degrees—Semi-square (stressful)

A transitional aspect leading into the Crescent phase. The conflict, or stress, in this aspect is the competing desires to generate ever more and new experiences (New phase), and the need to consolidate, internalize, and establish a personal meaning within the evolutionary intention of the Pluto aspect, so the new discoveries can be integrated (crescent phase). Balancing these two desires would serve to create a positive expression of this aspect.

Crescent Phase: 45–90 degrees

The evolutionary intention/purpose is internalized, inwardly established, and oriented to allow the evolutionary purpose to take root. This can only occur through a personal, or individual structure. Personal effort is required, which is a key lesson in this phase because of the fear that sliding back into past patterns of behavior can manifest.

45 degrees—Semi-square (stressful)

The evolutionary intention of the Pluto aspect now increases in intensity to be established, as the person struggles to make real the evolutionary intention in an individual way. The intensity is experienced because the person is trying to be free from all past conditions that bind him or her to past patterns of behavior that lead to a specific internal structure.

51'25 degrees—Septile (nonstressful)

The evolutionary intention/impulse of the Pluto aspect is now given a special purpose, or destiny. Actions are initiated in order to discover what the special purpose is. Action can be clear and consistent or sporadic and confused, depending on the planet aspect to Pluto. There can be moments of fadedness to this aspect relative to keeping the person aligned with the evolutionary intention of the Pluto aspect, and the intentions of this phase itself.

60 degrees—Sextile (nonstressful)

The process of consciously understanding the new evolutionary impulse/intention of the Pluto aspect is now effected through comparison and contrast. Isolation from the impact of the external environment must occur in order for the individual to realize from within what is special and individualistic. Withdrawal and isolation from the external world leads to inner contemplation and realization, which is then contrasted to the external world. Issues pertaining to the past can now be understood by the individual. This understanding leads to the natural awareness of the proper steps and experiences to generate in order to develop the evolutionary impulse/intention of the Pluto aspect in an individual way.

72 degrees—Quintile (nonstressful)

The meaning of the forming evolutionary purpose becomes highly individualistic in nature. It is ready for externalized action, though there may be a remaining tension relative to the pull of the past.

90 degrees—Square (stressful)

Transition from crescent phase to first quarter phase. As such, this aspect produces an intensified inner compression within the individual in the context of establishing specific forms through which the evolutionary intention/purpose of the Pluto aspect can manifest. The externalized integration and establishment of a specific form(s) of the evolutionary impulse is required in the first quarter phase. In this aspect, the awareness of what those new forms are, which have been progressively refined in previous phases and aspects, will emerge into consciousness. These forms, or structures must reflect the evolutionary intention of the new phase. There commonly exists a fear of failure, or of sliding back into past patterns of behavior because a person may fear that they do not know how to establish this form, or structure within the external environment, or society. There will be an inner push/pull within the Soul where the person will cyclically isolate themselves from the external environment, and then assert themselves in society in order to test and establish the new patterns, forms, or structures that have emerged into consciousness.

First Quarter Phase: 90–135 degrees

This phase often correlates with a crisis in action. The intention of this phase is to establish and make real the evolutionary impulse begun in the New phase. This requires that an external form or structure be established in society in order for the evolutionary intention and purpose to be integrated. The fear of sliding back into old patterns, or a fear of failure, can be quite intense. The need for an externalized form or structure often leads to a situation wherein the individual tries on many different hats, in order to discover which one most perfectly reflects the new patterns or forms. Each different structure or form will reflect a different way of being, and a direction that is highly unique and personal in nature. This describes the crisis in action of this phase.

90 degrees—Square (stressful)

The individual meaning of the evolutionary intention of the Pluto aspect must now be given a new form to operate through. This new form must manifest in order for the evolutionary intentions to be fully integrated and established. The specific form that needs to be established is relative to the planet that aspects Pluto. Creative tension manifests because there is commonly a compulsive temptation to slide back into old patterns of behavior versus allowing the new patterns to be integrated. Another cause of this tension is that the person may not know how to establish the new forms. However, these new forms must be established for further evolution to proceed.

102'50 degrees—Biseptile (nonstressful)

The new form that manifested in the square is given a special purpose/destiny that is highly individualized in nature. The special destiny/purpose that was identified at the septile is now remembered, or reawakened. The intention of this aspect is to exteriorize the evolutionary purpose, and to create a personal reality that reflects the special destiny given to the new evolutionary purpose. On this level, fate can be experienced relative to the Soul creating the necessary outer circumstances to point the way to the special purpose and destiny.

120 degrees—Trine (nonstressful)

The new evolutionary intention of the Pluto aspect must now be creatively actualized. This aspect symbolizes the potential for total conscious awareness of the entire process, or the past that led to the present. This awareness promotes a natural ability to create a personal reality that reflects the new evolutionary intention/purpose of the Pluto aspect, as well as integrating the evolutionary purpose/intention from within. The type of lifestyle this actualization would create within society can also be easily integrated, and will reflect the new evolutionary purpose.

135 degrees—Sesquiquadrate (stressful)

Transition from first quarter phase to gibbous phase, as such, is a very powerful aspect. Humiliation of the ego that has been willfully asserting the new evolutionary purpose of the Pluto aspect in the environment must now occur. This humiliation, or humility, must be experienced because the

Soul has been attempting to live only for itself, and the new evolutionary purpose/intention was not linked to societal needs. This humility will lead to an awareness, and an alignment of the evolutionary intention with social needs. Emotional shocks will be received via resistance to the individual if the alignment with societal needs and the overall social environment is not made. Analysis of why such resistance is occurring will lead the Soul to the understanding of what needs to be adjusted within to make this alignment possible.

Gibbous Phase: 135–180 degrees

This phase correlates with the need to learn personal humility, and in that sense, prepare to integrate into society as an equal. The evolutionary purpose started in the new phase must now be prepared to be integrated in a societal context. The inflated balloon of the ego must be popped, and humility will manifest.

135 degrees—Sesquiquadrate (stressful)

Continuation of the process when this aspect was in the first quarter phase. If the individual does not make the necessary inner changes to link the new purpose to social needs, then negative results will occur. The Soul will be thrown back on itself to re-experience the past, and confusion as to how to establish the new intention, and the personal reality, in a social context will occur until the changes are made.

144 degrees—Biquintile (nonstressful)

This aspect will realign the person with the original intentions of the evolutionary impulse if the sesquiquadrate was experienced negatively. This alignment is effected through relating the new evolutionary intentions to the individualizing process of the quintile. Analysis of how to link the new evolutionary purpose to serve the needs of the Whole, or society, must take place. Service promotes a deepening of the meaning given to the evolutionary purpose of the Pluto aspect.

150 degrees—Inconjunct (stressful)

This aspect promotes either clarity or confusion in the context of the Soul's self-concept, and how it is identified with the new evolutionary purpose of the Pluto aspect. There is an awareness of something special to do, yet the Soul does not know how to link the new evolutionary intentions to serve the Whole. An analysis needs to be made of what inner adjustments are necessary in order to allow such service to take place. Crisis commonly occurs in order to induce the analysis, and humility is effected in this way.

154 degrees—Triseptile (nonstressful)

Clarification of the person's self-concept is realized as the evolutionary purpose of the Pluto aspect is linked with the needs of others, and society. The analysis and inner purging of delusions of grandeur in the inconjunction created a natural humility. This humility allows the individual to prepare to integrate his or her evolutionary purpose/intention of the Pluto aspect in the social environment as an equal.

180 degrees—Opposition (stressful)

An opposition aspect always symbolizes that a Soul is throwing off patterns of behavior that are preventing further evolution. The gibbous opposition aspect is a key transition into the full phase, where integrating into society as an equal must take place. In this case, the opposition in this phase will reflect that the Soul is learning an essential humility via experiencing the voices and drives of others in society full force. The intention behind such an experience is to induce the awareness that the drives of others are just as strong as the individual's. The experience of other people's drives will occur, commonly, through others opposing the individual in relation to his or her values, needs, beliefs, and orientation. This experience can create anger and fear in the Soul, and then the Soul will react by attempting to oppose others that are opposing itself. This reaction manifests as cyclic withdrawal from social interaction, and then willfully asserting the ego. Such attacks and retreats will continue until balance is learned via integrating into society as an equal.

Full Phase: 180–235 degrees

This phase correlates with the need to complete ourselves through relationships, and in this way integrate as an equal with others. However, there is a competing desire to be free and independent from all forms of relationships simultaneously with the need to complete ourselves in a relationship. These two competing desires typically create a situation of extremes where the Soul immerses itself in social interaction, and then withdraws from social interaction and relationships altogether. The trigger for this withdrawing is when the Soul feels overwhelmed by the impact of so many people and the diversity of values, beliefs, and needs which these people represent. The person feels that they have lost touch with their own essence. When the other extreme of withdrawing totally from social interaction is reached, the individual will experience a personal implosion and a loss of perspective relative to him-or herself. This triggers the other extreme described before. Clearly, these extremes are not healthy, and the key is to learn balance. Balance is learned by honoring both drives, or needs, as they occur instinctually. When this type of balance is learned, then the true intention of this phase, which is the progressive socialization of consciousness, can manifest. These people learn what society needs from them, and how to socially integrate their evolutionary purpose.

180 degrees—Opposition (stressful)

The individual meaning of the evolutionary purpose of the Pluto aspect must now be given social meaning. A socialized framework, or context, must be given for the evolutionary intentions and purpose to operate through. The individual must relate to and integrate into society, specifically in relationships, as an equal, before this form can manifest. This person must learn to listen to others in relationships in order to evaluate his or her own individuality. The evolutionary purpose of the Pluto aspect can then be applied in a way that is needed by others, and is linked with a social need. Often, this opposition creates a collision of wills, and clashing desires, because the individual may feel that his or her personal power and sense of identity is being lost and absorbed through the necessity to interact with others. In a negative expression, the person may resist the necessity to develop a socialized consciousness, and shove their personal purpose down the throats of others in a willful way, in order to feel more powerful and secure. Until the person does successfully link his or her personal purpose to the evolutionary intention of the Pluto aspect, they will remain locked into this evolutionary gate.

206 degrees—Triseptile (nonstressful)

The personal meaning given to the original purpose of the Pluto aspect was given social meaning and application in the opposition. Now the Soul is ready to cooperate with a social or collective need.

210 degrees—Inconjunct (stressful)

The new social meaning/purpose of the evolutionary intent of the Pluto aspect promotes a clarification of the individual's awareness of social and personal limitations. The person must integrate the awareness of what he or she can and cannot do, and what is required of him or her from society, in order to express the social purpose. If the limits are not adhered to, then intense emotional confrontations and shocks will occur in order to enforce these lessons. This aspect promotes social humility and perfection, whereas the first phase inconjunct promoted a personal humility.

216 degrees—Biquintile (nonstressful)

The socialized evolutionary purpose is further refined through the awareness of the individual's innate capacities and abilities contrasted to the capacities of others.

235 degrees—Sesquiquadrate (stressful)

Transitionary aspect into the disseminating phase. As such, the individual is required to expand to include the awareness of the cultural, or societal, rules, customs, and norms. This must occur so the person can integrate the socialized evolutionary purpose of the Pluto aspect. For example, if a person wanted to become a doctor, then this aspect would promote the awareness of the proper steps that must be taken to actualize this (schooling, credentials, etc.).

Disseminating Phase: 235–270 degrees

The intention of this phase is for the ongoing socialization of the evolutionary purpose to continue. This progressive socialization occurs through learning all there is to learn about the society's or culture's rules, regulations, norms, and traditions. In addition, the person must now integrate the socialized evolutionary purpose in such a way as to fulfill his or her existing social obligations.

235 degrees—Sesquiquadrate (stressful)

A crisis now occurs, because the person must learn everything there is to learn about society's norms, rules, regulations, and traditions. The crisis is experienced because the individual is ready to disseminate the purpose, but must do so on society's terms before any establishment of the evolutionary purpose can take place.

240 degrees—Trine (nonstressful)

Symbolizes the refinement of the abstract and socialized consciousness. The person has the potential to understand how the society works, and can establish his or her socialized evolutionary purpose within the existing society. The person can easily understand and integrate what must be done in order to establish the socialized purpose, and others in society will not necessarily feel threatened by the individual.

270 degrees—square (stressful)

Key evolutionary juncture/transition into the last quarter phase. The creative tension or stress manifests because the Soul has now learned everything there is to learn about society and its regulations, customs, and rules— yet must now decondition, or liberate, from societal conditioning. This creates a crisis within consciousness. Socialization, or learning to establish the evolutionary intention in society has occurred previously. In this aspect, the Soul is now evolving toward embracing timeless, universal laws that are outside the consensus of mainstream society. Deconditioning, which is experienced in the last quarter phase, manifests in this way in the context of the Pluto aspect. However, commonly the Soul can't conceive of these new thought forms relative to universal laws. Thus, in this phase, rebellion against the consensus typically takes place because the beliefs, customs, and regulations are felt to be too restrictive and limited.

Last Quarter Phase: 270–315 degrees

This phase correlates with a crisis within consciousness, relative to belief systems. The Soul must now decondition from the influence of the consensus belief structure that is preventing further evolution. The intention behind this liberation and progressive deconditioning is to embrace timeless, universal truths that are not bound by any belief system. In this way consciousness is expanded. The crisis occurs because the cultural beliefs and conditioning of the consensus, which was learned in the previous phase, will no longer have any relevance or meaning to the Soul. The alignment with timeless, universal truths creates the crisis because, again, this liberation must occur in order for the Soul to grow. An additional intention in this phase is the beginning of the culmination process which follows this phase (which will be experienced in the Balsamic phase).

270 degrees—square (stressful)

Having learned everything there is to learn about society's laws, customs, and regulations, the Soul now experiences a progressive repolarization of consciousness to embrace timeless, universal truths in the context of the Pluto aspect. The creative tension of the square manifests as a crisis in consciousness as the Soul experiences such repolarization, and desires to liberate from the social conditioning of his or her belief system. The cultural beliefs and truths will no longer hold any meaning or value, and will no longer be the basis of creating personal and social meaning. What to believe, how to relate, and what to think become pressing issues.

288 degrees—Quintile (nonstressful)

The intention of transforming consciousness relative to social and personal identity occurs through the realization of the Soul's timeless, cosmic identity. Through this awareness, the Soul learns to relate inwardly in a totally different manner. A relationship and an awareness of the ultimate other, or the Source, must take place. Through such a relationship, the Soul will increasingly understand its cosmic role in the context of the duties performed in this life.

300 degrees—Sextile (nonstressful)

The cosmic identity of the individual is now given a productive purpose and understanding. The productive purpose allows the person to fulfill his or her social and universal role. The transition from the past to the future can be made easily, or easily resisted at this point.

308 degrees—Septile (nonstressful)

Individual action is now taken relative to the universal purpose given in the sextile via relating the purpose with a special destiny. Misidentification or misapplication of the special purpose can still occur in the context of existing delusions within the Soul. The Soul will create the necessary circumstances that will set the individual straight if misapplication occurs, and remind the person of the actual special purpose that is intended.

315 degrees—Semi-square (stressful)

Correlates with a transition into the Balsamic phase. As such, there is a tremendous amount of inner stress based on the need to withdraw from social interaction so that the seeds of universal and timeless truth can be sown. In addition, the need to fulfill the existing social obligations is intensified.

Balsamic Phase (315–360)

This phase correlates with the desire to embrace timeless, universal truths and laws. Culmination and completion of everything that was left unfinished or unfulfilled that proceeded this phase, which was started in the last quarter phase, must now occur. Commonly, this leads to a recreation of any behavior or pattern within the Soul in order for the culmination to take place. A brand-new evolutionary cycle can occur through such culmination (symbolized in the new phase).

315 degrees—Semi-square (stressful)

A new type of crisis occurs as the Soul accelerates the mutation between all that constitutes the past, personally and culturally, and the future. The future represents the unknown, and correlates with the timeless, universal, and unconditioned. The conflict is based upon conflicting desires as well. On the one hand, the Soul desires to withdraw from social interaction in order to internalize consciousness and allow new seeds of thought and experiences to manifest in the context of a new evolutionary cycle (which will be aligned with the timeless, universal truths that the Soul must learn). Yet, the thoughts, forms, and experiences themselves may create a conflict because of the desire to stay rooted in past behavior and the known, or to recover the past. New forms of social relationships must manifest. The person wants to withdraw from social interaction to experiment with new ways of being, yet must fulfill his or her existing social obligations. The key is to follow both rhythms or cycles as they occur.

320 degrees—Novil (nonstressful)

The seeds of a new evolutionary cycle, and timeless universal truths, create a gestation process. The Soul suddenly becomes aware of the nature of the new evolutionary cycle to come, and is now ready to implement the proper steps in order for this new cycle to actualize. Negatively, these new thoughts and perceptions may threaten the person's existing reality and emotional security, causing the individual to retreat into the past, or the known. Frustration can result from the knowledge that the cycle of evolution begun at the new phase must be culminated.

330 degrees—Semi-sextile (nonstressful)

The new evolutionary cycle is now clarified through complete conceptions, and ideas that the Soul may try to establish in this life. The Soul will attempt to formulate its life around the timeless, universal laws within the societal framework of the individual. The person is challenged to stay focused and committed to their vision of the timeless and universal because others in the society may not comprehend what he or she is trying to accomplish, and are thus perceived as strange or different. The new cycle begun in the new phase is now rapidly dissolving. Negatively, this will lead to experiences of emptiness and meaninglessness, and undefined personal identity or purpose. The key is to let go of the past, and allow the new thoughts, impulses, and conceptions of the new evolutionary cycle to occur on their own volition. These conceptions, thoughts, and impulses will then be the guiding light toward the individual's future.

360 degrees—Conjunction (stressful)

An entire cycle of evolution has been completed. From the Balsamic semi-square to the conjunction, the transition from egocentric consciousness to universal consciousness was initiated. Any Pluto aspect that is found (or any two planets) in these conditions, or aspects, has completed, or is completing, an entire cycle of evolution. The Soul will never again experience the Pluto aspect (or any two planets) in the way it was previously experienced. A brand-new cycle of evolution is about to begin. As such, a Pluto aspect in this phase can be a vehicle through which the timeless, universal, and the Source can be consciously experienced and expressed. However, the Pluto aspect in this condition may also be experienced as disassociation, disillusionment, and alienation. This experience is meant to teach the individual about the nature of his or her delusions and illusions. In essence, the person learns through disillusionment that ultimate meaning can't be found in any external condition or person.

6

Applying the Principles of Pluto Aspects

We have now described the core meaning of Pluto aspects from an evolutionary point of view, the specific evolutionary intentions of the planetary aspect to Pluto, and the meaning and manifestation of the specific type of aspect (stressful and nonstressful) that Pluto aspects can form.

We will now analyze two natal charts of real life case studies, in order to synthesize all of these principles. One case study will demonstrate a positive example of the manifestation of Pluto aspects relative to the individual's cooperation. The second case study will demonstrate a negative application of these Pluto aspects relative to the individual's resistance. These examples are meant to illustrate how to apply the core principles of Pluto aspects in an individualized context in any natal birth chart. These case studies are intended to emphasize the critical difference that the dynamics of cooperation and resistance will make in experiencing Pluto aspects in a positive or negative manner.

First Case Study: Richard Nixon

The first case study we are going to analyze is former president Richard Nixon. The very underhanded methods he used to achieve power through acquiring the presidential office are well known. Nixon continued to abuse the power and authority of the presidential office, and all his lies, manipulations, and deceptions were revealed before a horrified public during the Watergate investigation. Nixon resigned immediately after the Watergate scandal. This case study will clearly illustrate the negative application of Pluto aspects in the context of totally resisting the evolutionary necessities of Pluto aspects. Nixon experienced a cataclysmic event as a result of his resistance to his evolutionary intentions (impeachment), which demonstrates the close link between the four main ways Pluto affects the Soul's evolution, and the manifestation of Pluto aspects.

Nixon is in the third stage of the consensus evolutionary condition. This evolutionary state is determined through observation of his life, specifically in the context of his knowledge of how society operates and is structured. Souls who are in this stage have the desire and ability to actualize a career in the highest social strata because these individuals have thoroughly learned how the system, or society, operates and is structured in the evolutionary past. Nixon certainly had learned how society is structured and operates in his evolutionary past, and had this knowledge coming into this current life. His desire to actualize a career of high social prominence is evident. Nixon's obsessive need for social power lead him into some very dark and negative life experiences, which culminated in his removal from the presidential office.

In his natal chart, Nixon had Pluto ℞ in Gemini/10th house. The South Node is in Libra/1st house. The planetary ruler of the South Node is Venus in Pisces in the 6th house. Pluto's polarity point is in Sagittarius in the 4th house. The North Node is in Aries in the 7th house. The planetary ruler of the North Node is Mars in Sagittarius in the 4th house. Mars forms a conjunction with Mercury and Jupiter in Sagittarius in the 4th house.

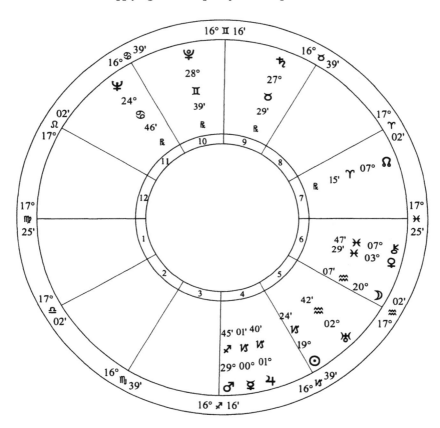

Richard Nixon—January 9, 1913, 9:35 pm, Yorba Linda, CA

Nixon has numerous aspects to Pluto, which correlates with the intention of an accelerated evolutionary growth pace in the current life. In this case, relative to his high degree of resistance, Nixon created a tremendous degree of cataclysmic and traumatic life circumstances. (Again, this is reflected in the numerous stressful Pluto aspects in the natal chart.) These events were intended to propel him toward his evolutionary/karmic requirements for the life in an accelerated manner.

In Nixon's natal chart, Pluto is square the nodal axis. Mars/Jupiter/Mercury are all in a full phase opposition to Pluto. Again, Mars is the planetary ruler of the North Node, which intensifies this aspect. Neptune ℞ is in Cancer in the 11th house makes a new phase semi-sextile to Pluto. Saturn ℞ in Taurus in 9th house is in a culminating (balsamic) semi-sextile to Pluto.

This natal signature reflects Nixon's obsessive and compulsive need for social power linked with a career. The desire and intentions of Pluto in the 10th house are to establish a voice of authority within society, and to adhere to the proper social methods to actualize a career through which a voice of authority can be expressed within society. Emotional maturity, and the need to learn to accept the responsibility of his own actions are intentions of the 10th house Pluto that were clearly not learned prior to the life. These lessons and dynamics are now being repeated in the present, in order to enforce these evolutionary necessities (Pluto retrograde). In this specific case, social status and social power equaled emotional security and personal power. Therefore, the career Nixon wanted to actualize was the presidential office, because it is the most powerful career one can have from a societal point of view. This compulsion led to blind ambition. In other words, Nixon desired a career of very high social status, solely for the sake of the social position and perceived power of such a career. Emotional security and the sense of identity were completely linked with social status, and the career that was actualized (Pluto in the 10th house).

With Pluto in Gemini, the types of facts, information, and data he collected would serve to support the methods he employed to achieve this position. Nixon would not take in any information that did not support some pre-existing notion of his own, or rationalize his abuse of power, as Nixon himself rationalized his behavior. The ends justified the means (Pluto in the 10th house), and he would only collect and absorb information that supported his justifications and rationalizations. Again, the retrograde position of Pluto correlates with the reliving of these desires and dynamics in order to resolve them. We can conclude that Nixon's prior refusal to resolve these issues led to reliving negative circumstances (Pluto retrograde). His knowledge of how society operates and is structured was meant, or intended, to be used in a positive and nonmanipulative manner. Obtaining a career of high social status should, and could have, been a vehicle through which he helped others actualize and establish their own voice of personal authority within society. His own personal evolution could have manifested through holding a meaningful social career by establishing his own voice of authority without being dependent upon, or overly identified with, his career from an egocentric point of view.

The South Node in Libra/1st house correlates with the need to initiate a brand-new cycle of evolutionary becoming relative to social and personal relationships. There is the need to have enough freedom and independence to initiate this new cycle. The intention of initiating a brand-new cycle of evolutionary becoming is symbolized in the South Node in the 1st house. However, in this case, Nixon's resistance to the evolutionary intentions was so compulsive it led into very distorted and extremely imbalanced relationship dynamics. Clearly, he dominated others in society in order to achieve the social and political power he desired.

Pluto is square the nodal axis, which reflects skipped steps from an evolutionary point of view. The 10th house Pluto retrograde now symbolizes the recycling, or reliving, of his past dynamics into the present because he has not initiated the new cycle of becoming that is intended for his Soul's evolution. Thus, he was instinctually acting (South Node in the 1st house) upon his past and known behavior linked with actualizing a career of social prominence for the sake of social power. He had the need to make others codependent upon him, and to be alter egos of himself, in order to fulfill his distorted need for social power linked with his career. This dynamic is reflected in the South Node in Libra in the 1st house.

The planetary ruler of the South Node is Venus in Pisces in the 6th house. This symbol reflects the need for Nixon to eliminate the psychology of victimization. The intention is to acknowledge the actual reality of his own inner reality, and how this inner reality is reflected in his relationships, as well as in his social behavior in general. As Watergate progressed, his constructed mask and persona were removed (South Node in Libra in the 1st house) and his true intentions and agenda were revealed. The personal and social humiliation he encountered (Venus/6th) was necessary because of his orientation to others in personal relationships and to others in society in general, in the context of his need to control and dominate others. Nixon earned an ongoing critical and negative public image as his lies and true agenda were exposed. The intention of experiences of this nature is to induce a vital humility, and purification. The need for self-improvement and to be of true service to society was intended as well (planetary ruler of the South Node is Venus in Pisces in the 6th house).

When Pluto is square the nodal axis, it correlates with an extremely important evolutionary juncture, because issues of the past and the future have not been fully resolved coming into the life. The individual has acted on both areas described by the nodes (the past and the future), yet the Soul has not fully resolved the lessons of either. Thus, the skipped steps symbolized by the square apply in both areas represented by the Nodes. The response that the individual has toward resolving these skipped steps will determine the evolutionary experiences that the Soul will have for a long time to come. This is why this aspect represents such a critical time, evolutionarily speaking.

In Nixon's chart, Pluto is applying to the North Node in Aries/7th because that is the node that Pluto last formed a conjunction with. This node then becomes the bottom line, or foundation, upon which all the unresolved issues described in the square can be resolved, and the current life's intentions can be integrated. The planetary ruler of the North Node will facilitate this process. In other words, the South Node, its planetary ruler, and the polarity point of Pluto must now be integrated through the North Node, with its planetary ruler facilitating the process.

The unresolved issues of this aspect are lessons of emotional balance, learning social and personal equality, and how to give to others what is needed, versus dominating others, and only taking from others what the subject wanted and needed. In essence, Nixon made everybody around him his own personal slaves, or servants, by telling them what they wanted to hear (Venus in Pisces/6th house). Specifically, this dynamic is based on what Nixon considered to be the most important path of all: social power linked with social status (South Node in Libra/1st house). In this way, he turned all those close to him into alter-egos of himself.

Nixon's exposure occurred in the public spotlight as Watergate unfolded, confronted by those who protested his political policies (specifically in the context of the Vietnam war). These confrontations were meant to induce the necessary lessons we have just discussed. Total inequality, dominance, and imbalances were created because of his orientation to personal relationships, and social interaction. Relative to the 10th house Pluto retrograde, social and personal responsibility were not learned previous to the current life, and were now unresolved lessons in this life reflected in the square to the nodal axis.

The North Node's placement in Aries/7th house correlates with these lessons being resolved through learning to be an equal with others, personally and socially (North Node in the 7th house). Inner emotional balance would be achieved, and a brand-new cycle of relationship patterns with others could be initiated (North Node in Aries). Nixon's career was forcibly taken away from him via public exposure and confrontations, as those in public office impeached him. It is important to state that this is an example of a cataclysmic event that is based upon karmic retribution.

The planetary ruler of the North Node is Mars in Sagittarius in the 4th house, which forms a full phase opposition to Pluto. This aspect reflects that the full force of society's opposition to him during Watergate was meant to induce the core lessons of personal and social equality, and to take full responsibility for his own actions (Pluto in the 10th house retrograde, opposing Mars, square the nodal axis). The full phase opposition also reflects Nixon's very forceful method of, to put it frankly, shoving his will and social dictates down the throats of others in society. As the public opposed such treatment, he was forced to retreat, or retract, from social interaction, which is a characteristic of how the full phase opposition will manifest if balance has not been learned.

All of his lies and dishonest practices were exposed during Watergate (Mars in Sagittarius/4th house opposing Pluto). The opposition is a stressful aspect, and because of Nixon's resistance to the evolutionary intentions for the life, this aspect was experienced in a negative manner through the cataclysmic event of impeachment. The opposition of Pluto to Mars is relatively old, which typically correlates with the Soul's enhanced, or developed, capacity to work through and resolve the issues symbolized by the Pluto aspect, because it has been an area of focused metamorphosis in the past. However, the resistance to his evolutionary intentions created a negative manifestation of this aspect. In this case, Nixon resisted the knowledge of the necessary changes he needed to make, and continued to act in the same old compulsive manner as in the past.

Mars is forming a balsamic conjunction to Mercury and Jupiter in Capricorn in the 4th house. This symbolizes that his intellectual patterns (Mercury) and belief system (Jupiter) that condoned justifying and rationalizing his abuse of social power needed to be eliminated (thrown off in the context of the opposition of all these planets to Pluto). His belief system, which condoned such behavior, and his compulsive need to justify his actions through the delusion that the ends justifies the means, operated simultaneously with the desires of a subjective nature that he acted upon (Jupiter/Mercury conjunction to Mars). The conjunction is in a balsamic phase, which symbolizes that these dynamics were intended to culminate in this life. Clearly, he resisted the evolutionary necessity for social and personal balance to manifest (extremes of the full phase opposition, North Node in the 7th house). The culmination aspect then manifested as re-experiencing negative past dynamics and life circumstances that were unresolved.

The polarity point of Pluto is Sagittarius/4th house, and the North Node is in Aries in the 7th house. The planetary ruler Mars is in Sagittarius in the 4th house, making the aspects described previously. The 4th house polarity point reflects the evolutionary intentions of learning to internalize emotional security, and eliminating all external emotional expectations and dependencies. The awareness of what constitutes emotional security, and for what reasons, is vital. Nixon needed to understand why he was operating on an emotional level in the way that he was, and purge all need for social prominence, and recognition linked with his career, to provide emotional security.

The Sagittarius polarity point correlates with the need to embrace the philosophies, and belief systems of others that he had previously judged as wrong, or invalid, because such beliefs did not conform to or support his own existing belief structure. The rigid and fixed intellectual structure that he had created, primarily because of his need to rationalize his own behavior in the context of his distorted need for social power, could be transmuted in this way (natal Pluto in Gemini in the 10th house ℞). Learning internal emotional security would allow Nixon to embrace the necessary beliefs, and align with natural law to create such a metamorphosis. The need to be completely honest in the context of his emotional conduct and motivations is reflected in the Sagittarius polarity point. Honesty and sincerity in helping others through his career would manifest.

The North Node in Aries/7th house, generally speaking, correlates with the need to become an equal with others, and to learn socialization. The need to learn emotional balance, and to treat others as we ourselves would want to be treated, is evident. Nixon was meant to initiate relationships with others in which equality, balance, and mutual independence could manifest. Learning these lessons would allow the intentions of the polarity point of Pluto to manifest. This is the resolution Node relative to Pluto squaring the nodal axis.

The planetary ruler of the North Node is Mars in Sagittarius in the 4th house making the aspects previously described. The placement of Mars re-emphasizes the evolutionary intentions of learning internal emotional security, emotional honesty, and throwing off all old conditioning patterns that were keeping Nixon bound to his compulsive need for social status and power. Mars makes a conjunction with Jupiter and Mercury in Capricorn/4th house, and a full phase opposition to Pluto. These aspects correlate with the lies (Jupiter) and hypocrisy (Capricorn) that Nixon used to rationalize (Mercury) his dishonesty—which was exposed through intense and heated confrontations with others in society (full phase opposition to Pluto). The intention of this type of experience, again, is to eliminate all old forms of emotional dependencies based on his social career, that lead to specific subjective desires (Mars), intellectual organization (Mercury), and beliefs (Jupiter) that were creating obvious limitations. In essence, these dynamics re-emphasize the lessons of Pluto's polarity point in Sagittarius in the 4th house of internalizing emotional security, eliminating all forms of external emotional dependencies (especially in the context of the need for social status and emotional honesty.

Neptune ℞ in Cancer/11th house forms a new phase semi-sextile to Pluto. This aspect reflects the evolutionary intention to dissolve all external emotional dependencies in order for internal security to manifest. The need to purge the delusion that emotional security will be derived from controlling a social group in an authoritarian manner is evident. The culmination of the past cycle of evolution would take hold through objectifying and liberating from all sources of external emotional security, and emotional dependencies in general. Deconditioning of the self-image would then take place, and this could be a potential way in which he could spiritually develop. In essence, through objectifying his self-image and dissolving all forms of external emotional dependencies to achieve emotional security, a culmination of old patterns of behavior would manifest. A new direction, symbolized by the new phase, could then be initiated in an increasingly conscious manner (semi-sextile). The emergence of the conscious awareness of what specific actions to initiate in order to discover the new direction and special purpose of this Pluto aspect will then manifest. Objectification would also take place through clearly understanding the severe emotional trauma he created for others relative to the dynamics discussed earlier. Again, the process of understanding what specific actions to implement to allow this culmination and transformation of the self-image to take place is symbolized by the new phase semi-sextile. The retrograde position of Neptune reflects that he has worked on this area of transmutation previous to this life, and is reliving or recreating the same emotional shocks (Neptune in Cancer/11th house) experienced in the past, in order to resolve these issues. This is a nonstressful aspect which tends to promote an ease of integration and understanding of the necessary evolutionary changes. In this case, this aspect was experienced negatively as an ease of resistance. However, the nonstressful aspect symbolizes that Nixon did understand the reasons why he was experiencing emotional shocks and trauma. It is a relatively new aspect, and Nixon clearly did not attempt to understand or resolve the issues symbolized in this aspect. This led to the egocentric shocks (Neptune in Cancer in the 11th house) in order to induce the necessary emotional detachment from his career, and objectification of his emotional reality in order to dissolve the past patterns of behavior that have been described.

Saturn ℞ in Taurus/9th house forms a balsamic semi-sextile to Pluto. This aspect re-emphasizes the need to establish his own voice of inner authority versus compulsively using social status and a career to provide him with a sense of power and authority. The 9th house placement of Saturn correlates with Nixon's dishonesty in his pursuit of social power. His lies were based upon his need to protect himself, or a very distorted form of self-preservation linked with the survival instinct symbolized in Saturn in Taurus. Survival, or self-preservation, in this case, refers to Nixon's need to keep his social position of power. The need to be honest, to align with natural law, and to become self-reliant is symbolized by this aspect. Again, the retrograde position symbolizes that these are unresolved issues that need to be resolved in this life. In the context of the balsamic semi-sextile to Pluto, resolution of these issues would create the required culmination of the past evolutionary cycle of behavior. The conscious awareness of how to culminate this cycle of evolution would then manifest. The need to align with timeless natural laws of the Universe instead of culturally based truths and anything temporal in nature is symbolized in these Pluto aspects. The balsamic semi-sextile symbolizes that the consciousness awareness of how to achieve this culmination relative to the evolutionary necessities reflected in his birth chart would be in place. However, Nixon's resistance to these lessons is evident (semi-sextile is a nonstressful aspect which, in this case, describes an ease of resistance to his evolutionary necessities).

As mentioned before, all Pluto aspects are meant to enforce the evolutionary requirements symbolized in Pluto's polarity point, North Node, and planetary ruler. Nixon's total resistance to his evolutionary lessons created the intense internal and external confrontations that culminated in the very humiliating experience of removal from office. (Nixon resigned after the truth of his actions was brought to the public's attention.) This case history is meant to demonstrate that resistance to the evolutionary necessities and requirements of Pluto aspects will create negative life circumstances and consequences. Of course, the exact opposite result will be experienced, i.e., positive experiences and

life circumstances, if a Soul chooses to cooperate with the evolutionary intentions reflected in Pluto aspects. This does not necessarily mean
that the Soul will not experience intense metamorphic, and sometimes
even cataclysmic events. The individual's response to those events and
attitude toward change will turn negative events into positive ones as
the necessary changes are made, and evolution occurs.

Second Case Study: Nostradamus

To illustrate this key point, next we will analyze the birth chart of the
famous and astoundingly accurate prophet, Nostradamus. He predicted
such events as the French revolution, Hitler's rise to power, and pos-
sibly the recent 9–11 attacks. Nostradamus was in the 1st stage of the
spiritual evolutionary condition which, again, is determined by his
life events and his capacities. He lived from the years of 1503 to 1566.
This time period was full of collective trauma and religious persecution (Catholic/Protestant wars). In his natal birth chart, he has Pluto
in Sagittarius/9th house squaring (first quarter) Uranus in Pisces/12th
house. Pluto forms a full phase inconjunction with Jupiter/Saturn/
Mars in Cancer in the 4th house, and all these planets are retrograde.
Pluto forms a new phase semi-sextile to Mercury (the planetary ruler of
the South Node) in Capricorn in the 10th house and the Sun in Capricorn in the 9th house. Pluto forms a crescent phase sextile to Venus in
Aquarius in the 11th house. Pluto forms a crescent phase semi-square to
Neptune in Capricorn in the 10th house. Neptune is the planetary ruler
of the North Node. He has the South Node in Virgo in the 6th house
and the planetary ruler is Mercury in Capricorn/10th house conjunct
his Sun in Capricorn in the 9th house. His North Node in Pisces/12th is
ruled by Neptune in Capricorn in the 10th house conjunct his Venus in
Aquarius in the 11th house.

   This natal signature symbolizes Nostradamus' deep devotion to the
Creator, and inherent understanding of natural laws (Pluto in Sagittarius/
9th house). His relationship to the Creator was very developed, and his
life was founded upon service to the Source (South Node in Virgo in the
6th house). Nostradamus is quoted as saying "everything proceeds from

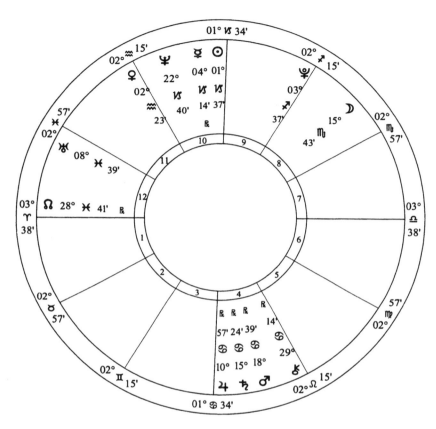

Nostradamus—December 14, 1503, 12:00 pm, Provence, France.
Note: The birth date of Nostradamus is calculated with the Julian calendar.

the power of God almighty, from whom all goodness emanates." His humility spoke for itself as he devoted many, many years of his life to serving humanity. Persecution of those who were perceived as different or radical was common practice during this time period, especially regarding religion (Pluto in Sagittarius/9th house). This dynamic can be seen in the nodal axis in the signs of Virgo/Pisces, and Uranus in Pisces/12th house squaring his Pluto (religious persecution). He lived in the time of the Catholic/Protestant wars, and the Inquisition. He was branded as a black magician by some who were threatened by the nature of his work, and he was summoned by the inquisitors. He escaped the inquisition by fleeing his home. Despite the personal pain to himself, however, he continued to help others through his prophetic writings. These writings transformed our vision and understanding of the nature of reality itself (Pluto in Sagittarius/9th house).

Nostradamas' accuracy of prediction is well documented, and has stood the test of time. He knew that if he could deliver the message warning of probable catastrophes that would occur in the future unless humanity changed its present course, these tragedies could be prevented from occurring in the first place. The Quatrains, or prophecies, that he wrote during his lifetime were intended to ensure that the horrific visions he had would never come to pass. He advocated that all humanity learn from the events of the past, in order not to relive them in the present and the future. In such a way, humanity could then create a better future and evolve as a species, from an evolutionary point of view.

The natal position of Pluto in Sagittarius/9th house correlates with Nostradamus' desire to understand himself in a cosmological/philosophical/metaphysical context. This natal signature demonstrates that he had a very advanced intuitive capacity (Pluto in Sagittarius/9th house), which allowed him to have visions of the future (Pluto square Uranus in Pisces/12th). It also correlates to his natural teaching abilities, and his innate capacity to assimilate knowledge very quickly. He studied and later practiced medicine for many years (South Node in Virgo in the 6th house). His medical knowledge and techniques were ahead of their time. He received a doctor's degree from a well known medical university which allowed him to apply his knowledge of new medical practices in society as an authority on this subject (South Node in Virgo in the 6th house, planetary ruler Mercury in Capricorn in the 10th house conjunct the Sun). Clearly, he was not bound by consensus religion to understand himself in a metaphysical context. He sought to align with natural laws that explain our connection to the cosmos, and not consensus or mainstream religion in any way. Nostradamus is known for his unorthodox beliefs such as astrology, and teachings of Eastern philosophers that were considered heretical at the time.

The South Node in Virgo/6th house reflects that his desire to improve, purify, and perfect himself was a natural point of gravitation. He used specific techniques to see the future, including smoke and a water bowl. This signature reflects that he would analyze the weaknesses and imperfections of his own beliefs (Pluto Sagittarius in the 9th house), and eliminate all beliefs within himself that were not in accordance with natural law. A negative and very critical self-image would be a point of stagnation and weakness that he would have to overcome. Nostradamus' humility is symbolized in the South Node placement as well. He was naturally aware of all his imperfections, faults, and weaknesses, and wanted to improve on these areas.

The need to purge victimization from consciousness is symbolized by the South Node in Virgo in the 6th house. Nostradamus advocated this teaching to humanity in his writings. Again, the key purpose of the predictions he wrote was to help humanity realize that we do have the power to change the future. The only way we can truly accomplish this is to learn from and accept responsibility for the past (planetary ruler of the South Node is Mercury in Capricorn in the 10th house). Nostradamus saw very clearly the repetition and recycling of history into the present and future because of humanity's refusal to accept responsibility for our own actions.

The potential trap, especially within this evolutionary condition, is one wherein he would never feel good enough, or perfect enough to do the tasks that he was being directed to do on behalf of the Source. Another dimension of the South Node is learning to adjust his own teachings and practices to reflect the needs and structure of the mainstream society (planetary ruler of the South Node in Mercury in the 10th house ℞). He could not merely criticize society and others for not understanding or adjusting to his advanced teachings and level of evolution. This is a reflection of his own negative, inner critical focus being projected outward. The dynamic of doubt, and undermining his own natural spiritual capacities would be very likely in this scenario. A common distortion in the first-stage spiritual condition is that the Soul does not feel worthy of the Creator's love, or the blessings that are received from the Creator. The South Node in Virgo in the 6th house correlates with feelings of inferiority, lack, and doubt. Thus, this dynamic of not feeling worthy of the Creator's love or blessings, which then reflects itself in the Soul's work function, is emphasized. The nature of the times he lived in were full of religious persecution, and emotional hysteria revolving around any individual who went against the norms and customs of that time. His self-determination to finish the work that he wanted to share with humanity is clearly an inspiration to us all. His self-determination is symbolized by the planetary ruler of the South Node, Mercury, in Capricorn in the 10th house ℞.

The need to accept responsibility in his own actions, and be emotionally mature, is reflected in the planetary ruler of the South Node in Capricorn in the 10th house, and Mercury being retrograde. This symbol also reflects his natural maturity and self-determination. In other words, he did have an innate maturity and desire to accept responsibility in his own actions. The unconscious cultural conditioning of victimization needed to be purged in order for him to reach his true capacity. The semi-sextile to Pluto intensified this need and intention. It is a relatively new aspect, which symbolizes that this evolutionary metamorphosis, or impulse, is new. It is clear that he was cooperating with his evolutionary intention by the nature of his life, and so this aspect would have been experienced in a relatively smooth manner, and the adjustment to the evolutionary impulse could occur quickly. As an adult he was offered a teaching position after he had graduated from a university with a doctor's degree in medicine. He was often criticized for methods that went against the traditionally accepted practices, such as his refusal to bleed patients (South Node in Virgo in the 6th house). Later on, however, he was hailed as a saint when his prescription of rose pills cured victims of the plague. These pills consisted of large quantities of vitamin C. Vitamin C is widely used today for aiding the immune system.

The orientation and desire to serve the Source naturally lead to the development of his healing capacities, his futuristic visions, and his ability to revolutionize traditional medical practices. This individual could intuitively analyze the deficiencies in current-day medical practices and suggest methods for improvement. His understanding of weakness and faults went beyond the field of medicine, and he could see the limitations of the prevailing consensus society as a whole (planetary ruler Mercury ℞ in Capricorn in the 10th house, South Node in Virgo in the

6th house). The Pluto/Mercury aspect symbolizes the need to adjust his ideas and philosophical wisdom to help the mainstream society evolve (Mercury in Capricorn in the 10th house retrograde).

The trauma of persecution that he suffered is symbolized in the Uranus in Pisces/12th square to his Pluto in Sagittarius in the 9th house. Uranus as a specific correlation with trauma, and the need to liberate from past conditioning patterns. This is why Uranus correlates with the future in a generalized sense. Uranus also correlates with humanity as a collective group, and the need to advance human consciousness as a group through the act of liberation. Thus, this signature reflects Nostradamus' gift to see the future and to help liberate humanity from the mistakes of the past, and to stop the recycling of past traumas into the future. In the context of persecution Nostradamus was condemned as a dark magician and a heretic by some in power in society because of the truth that he spoke, and simply for being different and refusing to maintain or conform to the status quo. Uranus correlates with projections. Nostradamus received many wounding projections by those who did not understand his work. Uranus is in a first quarter square to Pluto, which correlates to the crisis in action he then had in bringing his knowledge out into a society that was rampant with religious persecution, and social dictates to conform to the prevailing beliefs and customs. His own emotional fears stemming from persecution and being rejected wholesale by society (South Node in Virgo in the 6th house) needed to be worked through as well.

Mercury is conjunct the Sun, and Pluto makes a new phase semi-sextile to the Sun and to Mercury. The Pluto/Sun aspect symbolizes the evolutionary intention to identify and establish the Soul's creative purpose, or special destiny. This aspect symbolizes that a metamorphosis of the creative actualization process must occur through linking the special purpose to a socially relevant need. With the Sun in Capricorn in the 9th house, creative actualization must be based on the establishment of Nostradamus' own voice of inner authority within society, based on his innate understanding of natural law. His inherent teaching abilities will come to full actualization as he continues to align with natural law, and establishes a career that reflects these natural laws. An automatic regeneration, or transmutation, of his creative energy and purpose will manifest as these core evolutionary intentions are acted upon. This is a relatively new aspect, and nonstressful in nature, which reflects his ability to understand and make these necessary changes. The evolutionary impulse is new, yet if he desires to make the necessary changes the evolution intended in this aspect can occur smoothly.

The Pluto/Mercury aspect symbolizes the evolutionary need to re-formulate the intellectual structure or framework. This transmutation will occur through the elimination of all rigid and outdated intellectual patterns that are preventing further growth. Mercury is the planetary ruler of the South Node, which symbolizes that this has been a critical lesson from his past which has been carried over into the present. The semi-sextile is nonstressful, and this is a relatively new aspect. The semi-sextile correlates with the emergence of a conscious awareness of the new evolutionary cycle. The Soul begins to sense what the new evolutionary purpose or cycle is about. In this case, Nostradamus realized that for his own evolution to proceed, he needed to establish his own authority in society based on his intellectual capacities and knowledge of a metaphysical nature that reflect natural law (Pluto in Sagittarius in the 9th house, Mercury in Capricorn ℞ in the 10th house). Mercury is conjunct the Sun, which reflects that his creative actualization process will be based upon, and work simultaneously with, his ideas and information of this nature.

Pluto's full-phase inconjunction to the stellium of planets in Cancer in the 4th house consisting of Jupiter, Saturn, and Mars, all retrograde, symbolizes the crisis (inconjunction) he encountered in the context of establishing his visions and his work into society (full phase). The intention is to become aware of social and personal limitations. The individual must now become aware of what he or she can and cannot do, and what others require of the individual in order for the social purpose to be expressed. If these limits are not adhered to, then intense confrontations (crisis) will occur in order to enforce these lessons. One of the fundamental evolutionary lessons that is re-emphasized through this aspect is the need for Nostradamus to adjust his teachings and natural wisdom to fit the needs of society, in order for his teachings to be understood by the majority. The crisis symbolized in the inconjunction also reflects the damage to his self-image that persecution created. This aspect symbolizes that he must resolve insecurities in the context of bringing his work out into society as well. He was able to cure many, many people from the plague, yet he lost his wife and children to the plague. Thus, he was unable to save his family (stellium in Cancer ℞). Certainly, the wounds to his self-image are tremendous. A crisis revolving around the need to purge any insecurities and a negative self-image are manifested through this type of loss.

In the context of the South Node in Virgo in the 6th house, we can see that society was, at first, very critical, and undermined his abilities and wisdom for the reasons that have already been described. Certainly, the persecution and full force attacks Nostradamus received were very wounding to his self-image, and created a crisis in the context of integrating his social purpose into society. The intention was to establish his own voice of inner authority first (Saturn), and be secure within his own beliefs (Jupiter), initiating his own direction and own independent voice free from the dictates of societal conditioning (Mars). The retrograde position of these planets symbolizes that these are dynamics from the past that need to be resolved, and are being relived in some manner in order for the necessary resolution to take place. This Soul did cooperate with his evolutionary intentions as he continually improved and adjusted in whatever ways were needed in order to establish his visions and teachings in society. (He later remarried and reportedly lived a very happy life with his new wife until his death.) Thus, the stressful aspect was experienced positively, and the crisis of the inconjunction was resolved. It is an old aspect which symbolizes that this is an area of metamorphosis that he has worked on before, and is bringing to culmination in this life.

Pluto's polarity point is Gemini/3rd house. The North Node is Pisces in the 12th house. The planetary ruler of the North Node is Neptune in Capricorn in the 10th house conjunct Venus in Aquarius/11th house. Neptune is forming a gibbous opposition to his Saturn ℞/Mars ℞/Jupiter (all ℞) conjunction in Cancer in the 4th house. These symbols illustrate that Nostradamus' evolutionary intentions for this life were to expand upon his existing beliefs and knowledge of natural laws. Any old, outdated, and rigid beliefs that were not in conformity with natural law and inhibiting growth must be purged. In this way, all conditioned (man-made) beliefs will be eliminated. Certainly, his knowledge of natural laws and his beliefs were not necessarily wrong, or invalid, but his beliefs were limited in some way. This is symbolized by the natal position of Pluto in Sagittarius in the 9th house, and Pluto's polarity point in Gemini in the 3rd house.

The evolutionary requirement in this case is to embrace the viewpoints and ideas of other philosophies and belief systems that would promote further growth if these viewpoints did reflect natural law. Again, a common problem with the 9th house, or Sagittarian archetype is that the individual will be orientated to a portion of the total truth in the context of his or her existing belief system, yet will attempt to defend those beliefs as the only valid beliefs, and others as wrong. This will manifest as the widely known symptom of convincing and converting others. The natural truth of a diversity of paths leading to the same goal (God), or the many paths leading to the same end point, or the same natural laws and truth, is a vital lesson contained within the Gemini/3rd house polarity point. The need to understand the diversity of beliefs that express natural law, and the diversity of ways that natural laws can be expressed, was a critical lesson for Nostradamus. The relativity of truth itself could then be integrated.

Another crucial lesson symbolized by the polarity point is to discriminate the difference between fact and opinion, and truth versus indoctrination. Nostradamus did collect a diversity of facts, data, and information that allowed this expansion of consciousness to occur, which reflects his cooperation with his evolutionary intentions. He published a yearly almanac which was highly acclaimed, as well as completing his most famous writings of his predictions of the future (the Quatrains). Nostradamus traveled to different areas of the country, specifically from France to Italy, in which exposure to cultural differences enforced the necessary intake of information and viewpoints that would create the evolution of his own belief structure. In addition to traveling, he learned about different viewpoints and information in the context of the known philosophies and beliefs of his own culture by studying teachings and beliefs that were considered taboo and heretical from an early age. (If an individual was caught with such material it could lead to death in those times.)

Nostradamus was able to give specific examples of how history was repeating itself in the present, and how it would continue to do so if humanity did not learn from past mistakes. In other words, he had the ability to illustrate a single natural law, or spiritual principle, and demonstrate its diversity of expressions throughout history (polarity point Gemini/3rd house) by citing specific examples of historical facts. With this understanding he could then demonstrate that the same dynamic was still operative in the current times. He also applied his understanding of natural laws to medicine. These practices led to the improvement, expansion, and advancement of the medical field.

The specific type of information he learned provided a vehicle through which he could purge his own outdated beliefs that were preventing his evolutionary growth, and to expand upon his existing wisdom (Pluto in Sagittarius/9th house, planetary ruler Mercury in Capricorn/ 10th house re-expressed through the polarity point of Gemini in the 3rd house). He needed to communicate this knowledge with others in such a way that it could be understood from the other's point of view, and reflect the diversity of cultural truths and belief systems. His writing and contact with the patients he healed allowed this type of communication to take place. He was able to communicate with others in such a way that he would reflect the individual's own level of evolution, not just his own.

The North Node in Pisces/12th house correlates to the lessons of continual spiritual development, and of purging delusions from the Soul. His devotion to God was well documented. The lesson for this life would be to continue in that direction with an increased effort and singular focus. This symbol reflects that an entire cycle of evolution is coming to an end. Thus, all the unfinished, or unresolved dynamics contained within the entire cycle that is culminating must now be resolved. The information that he absorbed and communicated was timeless, and universal in nature. His writings transcended the cultural truths of his times because of the universality of his message, or the universal truths that he communicated. The spiritual knowledge that he expressed emphasized the need for unity in diversity, especially in the context of beliefs.

The need to simplify his life and to eliminate all forms of inner and outer crisis and chaos is symbolized as well (South Node in Virgo in the 6th house). The need to forgive himself for all his perceived faults and imperfections, and to love himself unconditionally, was very important in this life. In the context of the South Node in Virgo in the 6th house, all too often he could be excessively critical of himself—his own worst enemy. Any negative and critical self-focus needed to be eliminated. In this manner, he could then seek to improve and perfect himself without excessive inner criticism. The inner purity and clarity he would then attain could be passed on to others.

Relative to the North Node in Pisces in the 12th house, the described expansion and intake of necessary information would then be accomplished through spiritual development. The knowledge he would need to take in relative to the Gemini/3rd house polarity point would be of a spiritual nature. The need to merge the individualized ego with the Source of all creation, and to develop a direct and conscious connection to the Creator is reflected in the North Node. The need to absorb only the material and information that reflected what he intuitively felt to be true, which was relevant to his own evolutionary requirements, and reflected natural law, would allow a simplification in life in general to manifest (Planetary ruler of the South Node is Mercury ℞ in Capricorn in the 10th house, Pluto's polarity point is in Gemini in the 3rd house, North Node in Pisces in the 12th house).

Pluto forms a crescent phase semi-square to Neptune, which is the planetary ruler of the North Node. The evolutionary intention symbolized by Pluto/Neptune aspects is to dissolve all barriers that are preventing a direct and conscious merging with the Creator. The awareness of the nature of personal dreams, illusions, and delusions will manifest as the individual seeks such a relationship with the Source, and purges separating desires that are the cause of illusions and delusions. The realization that only a relationship with the Creator will create true and lasting ultimate meaning (Neptune) will then serve as the potential for Divine inspiration relative to the house and sign Neptune occupies.

Nostradamus certainly was inspired by the Divine in his work, which was accepted by mainstream society despite the struggles and opposition he received from some people (Neptune in Capricorn in the 10th house). It is a relatively old aspect, which symbolizes that this has been an area of focused metamorphosis in the past, and eased the stress of the semi-square. However, discrimination (South Node in Virgo in the 6th house) must be learned. The core lesson in this case is to discriminate whom to impart this knowledge to, and whom not.

Persecution is re-emphasized in this Pluto/Neptune aspect. He was dissolving all old conditioning patterns, and purging delusions and illusions relative to the nature of society in general (Neptune in Capricorn in the 10th house, semi-square Pluto). Any repression or suppression of his emotional body must be eliminated as well. He was establishing his voice of authority within society on his own terms, based on his own inherent wisdom, and not based on society's cultural conditioning. In others words, the need to establish his own voice of authority within society based on his own knowledge is intensified by this aspect. The crescent phase correlates with the need to give a personal application, or meaning, to the evolutionary cycle symbolized by the Pluto aspect. This is done by withdrawal from society in order for internalization of this cycle, or evolutionary purpose, to manifest. The stress in the semi-square is symbolized by the struggle he had with society's response when his work was not understood, and the need to purge his own delusions about the nature of society. In addition, there will be an intense need to create a career in which his spiritual capacities and wisdom could be actualized and communicated to society.

There is gibbous opposition from Neptune to Saturn ℞, Mars ℞, and conjunction to Jupiter, all in Cancer/4th house. This aspect reflects that a necessary humility was being learned through experiencing full force the voices of others in society who could not understand his work, and needed to adjust his work in order to be successfully integrated into the mainstream society. Also, the excessive criticism by people who simply did not accept those who were different is symbolized in the gibbous opposition. The disillusionment he then experienced would have been very painful, and certainly a dynamic that needed to be resolved in the context of actualizing his evolutionary intentions. The need to adjust his work to the level of the mainstream society, and to communicate it in such a way that it would be understood by the majority (Pluto's polarity point in Gemini in the 3rd house, Neptune in Capricorn in the 10th house) is symbolized in this aspect.

Another lesson reflected in this opposition is throwing off (opposition) all fears of persecution, and unresolved insecurities within his emotional body (stellium in Cancer in the 4th house). The negative effects to his self-image relative to persecution, and the trauma of the death of his own family members needed to be thrown off so he could continue to evolve. The extreme and intense opposition he encountered by some in positions of social power in authority was very painful, and hard to overcome (Saturn in Cancer in the 4th house ℞). We can see that disillusionment (North Node in Pisces in the 12th house) was an important, yet painful, aspect in propelling him toward his evolutionary intentions for this life. Also, any unresolved anger at authority, and at society for persecuting him needed to be settled as well. The use of anger in a constructive manner is a necessary lesson for this life (Mars in Cancer in the 4th ℞ inconjunct Pluto). The gibbous aspect manifested as this individual's ability to analyze the deficiencies of his own work. He was able to improve and adjust his work in the ways that were necessary so it could be understood by the majority at the time. Throwing off the described past patterns of behavior will allow his evolutionary development to continue, and the inner balance that is required in an opposition will manifest.

Pluto makes a crescent phase sextile to Nostradamus' Venus in Aquarius in the 11th house. This Pluto aspect symbolizes the evolutionary intention to create a metamorphosis of his inner and outer relationship patterns. With Venus in Aquarius in the 11th house the need to transform his existing inner relationship through the act of liberation of old patterns is highly emphasized. Relative to his South Node in the 6th house, and the other factors that have been described that correlate to a negative and critical self-image, the necessary liberation will resolve around the need to eliminate any aspect of old conditioning patterns that promote the negative self-image. Again, he lost his wife and children to the plague. The trauma that he suffered in his personal relationships and in society in general is symbolized by Venus in Aquarius in the 11th house, and the need to purge unresolved trauma in order to evolve (Pluto aspect Venus). It is a relatively new aspect which indicates that this evolutionary impulse is in its beginning stages of development, which typically creates stress because the evolutionary impulse is so new. Certainly, this tragic and very traumatic loss created stress. Yet, the sextile is a nonstressful aspect, which correlates with an ease of integration and applying these evolutionary intentions. In other words, the nonstressful aspect symbolizes his ability to overcome and work through the intense emotional trauma he suffered.

Venus is conjunct the planetary ruler of the North Node, Neptune. This symbolizes that in order to actualize the evolutionary intentions for this life, the unresolved trauma of the past must be overcome, and the necessary liberation from past patterns of inner and outer relationships must take place. Old, outdated, and crystallized patterns of behavior that were preventing growth will be transmuted. A direct and conscious connection to the Source will be established as these dynamics are brought to culmination. The conjunction of Venus and Neptune symbolizes that these dynamics will operate simultaneously, or as one function, within consciousness.

The case studies just analyzed are meant to illustrate how to interpret specific Pluto aspects in the context of any individual's natal birth chart (include all mitigating factors previously discussed). Clearly, the dynamics of cooperation and resistance to the evolutionary intentions symbolized in Pluto aspects will determine how any Pluto aspect (stressful or nonstressful) will manifest. Richard Nixon experienced very negative life experiences because of his total resistance to his evolutionary intentions. He did have numerous aspects to Pluto, and some were nonstressful. However, because of his refusal to implement the necessary changes, he set in motion the humiliation of forced removal from the presidential office, and the massive public disgrace he experienced after Watergate. Nostradamus fullheartedly cooperated with his evolutionary intentions, and his strength of will is demonstrated in his determination to complete the work that he knew he was meant to do, from an evolutionary point of view, on behalf of the Source. His service to others and devotion to the Creator is evident in his ceaseless efforts to heal those infected with the plague, and his completion of his predictions of the future. Even though he experienced a high degree of trauma and stressful metamorphic events in his life, his attitude toward growth and evolution created positive life circumstances.

7

Natural Archetypes of the Zodiac

What Do the Archetypes Symbolize?

In this chapter we will describe the core meaning of each archetype in the natural zodiac. Each archetype represents a specific function within consciousness—the archetypes symbolize the totality of human consciousness, and each individual archetype represents a specific psychological function within consciousness. When we have a comprehensive and thorough understanding of each archetype, we understand the structural nature of any Soul's consciousness, and the operative psychology within the individual.

We can then take these core archetypes and apply them to the birth chart. We will understand how to synthesize the archetypes together during chart analysis (Cancer on the 5th house cusp, Mercury in Pisces in the 2nd house, and so forth). This process will be described further in chapter 8.

In previous chapters, we learned that each archetype has a planetary ruler—the planet that rules the sign (Jupiter is the planetary ruler of the Sagittarius archetype). There is no difference between the archetypical meaning of Sagittarius and its planetary ruler, Jupiter. The planets describe any Soul's psychological make-up, while the sign and houses correlate with how each archetype is conditioned relative to the sign on each house cusp.

In addition, each archetype corresponds to a house (Taurus corresponds to the 2nd house, Gemini to the 3rd house, etc,) There is no difference between the meaning of the archetype and its corresponding house. In this chapter, the intention is to succinctly describe the core meaning of each archetype in the Zodiac. The main focus, or emphasis, in this chapter is the difference between the natural expression of these archetypes when the Soul is in alignment with natural law, and the distorted expression of each archetype when consciousness has become conditioned by man-made law. We can then take the core correlates of each archetype and adjust them to reflect the Soul's evolutionary state, or condition. The descriptions of the archetypes are taken from the Jeffery Wolf Green correspondence material and *Pluto Volume 1: The Evolutionary Journey of the Soul*.

The Meaning of the Natural Archetype of the Zodiac
Aries/Mars/1st house—Male/Fire/Cardinal

This archetype correlates with a brand-new cycle of evolutionary becoming. This implies that an entire evolutionary cycle has just been completed, or brought to culmination. It is fire, male, and cardinal. Whenever we see a male sign, or archetype, it represents an energetic pattern that emanates from within the center outward (energy moving from the center). Cardinal signs reflect the evolutionary need to initiate a new direction, or a new pattern in behavior. In other words, a cardinal archetype represents the need to initiate change in order for growth to continue. Cardinal archetypes manifest as the individual taking two steps forward toward change, and then taking one step back because he or she becomes insecure about the newly initiated action that reflects change. The net effect is change, despite this back and forth motion. In a distorted expression of this archetype the behavioral pattern described above can reach an extreme, and the individual is then blocking their own evolutionary growth. Clearly, consistency is the key toward achieving a positive expression of any cardinal archetype, and creating continual growth.

Aries correlates to a perpetual sense of self-discovery, and a continual state of becoming. It needs freedom and independence in order to act upon whatever desires and experiences it deems necessary, in order to realize the sense of special destiny (as do all other fire archetypes in the zodiac). The sense of special destiny that correlates with Aries is linked with the development, or discovery, of the intrinsic identity. The special destiny is connected with what is to come, because experience is a vehicle through which growth occurs in the context of the development of the identity. In other words, it is through the initiated actions, and instinctual responses toward any new experience that Aries learns more about its identity. In this way, the sense of perpetual self-discovery and a continual state of becoming is realized. Aries symbolizes our instinctual nature relative to the need for self-discovery, and the brand-new cycle of evolutionary becoming that must be acted upon. Aries correlates with our fears of all sorts, and Mars/Aries/1st house will all describe the nature of those fears.

The natural fire triad of the zodiac is symbolized by Aries, Leo, and Sagittarius. These archetypes form a trine to each other in the Zodiac. This symbolizes an ease of integration of these functions within consciousness in a general sense. The fire triad describes the Soul's full actualization process, or how the individual will act out and actualize the sense of special destiny in all its totality. Aries symbolizes that the sense of special destiny is linked with new experiences, self-discovery, and with what is to come, relative to a new cycle of becoming that is being put into motion. In Leo we have the principle of creative self-actualization based on the Soul's special destiny and creative purpose in life. In Leo, the creative purpose and special destiny are known, and complete. In Aries, the special destiny, again, is linked with perpetual self-discovery and a continuous state of becoming relative to the development of the individuality. In Leo, creative actualization of the special destiny must occur.

The archetype of Sagittarius correlates with the need to understand our connection to the universe in a cosmological, philosophical, or metaphysical context. Thus, Sagittarius correlates with our belief system, and our philosophical orientation in life. These beliefs are then linked with the sense of special destiny. The point in describing each of the fire archetypes is to illustrate that each fire sign in the zodiac has a sense of special destiny, yet what that special destiny is linked to is different in each of these archetypes.

Like all fire signs, again, Aries will need a high degree of freedom and independence in order to do what they must to discover or recover the intrinsic identity, and to discover what the new evolutionary cycle is all about. In this sense, Aries can act as a pioneer in whatever field they choose to work because of their capacity to break new ground. Aries learns on an action-reaction level, because it operates instinctively, or without forethought. Aries learns by the reactions to their generated actions. In its distorted form, Aries can manifest as extreme arrogance and self-centered behavior relative to delusions of self-importance. The sense of special destiny and the need to develop the identity becomes distorted in this way. The trine to Leo symbolizes the distortion of narcissism, delusions of grandeur, and the pyramid reality structure this psychology creates. Another distortion of Aries is that of domination, or of overpowering others. The individual will resent any perceived restriction of personal freedom and independence to act upon any egocentric desire they deem necessary. Of course, it is important to understand if distortions of this nature are based upon insecurities or a sense of personal superiority.

This archetype correlates to anger in any form. There are many reasons why we feel anger. Aries reflects anger at anything or anyone who restricts freedom and independence in order to grow, and initiate whatever experiences are deemed necessary. The crucial lesson in Aries is to use anger in a constructive way to affect the Soul's evolution, and eliminate all personal limitations that are preventing further growth. Anger of this nature truly emanates from within the individual at him- or herself in relation to inner limitations that are blocking further evolution. In its worst extreme, Aries can manifest as physical violence toward another.

It is through the archetype of Aries that we must find the inner courage and strength to create the essential steps toward a new evolutionary cycle of becoming in order to break away from past patterns of behavior that are inhibiting growth. We must find this inner strength so that we do not recreate the past in the present, or bring it into the future. Aries reflects the types of desires that we will hold at a conscious or subjective level. Aries forms an inconjunction to the archetype of Scorpio. Scorpio correlates to the Soul, and the dual desires within the Soul. The metamorphosis of the Soul as it purges its separating desires and evolves to greater heights is reflected in Scorpio. In essence, Scorpio symbolizes the confrontation between the ego and the Soul, and the need to transmute all our limitations that are preventing further growth. Aries symbolizes how the dual desires within the Soul will be consciously acted out, and our subjective desires that we will act upon in order to develop the identity. An inconjunction symbolizes crisis. The crisis that is experienced between Scorpio and Aries is the need to align the personal will and desires with a higher will. In essence, the individual must align his or her personal will and the development of the identity with his or her Soul nature, and cooperation with the evolutionary intentions for the life. Any willful, egocentric actions and separating desires that are inhibiting further growth will be met with intense internal or external confrontation in order for such desires to be purged. The crisis revolves around resistance toward changing past patterns of behavior relative to emotional security, and the effort to maintain the past (Scorpio) meets with the desire for continual growth, for freedom to create change and discover/recover the identity (Aries).

In addition, this inconjunction correlates to an emotional paradox linked with relationships.

Aries reflects the need for freedom and independence, and Scorpio then symbolizes the fear of entrapment in a relationship relative to other people's needs. This paradox revolves around the desire to be in a relationship, yet the fear of becoming entrapped or consumed by the partner's needs, and the need to commit to a relationship in general. The emotional paradox is then linked with these two seemingly colliding needs and desires—the need to be in a relationship and the need for freedom. When we have resolved this crisis within ourselves, the way in which these two archetypes operate within consciousness completely shifts. The inconjunction now reflects clarity rather than crisis and confusion, and our conscious desires (Aries) are now in alignment with our Soul's desires to grow and evolve (Scorpio). We will use positive will power to effect continual and constant evolution, and a desire to cooperate with the evolutionary intentions for the life. We will no longer overpower or dominate others, or have delusions of self-importance or an arrogant attitude toward others, and in life in general.

The question becomes this: what is the driving force or the underlying motivation behind our instinctual behavior? Mars (Aries) is the lower octave of Pluto (Scorpio). A lower octave is a denser, or condensed, expression of a higher vibration, according to *Pluto, Volume I*. In essence, the dual desires within the Soul are transmitted to Mars in order to be acted out. Mars correlates to the conscious and subjective desires that we have, and how we will act out, or act upon, these subjective desires emanating from Pluto. Thus, the evolutionary intentions for the life are given constant motion relative to the new cycle of becoming. This is how Mars operates as a lower octave of Pluto. In its pure form, Aries correlates to the purity of instinct in the context of the desire to align the personal will with the will of the Source. Aries also reflects the desire in each of us to separate, or the instinct to separate in terms of becoming our own individual. An important aspect to understand here is that Aries, itself, does not reflect the desire to separate from the Source. This desire is symbolized by Pluto relative to the two co-existing desires of the Soul.

There is a square from both the archetypes of Capricorn and Cancer. A square symbolizes creative tension/stress in some manner. The square from Capricorn to Aries reflects the creative tension/stress (square) of the restriction that cultural conditioning can create (Capricorn) relative to expressing our true identity (Aries). Cultural conditioning discourages the expression of our actual identity because we are expected to conform (Capricorn) to society's norms, rules, taboos, and regulations. The square may manifest in a negative manner because of unresolved anger at the culture or society of birth. Capricorn reflects the crucial lesson of accepting responsibility for one's own actions. In the context of the square to Aries, we must all learn to accept responsibility for our own desires, and how we have acted upon those desires. The square to Capricorn symbolizes the consequences that we face if we have acted out self-centered, egocentric desires. Positively expressed, anger can manifest at one's own inner conditioning and the desire and courage to break free from such conditioning patterns. In this way, the square can be experienced as the ability to use stress to create positive change (to resolve the tension within the Soul).

The square to Cancer reflects the creative stress/tension regarding insecurities relative to the self-image, and initiating the necessary actions in order to create growth. The new cycle of becoming creates fear and insecurities in the context of the individual's pre-existing self-image, and emotional security factors. The need to initiate change creates insecurities, which is reflected in the archetype of Cancer. The initial anxiety (Aries) of separation from the womb (Cancer) is symbolized in this square. In addition, an important dimension of the square from both the Cancer and Capricorn archetypes, which forms a T-square to Aries, symbolizes the issue of gender assignment. Any culture will have conditioned, prescribed, and socially accepted norms (Capricorn) for both genders, to which the individual is expected to conform. These norms then become a source of emotional security (Cancer) relative to conformity, and the need for social acceptance. These conditioning patterns, linked with gender, impact the self-image in a negative manner relative to insecurities in the context of not conforming to society, and embracing or integrating the anima/animus that is inherent in every Soul (Cancer). The T-square to Aries reflects the tension/stress that manifests relative to the need to develop and discover or recover the identity in an unrestricted manner, and the impact of cultural conditioning on gender assignment. Again, intense anger and rage may manifest because of the restrictions that cultural conditioning imposes on the development of the intrinsic identity, and the effect of cultural conditioning upon the self-image.

In order for evolution to occur within any archetype, it must embrace its polarity point. In this way, the archetype will transmute to higher levels of expression. The polarity point of Aries is Libra, which symbolizes that we all must learn to balance and harmonize our needs with the needs of another. It means that we need to balance our need for independence with the need to be in a relationship. In addition, it means that we must choose or select relationships that are mutually independent, or encourage coequality and coempowerment. Each person in the relationship will desire to actualize their own individuality on their own terms, and will be in the relationship to support each other. Libra symbolizes the necessary lessons of equality and balance, versus domination and overpowering others. Libra correlates with the natural law of giving, sharing, and inclusion. Libra reflects the need to objectively identify reality as it exists for another, not from our own reality. This lesson sets up the need to objectively listen to our partner, and others in general, in order to know what to give to others. Libra symbolizes learning to come from a place of true equality with others, and to give first rather than taking. When we operate in this way, the true beauty of Aries can shine, and we can encourage and motivate others to be and act upon who they intrinsically are as unique and special beings. (Actualize their unique and true identity in whatever way they deem necessary.) In addition, we will know which desires to act upon.

Taurus/Venus/2nd house—Feminine/Earth/Fixed

We are now coming out of Aries, where we were beginning a brand new cycle of evolutionary becoming, and discovering or recovering our identity. In the archetype of Taurus, we root or ground our sense of identity (earth sign), and we establish our inner relationship with ourselves, discovering or recovering our identity in Aries. Taurus is a fixed sign, which correlates with the static operation, or fixed nature, of this archetype. The resistance to change in the fixed signs can be quite intense in relation to insecurities we have when asked to change past patterns of behavior. In this archetype, the point is illustrated with the analogy of the frog in the well. The frog has identified the small part of the sky that it can see from the bottom of the well, and thinks this small piece of the sky is the total universe. The resistance to change symbolized in the fixed sign of Taurus is the resistance to jumping out of the well, and embracing more of the sky, so to speak. This need is reflected in the polarity point of Scorpio. Taurus has a fixed inner relationship based upon this orientation to life.

Taurus, on a bottom-line level, correlates our inner relationship with ourselves. It is a feminine sign, of energy returning to the center. It correlates with how we are inwardly vibrating, or our inner magnetism, and how we are inwardly listening to ourselves (our inner dialogue). Our inner vibration is then the causative factor of the nature of the relationships we attract (symbolized by the archetype of Libra, which is coruled by Venus). The law of attraction, or of like attracting like, is contained within Taurus relative to our own inner vibration and inner relationship.

Again, this archetype correlates to the need to root or consolidate what we have discovered/recovered of our identity in concrete form: we are now establishing our inner relationship with ourselves. The deepest aspect that determines our inner relationship with ourselves is what essential needs we have identified in order for survival to occur. Taurus, as such, correlates to the survival instinct. The survival instinct creates the need to become self-reliant, or self-sustaining. Thus, whenever we see Taurus, Venus, in the 2nd house in the birth chart symbolizes the need to become self-reliant on an emotional and physical level. Part of the survival instinct is the procreation instinct. On this level this archetype correlates to our sexual values: where we are coming from as sexual beings. Pheromones correlate to this archetype. Pheromones are a natural scent emanating from within our own body, which is based on our inner vibration. This inner scent determines whom we decide to be intimate with. This connects to the procreation instinct.

It is our values and the resulting meaning that we give to our lives that creates our inner relationship with ourselves and our inner vibration. The essential need for survival that we have identified determines what we will value and give meaning to, and our inner orientation to life itself. In its distorted form, this manifests as material values, or the desire to accumulate a vast majority of material possessions. These materialist values are then linked with the sense of survival. In addition, we have the distortion of relating to ourselves and others as objects, and possessions that create use and manipulation in relationships (Scorpio polarity point). In the worst case scenario, this dynamic creates the phenomenon of becoming a vicarious extension of another person's values in a relationship.

In a negative expression of Taurus, there is a resistance and laziness to identifying one's own values, and making a consistent self-effort to actualize the inherent capacities within the Soul. Thus, in a distorted expression of this archetype, we will attempt to live vicariously through the other person. Taurus is part of the earth triad, which contains the archetypes of Virgo and Capricorn. The earth triad symbolizes how we will establish and root our values, and the meaning in life that these values create (Taurus) in the type of service that we perform in society (Virgo) and in our career (Capricorn).

Taurus correlates with the inherent inner capacities and abilities we all have within us. The core issue to consider is if we have made a consistent effort to actualize these capacities from within ourselves. Naturally there exists a square between Taurus and Leo that reflects the creative tension/stress (square) in learning to creatively actualize (Leo) in a self-reliant manner (Taurus). Stress will manifest until we have learned this crucial evolutionary lesson. When we have resolved such tension, the square will be experienced positively as the necessary creative energy (Leo), due to effort (Taurus) manifested from within the Soul to resolve the issues described by the square. A core issue in this square is the need to be self-reliant and self-sustaining, versus expecting another person to actualize our capacities for us. Again, the distortion of living vicariously through other people will occur in the context of creative actualization. In addition, we must identify our own capacities, which reflect values of a nonconditioned nature that promotes helping others, self-worth, and self-effort. In other words, materialist values that promote self-interest and exclusion will create a narcissistic creative actualization process (Leo). The crisis of the inconjunction will then be experienced in order to induce self-reliance, self-sustainment, and identifying personal values independent from the consensus society in general. In a negative expression of this archetype, laziness or inertia will manifest in the context of the need to actualize our own lives by our own means. The distortion can also manifest as stubbornness and resistance to necessary change (fixed sign).

The archetype of Aquarius also forms a square to Taurus. Thus, the archetypes of Aquarius and Leo form a T-square to Taurus. The square from Aquarius reflects the crisis involving the need to objectify our inner relationship with ourselves, and adopt values that reflect the need to serve humanity, and are linked with a socially relevant need. The need to objectify ourselves, and liberate from the conditioning patterns of the consensus society triggers a crisis when we have not learned to identify our own values, and thus create a self-reliant orientation to life in general. The Aquarian archetype correlates to the peer group, and to our lifestyle on a mundane level. Thus, the tendency to adapt the values of the prevailing peer group will create intense crisis because of the evolutionary need to become self-reliant and actualize our inherent capacities. Aquarius also correlates with trauma. The square from this archetype to Taurus, then, reflects the crisis that trauma creates when a necessary self-reliance has not been learned, and the Soul must be thrown back on itself in order to learn this lesson.

Venus is the planetary ruler of Taurus, and shares a corulership with the archetype of Libra. Libra, again, is the archetype of the initiation of relationships with others, and emergence into the social arena in general. Libra is the projected, or external, nature of Venus relative to the relationships we form with other people. Taurus, then, correlates with the inner nature, or side, of Venus relative to our inner relationship. There exists a natural inconjunction between Taurus and Libra. As we become aware of what we possess in order to affect self-reliance we simultaneously become aware of what we do not have and need from other people. This dynamic is symbolized by the inconjunction of Taurus and Libra. Another dimension of this inconjunction is the crisis of learning self-reliance within a relationship. Again, to emphasize a critical point, the law of attraction, of like attracting like, is symbolized here. The underlying crisis of the inconjunction is the need to learn to meet our own needs (Taurus) from within ourselves instead of projecting these needs onto our partner and in relationships in general (Libra). The Libra archetype deals with the nature of projected needs and the expectations these projected needs create within relationships. Taurus symbolizes the need to become self-reliant, and to meet our essential needs from within. Thus, the inconjunction is felt when we have projected too many of our needs onto a partner and have become excessively codependent and needy (Libra). We are then thrown back on ourselves, and the vital lesson of self-reliance must be learned (Taurus). Of course, we can experience this same dynamic through our partner, who is projecting too many needs.

We can then manifest the other extreme (Venus, and the archetype of Libra correlates to extremity) of isolating ourselves from any social interaction. We then create an inner implosion because of the limitations this orientation creates (Taurus). Again, the critical dynamics that must be resolved in order to eliminate the crisis of the inconjunction is to meet our own needs from within, and stop projecting these needs onto our partners. Venus symbolizes balance that must be learned through its corulership of Libra. When we successfully learn the evolutionary lesson of creating self-reliant relationships by learning to meet our own needs from within and identify our essential needs instead of projecting these needs onto our partner, we will then eliminate the crisis of the inconjunction and the same aspect will manifest as clarity within consciousness. An inner vibration of harmony and inner balance will permeate our being. We will approach relationships in a totally different manner.

Venus correlates to the psychology of listening, and how we are listening to ourselves (Taurus) and to others (Libra). Taurus reflects the nature of our inner dialogues, and Libra symbolizes how we are listening to, or hearing, our partner and others, based on our inner dialogue. For example, if an individual is relating to him- or herself in an excessively critical manner, then that person will attract a partner who is critical, and reflects this inner dialogue in the relationship. In addition, the individual will project this critical dialogue onto others when listening to them. In other words, the individual will interpret the partner as criticizing him or her, when this may not be the case.

Taurus forms a sextile to Pisces. The archetype of Pisces correlates with the need to realize ultimate meaning, and transcend time and space altogether. Thus, this archetype symbolizes merging with the Creator, and the need to align with universal and timeless laws. The sextile from Taurus to Pisces symbolizes the need to establish ultimate meaning from within through a relationship with the creator. Neptune, the planetary ruler of Pisces, is the higher octave of Venus. Relative to the inconjunction to Libra, the common distortion that manifests when we have projected an ultimate meaning externally is to turn our partner into a defacto God/Goddess. We have, in essence, projected the ultimate meaning we are meant to find within, through a relationship with the Source, onto our partner. We then place the partner on a pedestal. However, at some point in time, we will realize that our partner is not perfect, and the partner will fall from that pedestal. Pisces symbolizes disillusionment, and we then experience disillusionment within the relationship in order to be realigned with actual reality. This experience is meant to induce the awareness that we must meet our own need from within, and stop projecting ultimate meaning onto our partner in relationships. We will then be able to see ourselves and our partner clearly (Pisces). In addition, this sextile symbolizes the need to develop a primary inner relationship with the Creator, in order to establish self-reliance, and find ultimate meaning from within through this relationship. We can then, again, approach relationships in a non-needy, self-secure manner.

The polarity point of Taurus is Scorpio. Scorpio, in general, correlates to the awareness of deeper levels of reality. Scorpio also correlates to the process of evolution, metamorphosis, and transmutation. Thus, this archetype symbolizes the need to confront and purge all internal limitations that are preventing growth. Scorpio correlates to the general field of psychology, and of psychoanalysis. Scorpio desires to penetrate to the core, or bottom line, of its own and others' psychology, in order to transmute limitations, and to become aware of its own and others' motivations and intentions. Scorpio is always asking the question "why?" Why life, why death, why am I behaving in this way, and another person in that way, and so on. This is why Scorpio correlates to internal and external confrontations. Scorpio also correlates with hidden, or ulterior, motives and agendas. This is why Scorpio symbolizes use, manipulation, and betrayal.

Remember earlier, we used the example of a frog in a well to illustrate how Taurus operates? Through the Scorpio polarity point, the frog is forced to jump out of the well due to the internal and external confrontations that manifest. These confrontations are meant to promote awareness of the limitations of the individual's pre-existing orientation to life. The polarity point promotes the awareness of why we are relating to ourselves in a specific manner, and why we have certain values. We must learn to merge ourselves and our resources with others in such a way that it adds to what we and others are. This demands that a fundamental self-reliance be learned. Through the metamorphic process of Scorpio, our inner relationship and values are transmuted to higher levels of expression.

Gemini/Mercury/3rd house—Male/Air/Mutable

Gemini correlates with the collection of a variety or diversity of data and information from the external environment. This archetype symbolizes the need to order and classify the world and information we collect in a logical, empirical manner (air sign-mentally oriented). We then make larger and larger connections to the world through the information we collect, so that ultimately we can come to a broader understanding of ourselves—where we fit in the grand scheme of things. Gemini comes after the archetype of Taurus where we were rooted inside ourselves, needing to withdraw in order to establish our inner relationship with ourselves. In Gemini, we re-expand outward into the physical, or external, environment (Male sign-energy emanating from the center). There is no limit in the context of how much information can be collected in this archetype. The need for perpetual intellectual growth and a diversity of experiences reflect the mutable nature of this archetype. The symbolic representation of the mutable archetype is a concentric spiral which reflects the adaptability to change. Gemini symbolizes the need to give names and classifications to the phenomenal environment. There is an emphasis on facts rather than on the deeper, metaphysical truths of these facts (Sagittarius polarity point).

The data that we collect will reflect our own mental orientation, attitudes, and opinions of all sorts. In other words, in the distorted form of this archetype we will leave out certain information or facts because it undermines our sense of inner security. This archetype reflects the way in which we communicate with others. This, of course, is a reflection of our inner thought process, or patterns. Gemini is left brained, rational, and empirically orientated. Mercury/Gemini/3rd house symbolizes a step by step, linear and analytical process. It is deductive logic and the process of one fact logically connecting to the next fact. This sign reflects the need in consciousness to logically and rationally explain the world around us. We need a diversity of experiences in Gemini in order to collect the type of information that will allow mental growth and expansion to occur. In addition, this sign reflects all sorts of opinions and mental biases that we may have, and need to grow past at this point in time. In the birth chart Mercury (which rules Gemini) reflects how we are mentally organizing the world around us, and our mental structure in total.

Mercury has a corulership with Virgo. This corulership correlates to the discrimination process—what information we take in and what information we leave out. In addition, the Gemini function in consciousness collects the information, and the Virgo function analyzes and organizes it. Both Gemini and Virgo correlate with the mental mind in these ways (air signs).

Gemini correlates the need to communicate what we have learned as a way of processing the information we have absorbed into the intellect (air sign). The risk in this archetype is to take in too much information, or too much data that connects in so many logical ways that we mentally implode. This occurs so the necessary mental adjustments can occur (Mutable sign). We must be willing to eliminate or let go of certain outdated or rigid opinions within ourselves that are creating blocks from an evolutionary point of view. Relative to the mutable correlation to Gemini, the mental adjustments can be made quickly when the need presents itself. Another correlation of this archetype is periodic restlessness and mental boredom or frustration. Restlessness is experienced when we are not getting the amount of information that we require, and reflects the need for continued mental growth. When this archetype is operating in a distorted manner, boredom is constant, and dominates our being. In a distorted fashion, when restlessness has not been resolved, we race out into the environment and collect one fact after the next without integrating or assimilating these facts. In other words, we read this book and that book, take this class and that class, yet no true assimilation of the information occurs. Superficial information and behavior in general is a common distortion of Gemini because of these dynamics. In addition, mental or intellectual defensiveness manifests if the pre-existing viewpoints and ideas are challenged. The individual will then react by attempting to assert that his or her views are right and others are wrong.

Gemini is connected to the natural air triad in the zodiac of Libra and Aquarius. The air triad reflects communication and collection of a diversity of information (Gemini) that will then determine with whom we form relationships, through comparison and contrast with others. We bond or socialize only with those who are of like mind (Aquarius), and who share our ideas, viewpoints, and mental orientation in general. In addition, the information we take in (Gemini) will allow us to compare/contrast ourselves against others through the attraction of a partner who mirrors or reflects our sense of individuality back to us (Libra). We can then form the appropriate social groupings/bonding with likeminded Souls and continue expressing our unique individuality through such liberation and the process of deconditioning (Aquarius). A crucial lesson reflected in the archetype of Gemini is that there is a limitation to what the rational and empirical mind can know. The intellect or intellectual mind does not know what is true and what is false. This realization triggers the need to embrace or evolve toward the polarity of Sagittarius.

The polarity point of Gemini is Sagittarius. Sagittarius correlates to the right brain and our intuition, and corresponds to the need to understand life in a metaphysical, cosmological, or philosophical manner. Thus, Sagittarius symbolizes our belief structure. Our beliefs are the determinant on how any of us will interpret life. Whereas Gemini reflects the process of collecting a diversity of information from the external environment, Sagittarius reflects the process of assimilation and interpretation of those facts into a holistic understanding (our belief system). Ultimately, we realize through the Sagittarius polarity point that the truth exists in and of itself, and cannot be known by the rational mind alone. The key here is to learn the difference between fact and opinion. When we can do this we can come to an understanding of how all the facts we take in connect to the bigger picture, or a larger concept. This is reflected in the Sagittarius polarity point.

Through the process of embracing the Sagittarius polarity we develop our intuition, which is firmly centered in our right brain. We become aware of, or focus on the larger picture in life, and conceptual wholes versus details and mental analysis symbolized by Gemini/Mercury/3rd house. In Sagittarius, we simply know what we know without knowing how we know it—this is the intuitive faculty in all of us. Another important point to address is that we must tune into this intuitive faculty in order to quiet the busy mind. As we embrace the lessons of the Sagittarius polarity point, we will pick one comprehensive system of knowledge that feels right, so that we can create a holistic and consistent way in which to interpret all the facts we collect. All unnecessary data, information, and facts that we have gathered will be eliminated in this way, and any mental chaos that we previously felt will no longer be experienced. The right and left brain become balanced within consciousness. As this balance is achieved, the ability to teach natural laws through illustrations of a diversity of facts that demonstrate the same natural principles will become unsurpassed. Sagittarius reflects the natural abilities that we all have.

Evolution takes place when we discriminate between facts that reflect the truth, and opinions that reflect our own mental biases. The realization that truth is relative is vital from an evolutionary point of view. Typically, this lesson will be learned through intellectual/philosophical confrontations with others in order to expose the limitations of the individual's viewpoints, and mental structure. Once we have realized this point, we will no longer have to label ourselves right and the other person wrong (Sagittarius polarity). The difference between a reaction and a response will be learned in this way. Again, through embracing the polarity point we can attain the capacity to intuitively grasp the connection of all the facts that we gather (Sagittarius polarity), and come to a holistic understanding of these facts. We can then become very adept at communicating and teaching this understanding to others. The polarity of the 9th house correlates to the archetype of the teacher, or the natural wisdom that any of us have and can then teach others. This is the true beauty of the Gemini archetype when it is expressed in its pure form.

Cancer/Moon/4th house—Feminine/Water/Cardinal

This archetype correlates to our self-image and egocentric structure. In Gemini we have projected ourselves into the physical environment to collect all the data and information that we needed for further evolution to take place. Now, in the sign of Cancer, we are forming a personal relationship to the information we have collected. In this way we form a unique self-image (feminine sign-energy moving back into the center). As such, the Soul's current egocentric structure and self-image will be described in the natal birth chart by locating the Moon by house, sign, and the aspects it is making. The function of the ego and resulting self-image in consciousness is analogous to a lens on a movie projector. If there was no lens on the projector, we would see only diffused images of light. In the same way, the egocentric structure of the Soul and self-image that manifests allows a conscious integration of our evolutionary lessons to take place through our emotional body (water sign). Cancer/4th house/the Moon will describe all the factors that imprint, or influence, our self-image. It also symbolizes the nature of our personal insecurities relative to pre-existing emotional security patterns.

Our early childhood environment has a tremendous impact on our self-image. This is exactly why Cancer has a correlation to the specific nature of our early childhood environment. Cancer correlates to the nature of the mother, or the key female, and the role she played in our lives. The crucial point within these correlations is emotional nurturing. Every child naturally expects to be emotionally nurtured and loved in the ways that they need. When these emotional needs have not been met in childhood, and left unresolved, we create displaced emotions in our adult life. This is why this archetype reflects the need to internalize emotional security. In addition, Cancer reflects our ability to nurture ourselves and, in turn, our ability to nurture others. Cancer symbolizes how we are living within ourselves, within our emotional body, on a day to day, minute to minute basis. In other words, this archetype reflects the nature of our inner home. The water triad of Cancer/Scorpio/Pisces describes the nature of our emotional body in total. When we carry these displaced emotions from childhood forward into our adult life we create the dynamic of emotional infantilism, or immaturity.

Cancer is a part of the natural water triad with Scorpio and Pisces. The water triad describes that totality of the Soul's emotional body and emotional dynamics, and reflects the metamorphosis (Scorpio) of the egocentric structure and self-image (Cancer) through uniting or merging with God (Pisces). In essence, the evolution within the Soul that occurs as the center of gravity within consciousness shifts from the ego to the ego to the Soul itself, as we merge and unite with the Source as reflected in the water triad.

A very deep dimension of this archetype is the anima/animus dynamic, or inner male and inner female. This principle reflects the natural truth that the Soul is simultaneously male and female (beyond gender). Cancer reflects how we will integrate and thus feel emotionally secure with both genders. The anima/animus dynamic, clearly, connects to our self-image relative to the need to integrate both genders. It is an absolute evolutionary necessity that we come to accept and actualize the anima/animus dynamic within our Soul during our evolutionary journey. Over a great length of evolutionary time and development, we arrive at a place of androgyny. In the context of the need to internalize emotional security, the need to become secure within both genders is symbolized in Cancer. Thus, Cancer deals with gender assignment issues of all sorts relative to emotional security and the self-image. The conditioning patterns of specific cultures relative to gender assignment is reflected in the Capricorn polarity point. Gender conditioning patterns are evident and promoted in many ways in our society. For example, here in the United States, if I am born as a man, am I not conditioned to be a "Marlboro" man? If I am a woman, am I not conditioned to be a "Betty Crocker" type person? What happens if I choose not to fit into these two generalized roles? Many of us will have to work through layers of insecurity in order to feel inwardly secure within both genders, and no longer play into these culturally prescribed roles. In this way, a natural femininity and a natural masculinity will manifest from within our Souls. Our self-image cannot help but transmute into higher levels of expression (trine to Scorpio) as we integrate the anima/animus dynamic.

Another aspect that triggers insecurity in Cancer is the need to conform with (Capricorn polarity) the expectations of the majority, or consensus, in society. Remember that Cancer is a cardinal sign, which means that there is a need here to initiate a new direction. The initiated change that is needed in Cancer revolves around internalizing emotional security and creating a positive self-image in the ways that have previously been described. Just imagine the damaging effects to our self-image after lifetimes of conforming to these incredibly binding roles, and being dependent upon another to provide emotional nurturing and security. Do we not, at some point, feel restricted and frustrated at the limitations of conforming to these prescribed roles? This is another dynamic that triggers the need to initiate a new direction symbolized by the cardinal nature of Cancer.

The natural square in the Zodiac from Cancer to Aries and Libra (forming a T-square) has been addressed in the description of Aries. Again, the square to Aries from Cancer symbolizes the need to break free from cultural conditioning patterns in order to discover/recover our intrinsic identity. Aries desires freedom and independence in order for self-discovery to occur on a continual basis. The tension in the square, then, reflects the insecurity that the need for self-discovery creates when our pre-existing emotional security is threatened relative to our self-image. Cancer also receives a square from Libra which, at its worst, can describe the extremity (7th house) of any ego (4th house) that has identified only with itself (1st house). In general, this square symbolizes the borders or boundaries (Capricorn polarity) of the identity (Aries) of any person and their egocentric structure (4th house), and of who they intrinsically are and who they cannot be (Libra).

When Cancer feels secure within itself, it can be one of the most emotionally nurturing signs of all. These people can encourage and motivate others to nurture themselves in the ways that they need so that they will not come into adulthood with displaced emotions of their own.

The polarity point of Cancer is Capricorn. The lessons of emotional maturity and of taking full responsibility for one's own actions are symbolized in the polarity point of Capricorn. Capricorn correlates with the structure of our consciousness, and symbolizes the need to actualize a personal voice of authority within society. We must learn society's norms, rules, regulations, and customs in order to integrate our personal voice of authority within society. As such, this archetype reflects the nature of our cultural or societal conditioning patterns. We need to conform to the consensus, mainstream society. Through the Capricorn polarity, we must take responsibility for ourselves and our actions, and learn to actualize our own lives through our own self-determined efforts. An important aspect of the polarity point is the career we choose to actualize. The crucial point is that we cannot choose a career simply because it is in conformity with the majority of society, if we desire to express our voice of authority within society in a meaningful manner. Our self-image and egocentric structure will be totally transformed in a positive way as we internalize emotional security, and mature emotionally through the polarity point of Capricorn.

As the core lessons of the polarity point are integrated, Cancer has the capacity to be emotionally nurturing and internally secure. We will have the ability to nurture ourselves in the ways that we need, and as a reflection, nurture others in the ways that they need. In the context of parenting, we will not be bound by the conditioning patterns of always needing to be an authority figure to the child, and in control of our emotions (repressing emotional expression via the Capricorn polarity). We will learn that the best way to be a parent is to be a friend, and to nurture the individuality of the child in the ways that are needed. This is the true beauty of the Cancer archetype when it is expressed naturally.

Leo/Sun/5th house—Male/Fire/Fixed

The core correlation of the Leo archetype is creative self-actualization. Leo symbolizes the need to take control of your destiny and actualize it out of the strength of the will (male sign). This is a fire archetype, which reflects the sense of special purpose and destiny within it. When in this archetype, the special destiny is known and complete, and it is time to creatively actualize this purpose (in Aries the sense of special destiny is linked with self-discovery and development of the identity).

Leo/5th house/Sun symbolizes the purpose for life itself. Coming from Cancer, when the egocentric structure and self-image were forming, in Leo it is time to creatively actualize that ego. The central distortions of Leo are the formation of the pyramid reality structure which creates a more or less narcissistic orientation to life, and delusions of grandeur. These distortions occur because of the special destiny and purpose within Leo, yet, most commonly, deep insecurities create the negative expression of this archetype. The critical point to address is that if any of us creatively actualize in an essentially self-centered manner, then we will remain locked inside a narcissist vacuum that will implode at some point in time. In addition, the dynamic of self-centered giving is a common problem within this archetype. This occurs when an individual only gives to another in order to have his or her own self-centered needs met. Another issue is that the individual will give to another according to his or her own self-centered reality, and not truly give to another what is needed. The individual may also project his or her own self-centered image upon another person, and attempt to control the creative expression and actualization of that person according to these self-centered images of the individuality of the other person. This type of conflict especially occurs between parents and children, and must be understood in this light when confrontations do occur.

There is a square from both the archetypes of Scorpio and Taurus. The square from Scorpio symbolizes transmuting the need for an external source of validation, and creating re-empowerment in this way. In the context of the compulsive nature of Scorpio, Leo correlates to a defacto compulsion to be externally validated as wonderful and special. In other words, insecurities within the Soul create a virtually bottomless pit of need for attention, flattery, and validation. Whatever the Soul receives is never really enough. This dynamic will not change until the Soul learns to provide this validation from within, and thus effect self-reliance (square from Taurus). A T-square also reflects the need in all of us to actualize ourselves (Leo) based on our own self-reliant and self-made efforts with our own inner resources (Taurus). The necessary inner metamorphosis can manifest relative to transmuting the need for constant external validation, and creating re-empowerment within the Soul (Scorpio). When we make these necessary changes, the way in which we creatively actualize will fundamentally transform. We can find the inner courage and will to take charge of our special destiny, and actualize a creative purpose that reflects our Soul nature and true capacities. Leo symbolizes leadership capacities that we all have. (Of course, these capacities will reflect the Soul's evolutionary condition.)

Leo forms an inconjunction from Capricorn. This aspect reflects the blocking force that will be experienced from society if we do not link our special purpose to a socially relevant need (symbolized by the polarity point of Aquarius). Capricorn symbolizes the need in all of us to find our own inner authority, and to actualize a personal voice of authority within society. A tremendous degree of frustration can occur when we are blocked by society in this way, and we do not feel acknowledged by as much recognition as we feel we deserve. Again, this will occur when we have not linked our sense of special destiny purpose with the needs of society.

The polarity point of Leo is Aquarius. The polarity point symbolizes the need to link our special destiny and creative purpose to a socially relevant need, develop an objective awareness of ourselves—in life in general—and detach from a pyramid reality structure. In so doing, we can acknowledge the creativity and special capacities of others without feeling threatened. We will be liberated from all conditioning patterns relative to an excessive, self-centered focus in life, delusions of grandeur, and the formation of a pyramid reality structure, as the necessary objectivity is developed. Objectivity means the ability to empty ourselves of emotion and dispassionately analyze or view any behavior or situation. Aquarius correlates with the need to liberate and decondition from cultural conditioning patterns. This need reflects the desire to express and actualize the Soul's inherent and unique individuality. It is through this archetype that we become aware of what is unique and different within. The desire to break free, or liberate, from all outdated and crystallized conditioning patterns creates the need to objectify ourselves and others, and remain essentially detached from the impact of the main society in general. Objective awareness leads to the ability to understand how an individual can positively contribute to a group, and how any individual's creative and special talents can best be used to serve humanitarian needs. Aquarius correlates to the individuated unconscious, which contains memories that are unique to an individual. This includes past life memories. As the awareness of our unique individuality becomes conscious, the desire to liberate from any past conditioning patterns that are preventing growth and expression of a unique individuality is triggered.

Once the Soul links the special purpose and destiny with a socially relevant need, the inherent leadership abilities and strength of will of Leo can shine. The Soul will have learned to provide inner validation, and will no longer be dependent upon others to provide this validation in a compulsive manner. In this way, the insecurities of the past that created this distortion will be purged. The individual will be able to objectively understand his or her own individuality, as well as the individuality of others. Leo can be truly generous, encouraging, and motivating to others in the context of creative actualization. The individual will give to others what is truly needed from their reality, rather than the individual's own, without any ulterior agenda or motive.

Virgo/Mercury/6th house—Feminine/Earth/Mutable

Virgo is a transitional archetype. In this archetype we are transiting from egocentric (subjective) focus and development (symbolized in Aries-Leo) into egoconcentric (objective) awareness and development (symbolized in Libra-Pisces). Egoconcentric awareness means that the Soul is progressively linking the identity to larger and larger wholes, and the universal.

In this archetype we become aware of all our lacks, imperfections, and faults. Feelings of inferiority, lack, and doubt manifest as a result. It is the awareness of all our lacks and imperfections that triggers the need for self-improvement, self-purification, and self-adjustment. Essentially, we must now deflate or pierce the balloon of the self-inflated ego coming from Leo. This is the reason this archetype correlates with the need to learn an essential humility.

In Leo, subjective development is at its maximum, and we are learning to actualize that which we are. In Virgo, we are learning what we are not, and again, piercing the balloon of the self-inflated ego. In its distorted form, this archetype manifests as an excessively negative and critical self-focus. We can truly become our own worst enemy.

This archetype symbolizes an existential void, which is more than just a basic aloneness that we can all feel at various points in our life. This is why Virgo correlates with a variety of avoidance and denial types of activities. The point is that until this void is faced, the individual will attempt to fill it with a variety of external activities. Examples of how this dynamic will manifest are as drug and alcohol abuse, or the "busy bee" syndrome. We create so many external obligations that we never get around to doing what we must do for ourselves. Sadly, the inner void lives on, and we compulsively try to deny or avoid it in any way we know how. This painful reality must be avoided at all costs.

Unfortunately, the negative and critical self-focus is all too often projected upon the external environment and life itself (always focusing on what is lacking and deficient in some way). The archetype of Virgo consciousness may suddenly turn inward, creating a self-analytical and self-critical focus. In essence, we are analyzing our own egos. This is a very important and necessary process, because true and sincere humility can then manifest.

In addition, Virgo correlates with the initial awareness of others. Ultimately, this leads to awareness of the Creator, or the Source (Pisces polarity point). It is through the self-perfection and purification process that we potentially become prepared for the next archetype of Libra, in which we learn to operate in society and in relationships as an equal. We also learn to achieve harmony and balance within ourselves and with others around us. In this way we become socialized beings. (Libra correlates with the initiation of a diversity of relationships with others, and embraces the social world, in general.) In other words, through critical self-analysis and self-purification, the Virgo archetype prepares to integrate in society and in relationships with others in a way that is based upon true equality.

In the broadest sense, this archetype symbolizes the need to be of service to the whole, or to society. We must learn to be of service in a way that is truly helpful to others, yet is not self-destructive. We learn these lessons through an inverted pyramid effect wherein our needs are now at the very bottom, whereas in Leo our needs were at the very top (no society will allow anybody to exist just for him- or herself). It is through the experience of the inverted pyramid effect that we learn the lessons of humility and personal purification. All delusions of self-grandeur and self-importance will be eliminated.

In addition, one of the deepest lessons of Virgo is a vital lesson of discrimination. On a bottom-line level, this discrimination means separating actual reality from any delusions or illusions that we may have (Pisces polarity point). In turn, this learned discrimination will promote the awareness of proper priorities. A critical lesson included in discrimination is aligning oneself with the actual work function that is meant to be performed from an evolutionary and karmic standpoint, and as directed by the Source (Pisces polarity point). This is meant to replace or eliminate any form of work done just to work, and is thus not in harmony with the individual's natural capacities, and evolutionary/karmic requirements.

Another dimension of this archetype is that we suddenly become aware of what we must work on (self-improvement) in order to reach our ultimate ideals or dreams of perfection (Pisces polarity point). Clearly, the awareness of what we are lacking symbolizes an ultimate standard of conduct or realization of ideals of some sort that we are attempting to accomplish.

The question becomes this: what is the basis of these ultimate or idealized standards? Are these standards based on a conditioned and false conception of the Source that is outside ourselves and, somehow, demanding perfection from us all? As we can clearly conclude, if we are judging ourselves and others based on standards of perfection that nobody can reach, then we will forever fall short of the measuring stick, and so will others. The point within this, especially in times like these, is to adjust and eliminate all unrealistic standards of perfection, and the chaos and pain they create. In essence, we must realize that nobody is perfect, and that we are all on this planet to evolve. We must adjust our conception of the Source as inherently perfect, and realize that the Creator is an evolving force (Pisces polarity point). This is exactly the evolution that must take place in order to reach the true purity and joy of this archetype. The danger in Virgo is to become so hung up on our imperfections, faults, and lacks that we become our own worst enemy. In the worst case scenario, we become too paralyzed to act at all.

The Garden of Eden myth is a very important correlation of this archetype. In this myth, we are told that man is superior to woman, and woman now, somehow, symbolizes the temptation or downfall of man. Man is then made to feel guilty for giving in to this temptation and angry because of it. Woman is then made to feel guilty and needs to atone for the guilt. This creates the dynamics of dominance and submission, or sado-masochism. In some individuals, these pathologies can operate simultaneously within consciousness.

In women, this myth creates the pathology of masochism. Again, masochism describes a psychology in which the individual feels guilty and inferior, and must atone for this guilt. When an individual is operating from a masochist pathology, he or she is, somehow, never good enough or perfect enough to do what must be done, and what the Creator is directing the individual to do in life.

The masochist will compulsively create one crisis after the next in order to avoid the pain that this psychology creates. This reflects the need for self-punishment relative to feelings of guilt and the need to atone for such guilt. On a positive note, crisis leads to self-analysis, which generates self-knowledge. Ultimately, the individual will learn what dynamics must be eliminated through the experience of crisis. Masochism creates a dynamic of perpetual undermining activity. This creates yet another source of guilt because of the feeling that we have copped out on ourselves in some way, because we have not fully actualized the true totality of our talents/personality (Pisces polarity point).

In men, typically, this archetype correlates with the pathology of sadism, wherein the individual feels guilty, yet superior, and then reacts from this anger linked with guilt. The sadist will hurt and humiliate others first in order not to be hurt, and punish others as a form of self-punishment. However, the sadist does not feel that they deserve this punishment as reflected in masochism—quite the opposite. The man now needs to get back at a woman for giving in to the temptation.

The behavioral results of both of these pathologies described above are truly horrendous, yet have astonishingly become a part of our living reality. In fact, sado-masochism has been a part of our emotional/psychological reality for so long that many of us do not even recognize these distortions for what they are any more. Obvious examples are the countless rapes and other abusive treatment of women by men that occur every day.

Another important aspect of this archetype is the psychology of victimization in which we either deny or are unable to accept the responsibility for our own actions. In this way, we feel victimized by the very reality we have created. Victimization is also a part of our cultural/religious conditioning that we must overcome. Many of us feel the inner call and yearning to throw off this conditioning for good, and to once again experience the joy of our natural selves. The inner call toward freedom from this conditioning is one of the deepest meanings of the Virgo sub-age of the Piscean age. This is why it is essential that we truly understand the conditioning of this archetype in sharp contrast to its natural expression of purity.

The polarity point of Virgo is Pisces. Pisces symbolizes the culmination of an entire cycle of evolution. As such, the Pisces polarity point demands that an emotional/mental simplification manifest in order to dissolve (Pisces) all old mental/emotional/spiritual patterns that are preventing direct and conscious merging with the Creator. In this way, an entire evolutionary cycle will be brought to culmination. In addition, this simplification process will create a clear and more holistic view of our self-concept. This knowledge will provide a crucial lesson of discrimination.

Pisces reflects the need to learn self-forgiveness and tolerance for all our faults, imperfections, and mistakes. Once we learn these lessons, it cannot help but be reflected in our external conduct with others. We will now be able to love ourselves and others unconditionally. The feelings of being absolutely alone are meant to guide us to the realization that only a relationship with the Divine, or the Source, can fill the existential void.

The Pisces polarity point, again, teaches us that only a relationship with the Divine will alleviate this condition. All feelings of aloneness will be dissolved, or brought to culmination, through a relationship with the Creator. We can then truly be of service to others. In addition, this archetype induces the transition from deductive to inductive reasoning—from attempting to build the whole out of all the separate parts, to the ability to grasp the whole first, and then allowing the parts to naturally reveal themselves. In this way, yet another dimension of the mental/emotional simplification process will be learned. We will arrive at a clearer and more simplistic understanding of ourselves (our own self-concept) and of life in general. In its pure expression, Virgo will manifest as a true and sincere desire to serve the Creator and others. We will allow the Divine to use us as a channel, and simply do the tasks we are being directed to do.

Libra/Venus/7th house—Male/Air/Cardinal

The archetype of Libra correlates with the initiation of a diversity of relationships with others. Libra evaluates its own identity through comparison and contrast with others. We become aware of our individuality in a social context. The initiation of relationships sets up the need to listen objectively to others in order to understand reality as it exists for others, not from our own reality (symbolized in Leo). This creates the awareness of the relativity of personal needs and values in life in general.

In addition, we are learning how to objectively identify reality as it exists for others, in order to know how and what to give to them according to their reality. This is a crucial lesson in Libra because of the need to integrate into society and operate in relationships as an equal instead of on a dominant/subservient basis (Virgo). Libra reflects the natural law of giving, sharing, and inclusion. Venus correlates to the psychology of listening, or how we are listening and hearing others. It is our inner dialogue that will condition how we listen to our partner. This is why the universal experience of not truly being heard by another manifests. When we are listening to others through the filter of our own needs, expectations, and reality in general, we cannot truly hear what the partner is communicating.

In the archetype of Virgo, we pierced the balloon of self-inflation, and potentially arrived at a place of true humility and inner purification. In the archetype of Libra we are now ready to interact or embrace the social world and integrate into society as an equal. In Virgo, we were preparing, or transitioning, into the initial awareness of others. Again, all traces of egocentricity and an overly subjective orientation to life were purged. The potentially purified individual can now enter the social arena as an equal. However, Libra correlates to psychological extremities and imbalances of all sorts, and the need to create or learn balance. Relative to the correlation of Virgo to sado-masochistic behavior leading to dominance and submission, Libra symbolizes that equality and balance within relationships, personally and socially, must be learned. (The common astrological myth is that Libra is inherently balanced.) It is in this archetype that we face the discordant and extreme aspects of our nature and try to reconcile them.

Libra symbolizes the need to complete the self through relationships. In its distorted expression it will manifest as the need to be needed. In essence, we have displaced emotional needs (square to Cancer) that we are projecting onto the partner to fulfill. This, obviously, creates codependent relationships. Until we have learned to meet our own needs from within the extremities, imbalances, and codependencies within relationships will be sustained.

There are two types of extremities that can be reached in this archetype. The first is when an individual dominates a partner with his or her own self-centered needs in such a way that other partner's needs are excluded. The individual expects the other to be an alter-ego of him- or herself. This type of individual will manipulate the dynamics of the relationship in such a way as to make the partner feel that he or she needs the individual in life to feel love, acceptance, and validation. The individual has clearly created a situation of extreme dominance over the other person. The individual has the need to make another codependent upon him or her in relationships. The other extreme is one wherein the individual becomes the alter-ego of the partner, and meets the partner's needs to the exclusion of his or her own needs. Again, the individual has become manipulated in such a way that he or she feels that by meeting the needs of the partner they are having their own needs meet.

Another central dynamic in Libra is that projected needs and expectations create the phenomenon of conditional love, and conditional giving. This is vastly different than unconditional love, and unconditional giving. (Neptune is the higher octave of Venus. Neptune correlates to unconditional love, and unconditional giving.) When projected needs in relationships are not met, then the withholding of love and giving will occur. In addition, we may not recognize the true giving that does come our way because of these unresolved emotional distortions.

Clearly, cultural conditioning dramatically impacts the relationship dynamics between men and women relative to these extremities. Women, again, are conditioned to feel inferior and subservient to men. This creates the expectation to be dependent upon the male partner, and that the female meet the male's needs to the exclusion of her own. The man is conditioned to feel superior to women, and thus, expected to create relationships where the female partner is dependent upon him. Again, until both partners have learned to meet their needs from within and not project these needs in relationship imbalances, extremities and inequalities will be experienced.

A very common distortion of Libra is what has been called "the chameleon archetype." This occurs when we adopt the persona of our partner, and unconsciously play into the expectations of others relative to the projected needs of the partner, and the persona that the partner projects upon us relative to these needs. Of course, we act in the very same manner. The point is that the need to be needed creates the appearance of one individual becoming many different people in relationships—depending on the current partner and type of relationship that he or she is in. This is why it has been called the chameleon archetype. Clearly, identity confusion is symbolized in the archetype of Libra.

The inconjunction from Libra to Taurus has previously been described under the archetype of Taurus. Again, the crisis that is reflected in this inconjunction is the need to meet our needs from within instead of projecting them onto a partner. In this way, we will become self-reliant in relationships, and encourage our partner, instead of creating codependent relationships. There is also an inconjunction from Pisces to Libra. Neptune is the planetary ruler of Pisces, which is the higher octave of Venus. This inconjunction symbolizes the crisis we will experience if we project our need for ultimate meaning (Pisces) upon a partner and, essentially, turn the partner into a defacto God/Goddess. If we place any person upon a pedestal in this way we will experience a crisis of disillusionment as the person falls off. This type of experience teaches us to meet our needs from within ourselves and create relationships of equality and balance. The sextile from Taurus to Pisces reflects the need to establish ultimate meaning from within through a conscious connection to the Source. We will become self-reliant in this way, and attract others who are vibrating in the same way.

The polarity point of Libra is Aries. Aries symbolizes the need to find the courage to strike out on our own and develop our identity in an independent manner. We must create relationships of mutual-independence in which balance and equality is realized.

The polarity point reflects the need to learn when to give and when not to give. These situations will always revolve around a partner who is asking for more to be given, yet has not integrated or acted on what was previously given. As the individual learns to withhold giving in these situations, he or she is actually practicing a form of supreme giving. The core lesson that must be learned is that by giving first, individuals will have their own needs met ten-fold. We must choose partners who have the capacity to actualize their own life by their own means, and who also encourage mutual independence.

As these lessons are put into motion, our orientation and approach to relationships will be totally transformed. We will be in relationships in a self-secure manner with a positive self-image. We will no longer be dependent on another to tell us who and what we are, and what we should or should not be doing in our life. We will be able to ask and answer our own questions from within, and thus discover or recover our identity. Our true identity can then shine as never before, as the pioneering capacity of Aries is actualized. We will, in turn, encourage and motivate others to have the courage to strike out on their own and discover or recover their identity.

Scorpio/Pluto/8th house—Female/Water/Fixed

The archetype of Scorpio symbolizes the Soul, and the process of metamorphosis and evolution. The common analogy used to illustrate the principal of evolution is a caterpillar that forms a cocoon and then transforms into a butterfly. This reflects transmutation, one form leading to another form. Pluto, Scorpio, and the 8th house reflect areas of deepest unconscious emotional security that any of us will have because of its correlation to the Soul. This is why this archetype symbolizes compulsions, obsessions, and resistance to growth (fixed sign).

The Soul contains two opposite, antithetical desires. One is the desire to return to the Source, the other to separate from the Source. The Soul evolves over a great period of time as we exhaust our separating desires. As we purge our separating desires, the desire to return and merge with the Source becomes stronger and more dominant within the Soul. It is the interaction of these two antithetical desires that determines the choices we make. This is why Scorpio symbolizes the phenomenon of choice making. The choices that we make will then create karma in general. Karma can be positive or negative, depending on the choices that we make relative to the desires we act upon.

In this archetype, we come face to face with our own limitations and points of weakness that we must overcome if we are to evolve. We experience power and powerlessness as a result. This archetype symbolizes the awareness of universal forces, and the desire to merge with these universal forces. Ultimately, these forces are those of God and Satan, or good and evil. Merging with universal forces allows personal evolution to occur. In a sense, the confrontation of the ego and the Soul is reflected in this archetype in relation to the two existing desires within the Soul. The Soul desires to grow, yet fear of the unknown related to pre-existing emotional security patterns creates the need to sustain separating desires and the old orientation to life in general.

Scorpio desires to penetrate to the core, or bottom line, of any dynamic that is preventing further growth. This creates the need for a psychological understanding of our own motivations, intentions, and desires, as well as the need to understand others in this same way. This is why this archetype correlates with the field of psychology. In essence, Scorpio is always asking "why?" Why life, why death, why do I operate in this way, and another person in that way? In addition, the need for evolution and transmutation creates the need to experience or challenge that which is labeled taboo, or forbidden by society.

Scorpio correlates with sexuality. Sacred sexuality is used to help the Soul evolve because of its transformative nature. Sexuality in its natural form is used in a ritualist manner to merge with the Source. The proper use of sexual energy must be learned. Sexuality is meant to be used to re-empower ourselves and our partner. The metamorphosis of sexuality is its transformation from profane and for procreational reasons to a sacred act that is used to merge with the Source, and with the divinity of another. We are all aware of the horrible sexual distortions that have manifested through the patriarchy. Sex used as a form of violence—to overpower or dominate another—is the unfortunate reality that has been created in current times. The worst form of this sexual distortion is rape and the other forms of sexual abuse that occur all too frequently.

Scorpio correlates with the dynamics of manipulation, use, loss, and betrayal. These distortions manifest because of unconscious emotional security factors, and the resistance to change. This archetype reflects the fear of abandonment, betrayal, and loss. These fears lead to the psychology of suspicion, and of knowing whom to trust and whom not to trust. There is commonly a fear of commitment—yet simultaneously, the desire to commit to one partner in a relationship.

The inconjunction to Aries from Scorpio symbolizes the fear of entrapment and the emotional paradox within relationships that this fear creates. The fear of entrapment, abandonment, loss, and betrayal are the causative factors that create a fear of commitment. Whereas Libra desires to initiate a diversity of relationships with others, Scorpio symbolizes the choice to share a committed, intimate relationship with, or not. This is the reason this archetype symbolizes marriage.

The water triad of Cancer, Scorpio, and Pisces symbolizes the emotional body in total, and the metamorphosis (Scorpio) of the self-image and egocentric structure (Cancer) as the Soul merges with the Creator

(Pisces). In addition, this triad symbolizes emotional security factors, and the experience of having the emotional rug of security pulled from underneath the feet. The intention of this experience is to internalize emotional security (Cancer) in order for evolution to continue (Scorpio) through a conscious connection to the Creator (Pisces). Emotional security is then linked with our connection to the Creator.

The polarity point of Scorpio is Taurus. This polarity point symbolizes the need to learn self-sufficiency and self-reliance. In essence, we must look within ourselves to find the inner symbols of power and transformation. In this way, all external dependencies for a source of personal power and transformation will be transmuted. The individual will view change and growth as a positive and necessary aspect of life.

As self-reliance is established, the ability to grow and change as necessary will manifest. The individual will learn to encourage and motivate others to grow and change as necessary in a nonmanipulative manner. All dynamics of use, betrayal, and violation of trust will be purged from the Soul. The ability to trust and commit to a partner in a sustained relationship (marriage) will manifest. Taurus symbolizes the need to identify our inherent essence, or identity, in contrast to other people that we have osmosed. We will be able to merge with others in a self-reliant manner, and this only adds to what we are. When these lessons are learned, the true beauty of Scorpio will manifest.

Sagittarius/Jupiter/9th house—Male/Fire/Mutable

Sagittarius correlates to the need to understand our connection to the universe in a cosmological, metaphysical, or philosophical context. This need then creates the belief system/structure of the Soul. In the archetype of Scorpio we are seeking to merge with a higher source of power, or universal forces, in order to effect evolution. In other words, through the archetype of Scorpio we become part of larger, universal forces, and desire to merge with these forces. In the archetype of Sagittarius, this connection is known. We now need to explain or understand our connection to the universe, or cosmos, in metaphysical context. There is a focus on the "bigger picture" and a higher purpose in life. In addition, coming out of Scorpio, psychological levity and humor occurs within Sagittarius. The ability to laugh at the absurdity of life in general manifests. This archetype symbolizes our intuition because we are aware that we are a part of the universe. The intuition simply knows what it knows without knowing how it knows it. It is not a product of the mental mind, or deductive reasoning. As such, this archetype symbolizes the right brain, which is conceptual and abstract in nature. We intuitively understand that there must be natural laws or truths that explain the existence of creation by the sheer fact that creation exists. This is why one of the deepest correlations of Sagittarius is to natural law. This archetype symbolizes our teaching capacity, and wisdom in general. However, an inherent problem within this archetype is the need to learn to communicate intuitive knowledge in a way that can be understood by the majority (Gemini polarity point). In other words, because this knowledge is intuitive, frustration commonly occurs in the need to communicate the knowledge in a logical language system that can be understood by most other people.

As with all fire signs, Sagittarius correlates with the need for freedom and independence. In this archetype, freedom and independence is needed in order for the individual to align with the beliefs that he or she is intuitively drawn to. In other words, this archetype will not allow restriction of whatever beliefs an individual feels drawn to experience. The sense of special destiny that Sagittarius feels is linked with the specific belief structure to which we are orientated. The belief system we have in place will then determine how we interpret any event—how we are, in truth, interpreting our very life. We can now clearly see the importance of this archetype and the issue of interpretation. In other words, if we are choosing to interpret our lives in a generally negative and critical manner, then we will not receive the true gift of what our lives are meant to give, nor are we learning from our prior mistakes. The issue of interpretation is an extremely important aspect in all our lives, and we must make sure that we are interpreting events, and our life, in a manner that is in alignment with natural law. Our interpretation needs to reflect natural law, and not conditioned indoctrination. On the deepest level, Sagittarius correlates to natural laws, or the natural principles that describe how creation itself functions. This is why the Sagittarian archetype correlates to truth and honesty. However, relative to the distortion of this archetype, Sagittarius can correlate with dishonesty and outright lies. In the worst case scenario, this can manifest as compulsive dishonesty, like master salespeople who can appear sincere, honest, and truthful to the observer, because of the belief in what is being sold.

Another common distortion of this archetype is the need to convince and convert others to the beliefs that the individual feels are true. Insecurity within the belief system is typically the causative factor that creates this dynamic. If we are truly secure within our belief system, then the need to convince and convert others will not manifest. The analogy that has been used to illustrate this distortion is the preacher at the pulpit. Intellectual and philosophical defensiveness toward any person who threatens or challenges the individual's existing beliefs can manifest. This is why the phenomenon of generalizations occurs in this archetype. Generalizations describe a situation wherein an individual attempts to apply his or her own limited personal beliefs to all people, and insists that these beliefs should be adopted by all others. The difference between true teaching and indoctrination must be learned through the Sagittarius archetype. This is why this archetype has been called the "Billy Graham" archetype. Sagittarius makes a sextile to Libra, which symbolizes the realization that truth is relative, and that we should not impose our personal beliefs on others. In addition, the sextile reflects our ability and need to harmonize our personal beliefs with natural law, and to work in harmony with nature. The extent of domination over nature that man-made indoctrination has created is evident, and must be brought back into balance.

The dynamic of compensation is a crucial factor. Sagittarius correlates to compensation relative to feelings of inadequacy and inferiority. Sagittarius makes a square to Virgo, which symbolizes the feelings of inadequacy and inferiority. The compensation for these feelings creates unconscious embellishments, exaggerations, and emotional dishonesty. The square symbolizes the creative stress/tension in the need to discriminate truth that reflects natural law, and indoctrination that reflects conditioned, man-made beliefs. The tension between aligning the left brain and the right brain is reflected in this square as well. Virgo correlates to health issues, and ultimately, through Sagittarius, Virgo realizes that health is a function of our inner vitality. Sagittarius also makes a square to Pisces. This square symbolizes the tension or creative tension in aligning our beliefs with universal, timeless truths. Through Pisces we realize that our personal beliefs are only a small portion of the total truth. The expansion symbolized in Sagittarius occurs as this realization is made, and embraces more and more of the total truth symbolized by Pisces. When we attempt to limit our beliefs to what we already feel secure with from an evolutionary point of view, then the square to Pisces will create the necessary tension in order to embrace the universal, timeless, and ultimate truths. Again, we must align our personal beliefs and truth with ultimate or universal truths that reflect natural law.

An important correlation of Sagittarius is the Daemon archetype, or the Daemon Soul. The word "Daemon" describes when consciousness in human form merges with all other forms of life, including plant and animal life, in such a way that an alchemic fusion with these life forms within consciousness occurs. The Soul then becomes a messenger of God, or the Source. The patriarchal Christian perversion of this word and of these Souls is clear in the word "demon." In addition, animals have been present as agents of evil, or of Satan. (This occurred as the delusion that human beings are superior to nature, and the rest of creation began to dominate the planet.) One of the greatest teachings of this archetype which has been expressed by daemon Souls who are well-known spiritual teachers, is to let nature be our greatest teacher.

The polarity point of Sagittarius is Gemini. The need to realize the relativity of truth, and that a diversity of paths lead to the same goal is reflected in the Gemini polarity point. The need to embrace different viewpoints that express natural law is symbolized as well. Outdated and rigid beliefs that are preventing growth can be purged in this way as the individual opens up to different intellectual/philosophical systems that allow expansion and growth to occur. Commonly, intense intellectual and philosophical confrontations will manifest in order to expose the weakest point in the individual's intellectual/philosophical system. It is not that the beliefs of the individual are necessarily wrong, but they are limited in some manner. As these lessons are learned, the need to convince or convert others will be eliminated. All emotional dishonesty and the need to embellish or exaggerate will be purged as well. Natural law will become the guide to know what beliefs and information to take in, and what to leave out. Natural law will also be the foundation of the Soul's belief system, instead of man-made indoctrination. In addition, the true teaching ability of Sagittarius can manifest. The ability to teach natural laws in a diversity of ways, and illustrate a variety of facts that demonstrate the same natural principles, is unsurpassed. The individual will now be able to communicate his or her knowledge in a way that is understood by the majority.

Capricorn/Saturn/10th house—Feminine/Earth/Cardinal

In the archetype of Sagittarius we are establishing our belief system, and aligning with the natural laws and principles of the universe. In Capricorn we now create an inner structure (feminine archetype) in which these beliefs are crystallized, or become concrete in our external reality (earth archetype).

This occurs through the laws, norms, and regulations that are established within any society (we must have laws and regulations in any society or country or else anarchy will manifest). This is why the archetype of Capricorn correlates with the country and society of birth, and all the cultural norms, regulations, taboos, and customs of the country of birth. Thus, this archetype symbolizes the mainstream, or consensus society. Capricorn symbolizes time and space reality.

This archetype symbolizes the structure of consciousness itself. Capricorn/Saturn/10th house function within consciousness is analogous to a cup that holds water. The water assumes the form of the container (cup) into which it is poured. In the very same way, our consciousness is conditioned by the nature of the society or country into which we are born, relative to the cultural norms, and taboos of that society. The phenomenon of consciousness itself is symbolized by Neptune/Pisces/12th house. The structure, or container, of consciousness is symbolized by Saturn/Capricorn/10th house. The archetype of Capricorn and Pisces forms a sextile, which reflects the relationship between these two signs that has just been described.

This archetype reflects the nature of our cultural conditioning patterns. Repression and suppression of our natural emotions is a distortion of this archetype relative to cultural conditioning patterns. It is the dynamic and need to conform to social/cultural norms that creates the suppression/repression of our natural emotions. Conformity to man-made doctrines now manifests relative to our belief system that is symbolized in Sagittarius. Conditioned guilt is created in this way because of the nature of religious indoctrination.

There are two kinds of guilt that we can all feel. One is acquired guilt, and the other is conditioned guilt. Acquired guilt is guilt that is linked with wrong actions in the past, and conditioned guilt is guilt that is linked with man-made, religious indoctrination. The difference between these two types of guilt is essential to understand, because of the dramatic impact guilt has within consciousness. Clearly, as we discriminate (trine to Virgo) the nature of guilt, we will know how to purge it from the Soul. Whatever is repressed or suppressed becomes distorted. When conditioning patterns of the consensus restrict our ability to express our natural emotions and our individuality, depression, frustration, futility, and pessimism manifest.

The dynamic of control, or of needing to control either our external environment, the people in our environment, or our own emotions (repression) manifests in this archetype as well. The fear of losing control over life's circumstances creates this reaction. A very important aspect of the Capricorn archetype is that the desire to access chaos, or to lose control, often creates the dynamics we have just described.

In addition, man-made indoctrination creates distorted judgments that are subjective in nature. The point in this is that there is a vast difference between what is naturally right, and what is naturally wrong, which is based on natural law. The conditioned morality that is promoted through indoctrination is not based upon natural law, and, in fact, induces conditioned guilt that is inhibiting to all of us. Judgment is intrinsic and natural to consciousness. We must judge our behavior as right or wrong in order to learn from previous mistakes and to grow. It is the nature of judgment, or the content that is being used to form judgments, that is the critical difference.

Capricorn symbolizes the need to express a personal voice of authority in society. This archetype has a direct correlation to authority relative to the external society, and the need to conform to societal rules and customs to actualize a career. The crucial lesson is to project a voice of personal authority from within, and not be dependent upon or dominated by a social role to provide a voice of authority.

Capricorn symbolizes the need to change or eliminate any component within consciousness that has become crystallized, outdated, and is preventing further growth (cardinal archetype). The common problem with this archetype is that a high degree of security is linked with the pre-existing structure of consciousness, and the need to change dynamics within consciousness that are preventing further growth creates insecurity. This creates the need to maintain the previous patterns of cultural conditioning. The common distortion is to become overly identified with a career or social role from an egocentric point of view. The dynamic that causes this is the need for social status linked with a social position. When this occurs, the danger is to desire a career because of the social status that it provides, and to neglect the responsibilities of that position (of course this can occur in varying degrees of magnitude and intensity).

Another vital lesson, or intent, within this archetype is the need to accept the responsibility for our actions, and mature emotionally. (The square to Aries from Capricorn symbolizes the consequences that we face relative to our initiated actions, and the frustration that occurs when we repress our natural instincts.) This is why morality correlates with this archetype.

Capricorn makes us aware of our mortality from an egocentric point of view. In other words, we become aware that we have a limited amount of time to accomplish our evolutionary goals. This awareness triggers emotional maturation. The psychology of self-determination is created as we motivate ourselves to do the necessary inner work that will allow our inner and outer structures to change in a positive manner. The need reflected upon past conditions of an internal and external nature is symbolized because of the need to change aspects within consciousness that are preventing further growth. Reflection promotes the awareness of what we need to change, and how to implement the proper steps to actualize the necessary changes. Reflection is a positive expression of the Capricorn archetype in contrast to depression, because there is no negativity in the emotional expression.

The polarity point of Capricorn is Cancer. Cancer describes the fundamental lesson of internalizing emotional security. Emotional security cannot be dependent upon social status, and thus the social career one has actualized. A personal voice within society will then manifest what is not defined by a career.

Another aspect of internalizing emotional security is integrating the anima/animus dynamic. This occurs in higher evolutionary states, but the need to not conform to socially prescribed roles relative to gender is crucial in all evolutionary states.) This archetype reflects the need to become aware of our emotional dynamics, and why we operate emotionally in the ways that we do. Opening up to our natural emotions, and allowing these emotions to be expressed will create emotional maturation. All repression/suppression of the emotional body and the emotional distortions that repression creates will be eliminated in this way. The need to allow ourselves to be vulnerable is also reflected in the polarity point. The ability to nurture ourselves and others will then manifest. As these lessons are learned, we will be able to hold a meaningful career in society without overly identifying with the career from an egocentric point of view. Internalization of emotional security fosters the ability to use a career in a constructive manner that supports our ongoing evolutionary needs.

Cancer correlates with family, and the family environment. As such, the family will play a crucial role in creating these necessary lessons. The individual must be available to his or her family on an emotional level. Thus, a balance between the social and family obligations will be learned. In other words, the family environment will be a primary vehicle through which these evolutionary lessons can be integrated and acted upon. When Capricorn operates in its natural state, the ability to make others feel respected and dignified is unsurpassed. We can then help others actualize a personal voice in society as well.

Aquarius/Uranus/11th house—Male/Air/Fixed

In Capricorn we are establishing a crystallized or concrete structure of consciousness, and actualizing our own voice of authority in society. The nature of cultural conditioning, and the dynamic of conformity to the consensus, is symbolized in Capricorn. We have gained an understanding of how conditioning patterns operate individually and collectively. We have the awareness of how society works, and the nature of our own structure of consciousness.

In the archetype of Aquarius, we must now liberate and decondition from all of our conditioning patterns, in order to arrive at our own unique essence. The Buddhists have termed this the "diamond self." The analogy that has been used to illustrate the individuation process is the peeling of an onion to arrive at its core. Conditioning is progressive over lifetimes, not just the current life. Thus, Aquarius reflects a need to liberate from past life memories that are influencing our present behavior. The natal location of Uranus, the house that the sign of Aquarius occupies, and planets in the 11th house or in Aquarius in the natal birth chart, all symbolize dynamics that the Soul intends to liberate from in this life.

Aquarius symbolizes an acceleration of evolution because of the need for liberation. For example, if a Soul has Uranus in the 9th house, then that Soul desires to liberate from all man-made religious beliefs that are inhibiting further growth, and the expression of individuality. In addition, all emotional dishonesty must be eliminated. Liberation and deconditioning will occur through aligning with natural law, and expressing the Soul's true individuality through beliefs that reflect natural law.

Clearly, in this archetype, the need for liberation is essential, because the conditioning patterns of the consensus are often very restrictive to growth, and to our intrinsic individuality. However, relative to Capricorn which proceeds Aquarius, this need may be suppressed because of the fear of being ostracized for being different, and not conforming to mainstream society. In the consensus evolutionary condition, the need to decondition from cultural conditioning patterns and the feeling of being different is most often repressed. This commonly manifests as an individual attempting to maintain the status quo's method of operation, and resistance to any departure from social norms of the current time. Again, this reflects insecurity and fear linked with the need to change inner societal conditioning patterns that are inhibiting further growth.

In the individuated state, generally speaking, there will be a high degree of resistance to any external agent that arbitrarily attempts to mold our personality and tell us who we "should" be or how we "ought" to behave. Those in the individuated state will feel very different than those in the mainstream society, and the desire to liberate from cultural conditioning patterns intensifies. In this evolutionary state there is a growing sense of alienation from the consensus. However, especially in the 1st stage of the Individuated state, compensation may still manifest through external conformity to the consensus.

The Aquarius archetype is an important one because it triggers transformation on a personal and collective level. If all of us were simply to conform to these social norms, evolution would not occur. We need to question societal norms, customs, and taboos in order for individuation and liberation to manifest. We must find the inner strength to be unique individuals, and not conform to cultural conditioning patterns. One of the deepest lessons of this archetype is to learn to be a group of one, if necessary. On a mundane level, this archetype symbolizes our lifestyle.

The psychology of liberation requires that we develop the capacity to objectify reality in general, in order to eliminate any behavioral dynamic that is restricting further growth. Any cultural conditioning patterns that do not reflect our true essence, or individuality, will be eliminated in the same way. We must learn to empty ourselves of emotion in order to dispassionately and objectively understand the dynamics that need to be purged in order for liberation and individuation to manifest. This is why the archetype of Aquarius reflects the ability to detach from the environment and from the emotional body. In essence, we are detaching from the immediacy of our own ego (Leo polarity point), and learning to view life and ourselves in an impersonal and objective manner. We are learning to detach from the mainstream of society as well. The negative application of Aquarius is detachment from the emotional body, and from emotional interaction with others. In addition, there is very little, if any, participation in society, in the context of helping society evolve through the act of transformation of the existing societal structure.

An important correlation to this archetype is trauma. Trauma often occurs in order to induce the necessary objectification and liberation from past conditioning patterns that are preventing growth. When trauma is unresolved, it creates detachment from the emotional body, and emotional/mental/spiritual fracturing, because the traumatic event(s) has not been resolved. Thus, the individual cannot integrate into the current moment in time, or into the present reality. Unresolved trauma creates the dynamic of post traumatic stress disorder (PTSD). Jeffrey Green states that approximately 80 percent of all Souls on the planet are born with PTSD (Jeffrey Green, Boulder, CO class, 2004).

When trauma has not been resolved, the phenomenon of projections occurs. The trauma is unconsciously projected upon others, with the resulting fear of experiencing this trauma again in the present moment in time. The core issue within this is that the past is forever being projected outward into our current reality in such a way that we cannot fully integrate into the present moment. We will recreate the past, including traumatic events, because of the projections that are in place. Projected judgments (Saturn) that emanate from the unconscious manifest until such judgments are purged through liberation. The way to resolve this viscous cycle is to make the consciousness effort to accept responsibility for our past. We must liberate from the impact of previous trauma, and purge projections of the past. In this way, we can integrate into the current moment in time, and truly shed skins from the past that are preventing further growth.

This archetype, again, makes us aware that we are different than most others around us. It promotes the awareness within consciousness of what is unique and different within ourselves. Along with this knowledge, we need to have the inner courage and strength to be secure within our own unique essence, and create the necessary liberation from past cultural conditioning patterns in order to actualize our individuality. This is why the need to bond with others of like mind is reflected in Aquarius. We find natural strength and support when we bond with others who are also different, and trying to actualize their unique individuality independent from the mainstream society.

There are commonly three main types of social bonds formed.

1. The first are those who are suppressing the inner impulse to change (Saturn). These types will project a tired old vision of the past to solve the problems of modern times. These types are called social dinosaurs. This orientation reflects that these individuals are resisting the inner impulse to liberate and move on. These individuals are threatened by any signs of outward change because it triggers insecurity and fear about liberating from past cultural conditioning patterns. Many of these types are invested in maintaining the status quo, because any change undermines their sense of personal security and power.

2. The next group of individuals are those who delusively feel that they are rebelling, and standing outside the mainstream of society—but actually are just conforming to the latest trends in society, simply following the prevailing peer group. Insecurity relative to the need for peer group acceptance creates this dynamic.

3. The last type of social groups are those who are actually making a real effort to initiate personal and collective change. These types are often termed "social revolutionists," and can be ahead of their time, orientated toward making the necessary changes on a personal and social level while liberating from cultural conditioning patterns. We can now clearly see the differences in these subgroupings in society and how the vibration of like-mindedness serves as the determinator of attraction. The principle of "like attracting like" is symbolized in the archetype of Aquarius.

Anatomically speaking, this archetype correlates with the formation of dendrites in the brain. Dendrites essentially function as synapses in the brain that trigger electrical impulses. The more advanced, or evolved, consciousness becomes, the more dendrites form, reflecting a more active area within the brain, itself, and the evolution of consciousness relative to the psychology of liberation. The electrical structuring of the entire brain is also symbolized in this archetype. Any imbalance or dysfunction within the brain will be reflected in the Aquarius archetype.

This archetype functions as a master computer, with smaller computers plugged into a master computer. The Source is symbolized by the master computer, and symbolically, we are the smaller computers. The plug that connects the smaller computers to the master computer is the Aquarius archetype's relative thoughts, electrical in nature, that we receive from the Creator. The thoughts we receive from the Creator via Aquarius, revolve around the need to liberate, decondition, and revolutionize ourselves. This occurs on a personal and collective level.

Aquarius correlates with genius capacity, which manifest as more of the brain becomes active and developed (only 10 percent of the human brain has currently been developed by most individuals). We develop the capacity to transform the structure of our consciousness through the psychological act of liberation. We can then naturally transform the existing social structure. We are not bound by the conditioning patterns of mainstream society (Saturn), or the current moment in time in general. In other words, we can separate ourselves from the time we are living in, and objectively understand what lessons on a personal and collective level need to be learned. We can project ourselves into the future in such a way that we can implement the changes that are needed to revolutionize society and our personal lives.

Mercury is the lower octave of Uranus. Uranus correlates to long-term memory, and Mercury to short-term memory. Uranus correlates to the liberation process and our thoughts relative to how we will act upon this process. Mercury correlates to the physical process that we must go through in order to accomplish liberation. In other words, if I am shown that I am meant to teach, or to be an author, then Mercury symbolizes the actual writing or speaking process that will allow the necessary transformation and deconditioning to occur (Uranus). In addition, Mercury correlates with how we mentally process, analyze, and organize all the information we receive regarding our liberation process.

Aquarius/Uranus/11th house reflects the individuated unconscious. This part of the unconscious is where memories unique to us as individuals are stored. It holds the entire blueprint of our future. Whatever has been repressed (Saturn) is stored in this part of the unconsciousness. Memories that are stored in the individuated unconscious include memories of past lives, and the traumas we may have suffered. As we liberate and decondition from these repressed memories and emotional traumas, they are cyclically released into consciousness awareness. We then know what actions to take in transforming our current inner and outer reality, if necessary. We can work through traumatic memories, as well, in order to purge the negative impact these memories often create in our current reality.

The polarity point of Aquarius is Leo. This polarity point reflects the need in all of us to creatively actualize what is unique and individualistic within ourselves. A common problem is that we can feel insecure relative to expressing what is different and unique about ourselves. This insecurity is linked with the pressure to conform to the social norms and conditioning patterns of the mainstream, or status quo, society.

The thoughts about how to actualize our own uniqueness can, unfortunately, be left unmanifested. Another problem that is created is a dependency upon the peer group in the context of creative self-actualization. The individual will not act to actualize him- or herself if the surrounding peer group has not acted first. The polarity point reflects the need to take charge of our special destiny and to shape it out of the strength of our own will. The creative purpose and special destiny will be actualized in such a way that it reflects the Soul's true individual nature.

Personal and collective evolution is accomplished as we translate our thoughts about the liberation and deconditioning process into action (creative actualization). If we transform our inner nature and structure of consciousness, then this liberation process can not help but be reflected externally in society. Our social interactions with others will be drastically different once we have found the inner security to actualize our own unique essence free from the conditioning patterns of mainstream of society.

We will attract others of like mind who are also different and working to actualize their own individuality. These types embrace inner and outer change, and understand that change is a necessary part of life, as it promotes evolution. We will not feel so isolated, and see that the value of attempting to create social change is in the effort itself. When we are in alignment with our true individuality and working to actualize it in our personal lives and in society, then we will see the true beauty of the Aquarian archetype. It is now being expressed in its natural form. We will deeply appreciate and encourage others to actualize their own unique Soul essence, free from the conditioning patterns of the past.

Pisces/Neptune/12th house—Feminine/Water/Mutable

In the archetype of Aquarius we are liberating and deconditioning from past cultural conditioning patterns that are inhibiting further growth. The unconditioned, or diamond, self is actualized through liberation, and the individuation process. Transformation of the Soul's pre-existing structure of consciousness manifests through the act of liberation. Social transformation and revolution occurs as well.

In the archetype of Pisces, we are now ending an entire chapter or cycle of evolution in order for a new cycle to begin. (This new cycle is symbolized in Aries.) As such, all old and unresolved dynamics will be recreated and relived until brought to culmination. Pisces is a composite of all the other archetypes that have preceeded it. In the context of the dual desires within the Soul (Pisces forms a trine to Scorpio), all separating desires are now being brought to an end.

All egocentric barriers and old emotional/physical/spiritual barriers that are preventing a direct and conscious connection with the Source must be dissolved. In essence, any area or dynamic with which the Soul has become overly identified, from an egocentric point of view, will be dissolved. In this way, the Soul can experience its cosmic identity as an individualized reflection of the Source.

Pisces correlates with the transcendent impulse with consciousness. Transcendence means transcending the confines of time and space altogether. The transcendent impulse reflects the desire to return to the Source, and promotes the need to spiritually develop. This is why this archetype symbolizes timeless, universal truths, and the absolute and infinite. The Soul's immortality is experienced in this archetype. Wherever Neptune, Pisces, or the 12th house is located in the natal birth chart symbolizes the natural way any Soul is meant to spiritually develop. (For example, if an individual has Neptune in the 7th house, then initiating relationships are a natural way to spiritually develop.) The desire for ultimate meaning is reflected in Pisces because of the desire to merge and unite with the Source. This is why this archetype reflects ideals of all sorts. In the context of the need to spiritually develop, as Souls evolve, this archetype correlates with psychic abilities and capacities of all sorts, such as telepathy, clairvoyance, and audiovoyence.

Pisces symbolizes the phenomena of consciousness itself. Remember that Capricorn/Saturn/10th house correlates to time and space reality, the structure of consciousness, and to mortality and the finite. As such, the relationship between these two archetypes is the need to dissolve (Neptune) the barriers (Saturn) of egocentric or subjective consciousness from Soul consciousness. Again, the center of gravity of consciousness in most people is in the ego, not the Soul. The ultimate intention of spiritual life in the shift the center of gravity from the ego to the Soul.

Consciousness is analogous to water. It is important to state that consciousness is not limited to the human being, but to all forms of life. The specific life form creates a structure (Saturn) that conditions consciousness (Neptune) just as water assumes the form of the container it is poured into. The only difference is the self-awareness within consciousness. (A simple example to illustrate this point is that animals are aware that they are a specific animal, whereas plants and rocks clearly do not have this self-awareness.) The awareness of the unity of all life, or the interrelatedness of all of creation promotes Gaia psychology. This awareness is reflected in the knowledge that every form of life has been created by a Universal Source, eliminating the destructive belief that human beings are superior to nature and to creation.

An important correlation to this archetype is illusions, delusions, and fantasies. The causative factors that create illusions and delusions are separating desires linked with ultimate meaning. In other words, separating desires within the Soul become the ultimate meaning that the individual is seeking in life. These dreams and illusions are then actualized. At some point in the evolutionary journey, these illusions are seen for what they are, as the individual experiences them as something less then he or she had hoped they would be. Disillusionment then manifests in order to align the Soul with actual reality (Virgo polarity point). The key point within this is to interpret disillusionment in a positive manner. We learn the crucial lessons that we are a co-creator with the Source, and that ultimate meaning can only truly be established from within the Soul through a direct connection to the Creator.

The painful experience of disillusionment is intended to promote this wisdom. Disintegration, meaninglessness, and a sense of emptiness occurs when ultimate meaning cannot be found in the illusions and delusions that have been actualized. These experiences are also intended to promote the awareness of specific dynamics of the previous cycle of evolution that is now being brought to completion.

A negative manifestation of the archetype of Pisces is the psychology of escapism and/or avoidance. A common type of behavior that is linked with escapism is substance abuse (drugs and alcohol). Of course, this type of behavior can manifest in varying degrees of magnitude. Any behavior that reflects the psychology of escapism and/or avoidance will clearly have a negative impact on any individual's life, and must be eliminated from the Soul. The causative factor that creates this distortion is the feelings of meaninglessness, emptiness, and worthlessness.

The core issues that are projecting ultimate meaning outside oneself, and the resulting disillusionment, causes the emotional pain that these dynamics create that are being escaped from and avoided. Another manifestation of this distortion is to create an active fantasy life in an attempt to escape actual reality. The proverbial rose-colored glasses create the illusion that nothing is wrong, and that reality isn't so bad. Again, the need to accept and acknowledge actual reality is critical. In addition, a vital lesson in the archetype of Pisces is to eliminate victimization (Virgo polarity point). When ultimate meaning has been established from within through a connection with the Source, and the psychology of victimization has been eliminated, there will no longer be a need to escape or avoid reality.

Pisces correlates to our sleep cycles and to dreams. There are three types of dreams: junk dreams, past-life dreams, and super-consciousness dreams. What function do sleep and dreams play within consciousness? Consciousness operates like a sponge, and is thus hypersensitive to stimulus in the environment. TV, radio, and loud noises all are absorbed into consciousness. Excess stimulus, or content, must be purged (trine to Scorpio) in order for consciousness to be psychically stable. Sleep allows such purging to occur.

One way this manifests is through junk dreams, which mean nothing. Sleep creates regeneration within the brain, and to minimize the intake of stimulus. Past-life dreams are dreams resolving around events of past lives. These dreams will manifest at key points in the Soul's life and will have a direct connection to the current life circumstances. These dreams will always have a dark halo of light in them. Super-consciousness dreams are dreams in which the Soul is transported to a higher realm (astral or causal), and given divine knowledge or advice of some nature. Most often, this occurs when a Soul has been asking the Creator for guidance or help. These dreams will have the sensation of flying or falling as the Soul is transported to a higher realm.

Anatomically, Pisces correlates to a substance called melatonin. This substance is secreted by the pineal gland. Melatonin regulates our sleep cycles, and is only actively secreted when the light around the pupil is very dim. This is why meditation will stimulate its secretion. This substance facilitates spiritual development, because its function within consciousness is to dissolve the barriers of egocentric or subjective consciousness from Soul consciousness. In a very negative application of this archetype, this correlates with mental disorders of all sorts such as schizophrenia, psychoses, and neuroses. Jeffrey Green's personal research in mental institutions demonstrated that 90 percent of all individuals in such institutions have a highly emphasized Pisces/12th house/Neptune signature in the natal birth chart (Boulder, 2004). Insanity means the inability to discern illusions/delusions from actual reality. The individual cannot discern unconscious illusions and delusions that have come into consciousness awareness from actual reality. We can now understand how melatonin connects to this phenomenon.

This archetype correlates with the collective unconscious. Collective unconsciousness contains memories specific to the human species since its origin. These are memories that we all share because we are all human-beings, and they reside in every individual. Pisces correlates with the collective consciousness as well. Collective consciousness simply reflects the totality of all thoughts and vibrations of every being on the planet at the current moment in time. We can all tune into the collective consciousness via the Neptune function, and osmos it into ourselves relative to a trine to Scorpio. There are three main types of collective consciousness. The first is racial consciousness. There is a difference between the structure of African-American consciousness and Caucasian consciousness. The second type is national consciousness, with a sub-category of national consciousness called regional consciousness. National consciousness, for example, describes the difference between the collective consciousness of an American and a European. Regional consciousness, then, describes the difference between the collective consciousness of individuals who live in southern Germany, versus those who live in the northern region of Germany. The third type of collective consciousness is that of the human-being since its origin, which again, we all share in common.

The polarity point is Virgo, which symbolizes that we need to create specific rituals, techniques, and methods in which spiritual development can be advanced in a practical manner. Virgo correlates with the need to be of service to society, and thus, the work function we perform. Karma Yoga is an Eastern term that describes aligning the work function with the Creator's will in such a way that the Soul becomes a channel for the Divine (Pisces). The Soul's work will then allow purification and expansion of personal horizons to manifest. The form of service will be in alignment with the Soul's evolutionary/karmic intentions for the life, and will truly be beneficial to others. In addition, the work function can become a vehicle through which the often unfocused and diffuse energy of Pisces can be brought into focus.

Virgo symbolizes the need for self-improvement and self-perfection. Thus, any old mental/spiritual/physical patterns of behavior that are blocking spiritual development, and a direct and conscious connection to the Source must be eliminated. Any aspect or component within an individual that is imperfect or inadequate in the context of spiritual development will be analyzed and eliminated.

The need to discern actual reality from illusions and delusions is critical. As mentioned earlier, the delusion of victimization must be purged from the psyche. The awareness of proper priorities must manifest as well. One dimension of the need to align with actual reality through discrimination is discernment of the actual emotional reality and dynamics within an individual. All too often, the Pisces archetype reflects difficulty or confusion relative to identifying the actual emotional reality and dynamics that are occurring within ourselves. Another problem that commonly manifests is confusion or disassociation relative to unconsciously osmosing and duplicating the behavior of others.

As these lessons are learned, the Pisces archetype will be expressed as a divine illumination, and continued spiritual progression. The ability to empathize and help another person develop spiritually is unsurpassed. The individual has purged, or seen through, his or her own delusions. The Soul, in turn, can now help others purge their own delusions. The highest and brightest expression of this archetype is a natural innocence, purity, and unconditional love that reflects the Creator's love. Divine inspiration and cosmic revelations can then manifest. In the highest forms of evolution, Pisces manifests through the great spiritual teachers and Masters of our times.

8

Chart Interpretation: The Planetary Method and House System of Chart Analysis

Chart Interpretation: Signs, Houses and Planets

There are two methods, or systems, of chart interpretation. One is called the planetary method of chart interpretation, and the other is called the house system of chart interpretation. The planetary method is a linear, step by step process in which a specific order, or sequence, is followed, based on all the planets in the birth chart. The house system of chart interpretation analyzes the specific and individualized application, or expression, of the houses in a birth chart by analyzing the planetary rulers of the sign on each house cusp. When these two methods are used in combination, we arrive at an incredibly in-depth interpretation of any birth chart.

These two systems will, of course, be founded upon the Pluto methodology and principles already described in previous chapters. In other words, Pluto, the nodal axis, and their planetary rulers are still the bottom line in chart analysis. Every other contributing factor in the birth chart will be interpreted and given meaning in the context of the main evolutionary/karmic dynamic in the birth chart. The methods that we will be applying in this chapter are the next step in the context of a total chart analysis. This process will culminate in the ability to accurately and thoroughly interpret any natal birth chart. This in-depth interpretation is based on uncovering repeating or recurring themes. When we identify recurring themes, we are identifying the core, fundamental archetypes within consciousness that are in operation. In this way, a foundation, or context, for the birth chart is developed.

Using these two systems eliminates the common problems that most people encounter when beginning astrological interpretation: 1) feeling overwhelmed by the numerous symbols to interpret, 2) struggling to understand the proper beginning point for the chart analysis, and 3) how to synthesize all the isolated symbols into a holistic interpretation. The planetary method and the house system of chart interpretation, used in combination with each other and incorporated with the Pluto methodology, will give the chart a solid context for interpretation, and will reveal core, repeating themes that can be continually referenced when interacting with a client.

Houses, Signs, and Planets

Before we discuss the specific sequence and procedure of the two methods of chart analysis, we must first understand how to interpret any isolated symbol in the birth chart. Remember that the house which any planet occupies must be analyzed first, and then the sign is added, or incorporated, into that house in order to arrive at an accurate interpretation of any planet in the birth chart. In astrological terms, we say that the sign *conditions* the house. This is true for all the signs on each house cusps, in every natal birth chart. The house will dramatically alter how the sign of the planet, or that house cusp, will be expressed. This same principle applies to planets in the context of house and sign locality. It is important to understand that there is no difference between the archetypical meaning of the planet and the archetypical meaning of the sign that rules that planet. Therefore, the chapter that describes the correlation, or meaning, of the natural archetypes of the Zodiac will apply to the planetary ruler of each archetype.

However, the crucial distinction to make during chart interpretation is that the planets, by house and sign locality, correlate to the actual psychological structure, or make-up, of any Soul (again—the archetypes symbolize the totality of human consciousness). The house that any sign is in symbolizes how each natural archetype is conditioned, and thus expressed, in any given consciousness.

For example, if an individual has Cancer on the 2nd house cusp, but no specific planet in that sign or house, we can determine that, in this individual's consciousness, the archetype of Cancer is conditioned by, or expressed through, the archetype of the 2nd house. The Moon (planetary ruler of Cancer), specifically correlates to the Soul's current egocentric structure by house and sign locality. In the case of a planet that has a corulership, i.e., Venus as a coruler of Taurus and Libra, we combined the meaning of both signs into the single planet. The planet will symbolize both archetypes that are contained within the corulership. We can now understand why the planet Venus correlates with any Soul's inner relationship, and the nature of the Soul's external relationships. The inner side, or function, of Venus correlates with the sign of Taurus (inner relationship). The outer side, or nature, of Venus correlates with the sign of Libra (external relationships).

Let's demonstrate the principles we have just described by using the brief example of a Soul that has Sun in Sagittarius in the 1st house. Where would we begin to interpret this isolated symbol? We must synthesize the archetypical meaning of the Sun, the 1st house, and Sagittarius. The core essential intentions and meaning of the Sun is creative self-actualization of the special purpose (the Sun is the planetary ruler of the 5th house, and Leo). The Sun in the chart will correlate to how we integrate and give meaning to the evolutionary purpose for the life. Thus, the Sun symbolizes the very purpose for our life.

Now, we must put the Sun in the 1st house. How will this operate within consciousness? Simply stated, the Sun in the 1st house will operate instinctually to creatively actualize its sense of special purpose and destiny. The feeling of a special purpose and destiny, and the instinctual desire to creatively actualize that purpose will be very intense. Freedom and independence to creatively actualize the special purpose, and to act to generate the necessary experiences in which self-discovery can occur, is necessary. The Sun in Sagittarius correlates with this integration process occurring in metaphysical, cosmological, or philosophical context. The development of the intrinsic individuality and self-discovery will be given a philosophical meaning, and interpretation. The person's creative self-actualization process would revolve around the need to understand his or her connection to the universe in a philosophical or metaphysical manner. The expression of the person's creative purpose will reflect the archetypes of the 1st house and Sagittarius that have just been described.

We can now adjust the basic correlations of these archetypes to any evolutionary condition of the Soul. For example, if the Soul is in an individuated condition, then the instinctual self-discovery and the self-actualization process will revolve around asserting and expressing intrinsic individuality, free from previous conditioning patterns of conformity to the mainstream (consensus) society. Mainstream religion will no longer be gravitated to, in order to provide life with a metaphysical context, or interpretation. Thus, the Sun in Sagittarius will integrate its life intentions and purpose, founded on a philosophical and metaphysical understanding of the need to individuate, and to express an individual and creative purpose. With the Sun in the 1st house, the Soul will manifest anger at any restrictions to expressing the creative purpose in an independent manner, or any restriction of personal freedom of expression. If the Soul was in the consensus state, then the Sun in Sagittarius would be put in the context of the mainstream religion, and most commonly, willfully assert (1st house) these beliefs upon others (the dynamic of convincing and converting others).

Let's take the same Sun in Sagittarius, but put it in the diametrically opposed house, which is the 7th house. How will the Sagittarius Sun manifest in this specific case? Creative actualization will take place through initiating relationships in which comparison and contrast with others takes place. Relationships will be a vehicle through which creative actualization of the special purpose and destiny relative to the evolutionary intentions for the life occurs.

The philosophical context and integration of the purpose of the life will resolve around the need to learn balance, equality, how to give and receive, and to develop an objective sense of individuality in a social context. Creative actualization will be realized through a relationship of mutual independence and honest communication. The partner and the individual must share a mutual philosophical orientation to life. Dependencies, compensation, and extremes of any nature relative to the creative actualization process must be eliminated. We can now interpret any isolated symbol in the birth chart by following this same procedure, or principles. We can now move forward to applying the two methods of chart interpretation, because the core principles of how to interpret and synthesize planets, houses, and signs have been illustrated.

Of course, Pluto and its polarity point will always be the starting point to analyze the evolutionary intentions of the birth chart. We then determine the main evolutionary/karmic dynamic of the birth chart by adding the North and South Nodes, and their planetary rulers by house and sign locality. As described before in the chapter that illustrated the specific procedure to determine the main evolutionary/karmic dynamic, these symbols form the foundation of the entire birth chart. Every other planet and contributing factor in the birth chart will be interpreted and given meaning based on the main evolutionary/karmic dynamic in the birth chart. The analogy of the foundation of the house was used to describe how the main evolutionary/karmic dynamic in the birth chart operates within consciousness.

The planetary method of chart interpretation will provide a system of analysis that gives every other planet in the birth chart a context in which an in-depth interpretation of the entire birth chart can occur. This method will demonstrate how all the symbols in the birth chart interrelate, or interact with each other by providing a step by step, linear sequence. The house system will then add further insight and clarity into the specific application, or expression, of the birth chart of any Soul. It describes how the houses of the chart are specifically conditioned by analyzing the planetary rulers, by house and house locality, of the signs that occupy each house.

This system of interpretation provides an amazingly detailed and personalized picture, or understanding, of the unique expression of any birth chart. We will describe and illustrate how both systems are used, by applying these methods in detailed examples. The other mitigating factors to include when interpreting a birth chart are the individual's gender, evolutionary condition, cultural/religious conditioning relative to the country of birth and family environment, and economic status. In this chapter we will determine the core, underlying dynamics and themes within a chart by applying the two systems of chart interpretation. We can then adjust the chart to incorporate, or reflect, these crucial mitigating factors.

The Planetary Method of Chart Interpretation

The planetary method of chart interpretation is a linear, step by step process that is based on a sequential order of all the planets in the birth chart. This eliminates the problem of feeling overwhelmed by the numerous symbols and aspects in the birth chart, and provides a foundation upon which the entire chart can be accurately interpreted. It is deductive understanding, leading to an inductive understanding. This occurs as the linear sequence is followed and the underlying, core themes in the birth are revealed in a holistic manner (Virgo leading to Pisces).

We will now go through the specific procedure, or sequential order, of this method of chart analysis. The best way to integrate this method is to write a few brief paragraphs on the core meaning of each planetary archetype that we discuss in your own natal chart. We will apply this method by using a hypothetical birth chart illustrating how to use the planetary method after the sequence has been explained. Once we grasp the underlying themes in the birth chart we can then adjust for the other mitigating factors such as the Soul's evolutionary state, cultural conditioning, and economic status.

1. Pluto (A) and Its Polarity Point (B)

Of course, the very first symbol to use to arrive at an accurate chart analysis is Pluto, by house and sign position, and the aspects it is making. This graphically describes the core dynamics within the Soul, and its past intentions, desires, and patterns of identity association. This orientation will be a point of natural gravitation coming into the life. Pluto's polarity point, then, will correlate to the evolutionary cause, or intentions, for this life, by house and sign position. The dynamics described by Pluto and its polarity point will constitute the bottom line, or core theme, of the entire birth chart.

As an example, let's use a Soul who has Pluto in Libra in the 3rd house, without any determined evolutionary condition. The description of the core archetypes will provide a very clear example to illustrate how the planetary method works. If you have trouble adjusting these archetypes to the individual's evolutionary condition, refer to the chapter titled "The Four Natural Evolutionary Conditions of the Soul."

We will write out a few brief paragraphs describing the core dynamics and correlations of Pluto in Libra in the 3rd house. After we do this, we will use the same procedure for interpreting the polarity point of Aries in the 9th house. We have just described the Soul's past desires, intentions, and deepest points of unconscious emotional security. Pluto's polarity point now symbolizes the evolutionary cause, or evolutionary intentions, for the current life. Pluto correlates with all the limitations, points of stagnation, and weakness that we all have. Pluto's polarity point describes the path to change, and the areas that we must embrace in order to purge old patterns of behavior that are causing stagnation, and inhibiting further growth. There will be an on-going metamorphosis of the areas symbolized by Pluto's natal position relative to its polarity point throughout the life. The expression of the areas symbolized by the natal position of Pluto will generate, or transmute, to higher levels of expression.

1A. Pluto in Libra in the 3rd house

Pluto in the 3rd house correlates to the desire and need to collect a diversity, or variety, of information from the external world in order to build a logical, and rational understanding of the world and the Soul's connection to the world. The Soul understands its connection, or place, within the world through the nature of information that is collected from the external world. There is a focus upon the physical environment, and the collection of facts and ideas rather than a metaphysical orientation and the formation of a belief system (9th house polarity point). In other words, there has not been a focus upon understanding the deeper truths, or metaphysical laws, of the facts that are absorbed into the psyche. There has been, and will be, a very deep need to develop the intellect as a result of this past evolutionary intention. These Souls will have a very highly developed intellectual capacity coming into the life. In essence, the evolutionary limitations in all cases will revolve around the nature of the information that is collected relative to the pre-existing notions that the Soul has of what is true and what is false. The Soul's pre-existing belief system creates a filter as to what information will be absorbed, and what will not. Limitations and evolutionary blocks are created because of this dynamic. The need to transmute all intellectual opinions, biases, and the need to defend these viewpoints as right and others as wrong is symbolized by Pluto in the 3rd house.

Pluto in Libra correlates to the initiation of relationships in order to understand the sense of individuality in a social context. The Soul will evaluate its own identity through comparison and contrast with others in the context of the relationships that are initiated. The need to learn balance, equality, and how to give and receive are central dynamics that the Soul is learning from an evolutionary point of view. Extremities and imbalances in personal behavior and in relationships are blocking further growth. In essence, the core distortion symbolized in Pluto in Libra is the need to be needed, which creates the formation of codependent relationship types.

In addition, there are projected needs which create expectations that the Soul is looking for another to fulfill. When these projected needs are not met, very deep and intense relationship conflicts occur. Turning either the partner or the self into a defacto god/goddess commonly occurs because of the projected needs within relationships. The evolutionary need is to eliminate any dependency upon another to fulfill these projected needs, and to tell the individual who or what to be, or what he or she should or should not be doing in life. In this way, codependent relationships will be transmuted.

With Pluto in Libra in the 3rd house, the Soul will initiate relationships with others in order to communicate and receive intellectual knowledge. The Soul will desire a partner with whom intellectual ideas and notions are mutual, or commonly shared. The desire to expand the intellect, or mind, will occur through relationships. The partner will be a key influence in the context of collecting and communicating information.

With Pluto in Libra there are extremities of dominating and being dominated within relationships relative to ideas, notions, and viewpoints. The need to defend pre-existing intellectual knowledge as right and the partner's as wrong will have manifested. There will be a dependency upon the partner and the relationship as a means of knowing what information is true, and what is false; what to think, and how to think about it. Of course, the Soul's evolutionary condition will determine the nature of the information and the type of relationship that the Soul will desire to create. For example, in the consensus state, the information that will be gravitated to will resolve around mainstream understanding, ideas, and notions in the external world in general. The Soul will desire this information in order to learn how society operates in order to get on top of that system. With Pluto in Libra, any individual who does not conform to these socially accepted norms will be excluded. Relationships with those who also gravitate to the mainstream society will be formed, and whose ideas and notions about life in general are shared.

In the individuated state, the Soul will desire to intellectually grow with his or her partner, and be intellectually open to explore a variety of different areas in life and different points of view in society that go outside the mainstream. The individuation process will occur in this case through being intellectually open in the context of embracing viewpoints and information that expresses individuality versus the consensus notions that one size fits all. The Soul will then compare and contrast the diversity of information and points of view that are collected in order to discover which reflects the Soul's true identity, or individuality. In the spiritual state, these core dynamics that correlate with Pluto in Libra in the 3rd house will be put in the context of forming relationships with others in this same evolutionary condition, and collecting information that is based on natural spirituality in order to merge with the Creator.

1B. *Pluto's Polarity Point in Aries in the 9th house*

The evolutionary cause, or intention, for this life is to align with a comprehensive metaphysical/philosophical/cosmological system that will allow all the facts and information to be given and consistent interpretation. Merging with natural laws that this system must promote will induce the awareness that truth is relative, and that there are a diversity of paths that lead to the same truth. In this way, the need to defend viewpoints and opinions as right and others that do not agree as wrong will be eliminated.

The revolving door of perspectives that is commonly created within 3rd house Pluto Souls will be transmuted if a comprehensive metaphysical system becomes the bottom line in interpreting all the facts and information in the environment. The 9th house polarity point symbolizes the need to learn that there is a limit to what the empirical mind can know in and of itself. The intellect does not know what it true and what is false. This realization induces the awareness that the intuitive faculty, or component, must be developed in order for evolution to proceed. The truth simply exists, it is not a product of rational thinking, or mental construction.

With Pluto's polarity point in Aries, the Soul must learn to strike out on his or her own, and ask and answer their own questions from within the self. The Soul must learn to independently initiate a self-motivated direction in life outside of a relationship. Relationships of mutual independence and coequality will be created if these evolutionary intentions are acted upon. Balance, equality, and the knowledge of when to give and when not to, and how to receive from others will manifest.

Relative to the 9th house polarity point, the identity and independent voice will be developed through the metaphysical/philosophical principles that the Soul is drawn to on an intuitive level. The Soul will have a very intense need for freedom and independence in order for self-discovery to occur in the context of the belief system. In other words, the Soul must have enough freedom and independence in order to generate the necessary experiences to discover the specific belief system that intuitively resonates with the individual. The Soul must use natural law as a guiding light to develop the identity, and interpret all the facts and information that have been collected. The Soul's partner must support this evolution, and allow individual growth to occur within the relationship. We can take these core correlations and adjust them to reflect any evolutionary state, or condition of the Soul.

2. South Node

We must now locate the South Node by house and sign position, and aspects it makes with other planets. The South Node correlates with the past egocentric structure of the Soul, and the past self-image that the Soul created in order to consciously actualize the desires and intentions symbolized by the natal position of Pluto. The dynamics represented by the South Node will also correlate to a natural point of gravitation because, like Pluto, it is known and familiar. The Soul has gravitated to these dynamics in the past for emotional security reasons, and will do so again coming into the life. Just as in the prior example of Pluto and its polarity point, write out a few paragraphs describing the core dynamics that correlate with the natal position of the South Node, and aspects it is making to other planets. It is important to remember to interpret the South Node in the context of the natal Pluto, and not as an isolated symbol. (In other words, relate the dynamics of the South Node to the actualization of Pluto.)

To continue with our example, let's use a Soul that has the South Node in the 4th house in Scorpio. This will symbolize that this Soul has used his or her family environment, and emotional body, in general, to develop the intentions reflected by the natal position of Pluto. With the South Node in Scorpio, the individual will naturally desire to psychoanalyze the nature of his or her emotional body and self-image.

The individual will penetrate others in this same way, especially those in his or her family and personal environment (South Node in the 4th house). The metamorphosis of the emotional body, and the self-image, are the underlying dynamics that have been, and will be, used to consciously actualize the desires and intentions of the natal Pluto in Libra in the 3rd house. The Soul will desire to initiate relationships with others who provide emotional depth, and emotional nurturing.

Most commonly, the Soul will be deeply insecure, and manipulate others in the personal and family environment in order to receive nurturing, attention, and reassurance that have not been found, or established, from within. There will be a deep need to internalize security, and to eliminate all forms of emotional dependencies that are preventing further growth. In the context of the 4th house South Node, the dependencies will be upon those in the family environment. Relative to Pluto in Libra in the 3rd house, the need for the other family members to tell the individual what to think, what is true, and what is false, will be very deeply ingrained. Attracting others who are very emotionally manipulative and dominating in nature, especially in the context of intellectual growth and formation, will be very likely. The individual will osmos the intellectual patterns and relationship model of his or her family environment, and defend the intellectual patterns and resulting psychology as right and others as wrong.

Of course, the other extreme that could manifest is that this individual will unconsciously attempt to make others dependent upon him or her, and emotionally manipulate the other in the context of intellectual development. This will be a reflection, or mirror, of what the individual has learned in early childhood. The Soul will most likely be emotionally immature. This is caused by displaced emotions from childhood, when the individual was not nurtured in the ways that were needed.

The South Node in Scorpio symbolizes the experiences of abandonment, betrayal, and loss that must be resolved in order for internal security to manifest. There are unconscious fears of this nature that create the distortions that have been described. The Soul will simply expect to be nurtured. These displaced emotions are now carried into adult life. Relative to Pluto in Libra, the issue of relationships and the need to resolve these displaced emotions is critical. The limitations are evident, and must be transmuted if evolution is to continue.

3. Locate the Planetary Ruler of the South Node

The planet that rules the South Node will describe by house and sign position and aspects it makes to other planets, the dynamics that have been used by the Soul to consciously develop the areas symbolized by the South Node. Just as Pluto used the South Node to actualize itself, the South Node will use the planetary ruler to develop itself in a conscious manner. Again, interpret the planetary ruler of the South Node in the context of the actualization of the South Node.

In this example the planetary ruler of the South Node would be Pluto in Libra in the 3rd house. The Soul's relationships, and intake of intellectual facts, ideas, and information from the external environment will be the core dynamics that are used to actualize the South Node in Scorpio in the 4th house. The individual will be unconsciously looking for a teacher type (Pluto in Libra) to provide intellectual information, ideas, and to tell the individual what to think, what is true, and what is false (Pluto in the 3rd house). Codependent relationships, extremities, and imbalances of all sorts will be created because of these dynamics. Again, the Soul will simply expect to receive emotional nurturing from the partner. Psychological penetration of the emotional body will be based upon the information and ideas that are communicated by the individual's partner, and absorbed from others in society in general. The partner that the Soul attracts will mirror those in the early childhood environment, and reflect the identity, psychology, and emotional vibration of key people in the individual's family.

Positively expressed, the Soul will desire to attract a partner with whom deep emotional nurturing and psychological empowerment can occur. The information that is collected and communicated will revolve around this theme. In this way, emotional expectations to be nurtured, and fears of abandonment, betrayal, and loss will be purged from the psyche. A positive self-image will be created in this way. The individual now has the ability to deeply nurture him- or herself from within.

Having interpreted these three symbols, we have just described the core dynamics that have been, and will be, in operation within the Soul coming into the current life. The limitations within the Soul that are preventing further growth are also clearly described.

4. Locate the North Node

This will graphically describe, by house and sign locality, how the Soul will consciously develop, or actualize, the evolutionary intentions for the life symbolized by Pluto's polarity point.

In our example, the North Node is in Taurus in the 10th house. The evolutionary intentions symbolized by Pluto's polarity point in Aries in the 9th house will be consciously actualized by the North Node. Simply stated, the evolutionary intentions for the life will be actualized through developing self-reliance, and creating a positive inner relationship. The person must identify his or her own inherent resources and capacities in order to effect survival on an emotional and physical level. Identifying personal values, and establishing a positive inner relationship will create self-reliance and self-sufficiency. The 10th house North Node symbolizes that these lessons will be learned through establishing a voice of authority within society through a career. Emotional maturity, and self-determination will manifest as the Soul accepts responsibility for his or her own actions. The emotional expectations of the past in the context of relationships will be eliminated as the Soul purges insecurities, and creates a positive inner relationship. Again, self-reliance will manifest as the Soul learns to identify his or her own resources and capacities from within. There will be a necessary withdrawal from the external environment in order to establish a self-reliant orientation in life in general, and to deflect the impact of the external environment.

The evolutionary requirements represented by Pluto's polarity point will be consciously actualized in this way. As a critical self-reliance and a positive inner relationship is established from within the Soul, the courage to strike out on the individual's own in order to develop his or her own independent voice and identity will manifest. Relative to the 9th house polarity point, the Soul must align with natural laws in order to develop the identity. This will be done primarily through aligning with a comprehensive metaphysical/philosophical system that allows all the facts to be interpreted. In this way a belief system that is founded on natural law, and the development of the intuitive faculty will manifest. An emotional maturation must occur as well, as the individual accepts responsibility in his or her own actions (North Node in the 10th house).

The Soul will now approach relationships, and the method of gathering and interpreting facts in a transformed manner. Relative to the North Node in Taurus in the 10th house, the Soul will have developed the capacity to establish his or her own voice within society, and be self-reliant within a relationship. The Soul's career will reflect its inherent capacities and values.

5. The Planetary Ruler of the North Node

The planetary ruler of the North Node by house and sign position correlates to the dynamics that the Soul will use to develop, or actualize, the North Node. The planetary ruler of the North Node in our example is Venus.

Let's put Venus in Virgo in the 3rd house (not conjunct Pluto). This will correlate with the need to collect a diversity of facts, information, and viewpoints from the external world and of the individual is essential, as well as intake of information from others. The individual's intellectual structure, or framework, will then be analyzed in order to determine what is lacking or deficient in some way.

Humility will manifest as self-analysis takes place. Self-improvement and purification will manifest through the collection of ideas, facts, and information in the external environment (Venus in Virgo). The Soul will take in and share information that revolves around the need to be of service to society. Most commonly, the individual will have a very critical and negative inner relationship. This will manifest as either a masochistic or sadist pathology that is reflected in external relationships.

Relative to the North Node in Taurus in the 10th house, the Soul must only take in information that is relevant to its ongoing evolutionary needs, and reflects the individual's personal values. Crises will be experienced relative to the need to discern what information is true and what is false. Facts that reflect actual reality in general, and the actual nature of the individual's internal and external reality, must be the only information that is taken in. Information must be eliminated that does not reflect the nature of actual reality and, specifically, promotes victimization.

Again, the natal Pluto in Libra in the 3rd house symbolizes that there has been a dependency upon relationships in order to know what information is true and what is false. The crisis now symbolized in Venus in Virgo in the 3rd house is the need to discern who is right and who is wrong, relative to the differing points of view that are expressed within different relationships. In this way, an essential discrimination symbolized by Venus in Virgo will be learned.

In addition, the nature of the information that is collected must encourage self-reliance, emotional maturity, and allow the individual's voice of authority within society to be expressed. Self-analysis and self-improvement will revolve around the need to eliminate all irrelevant information that the Soul cannot relate to, and does not support the necessary evolutionary growth needs of the individual. The Soul will also have developed the capacity to understand who to communicate with and receive information from, and who not. Any person who attempts to create a codependent relationship, or a dependency upon him -or herself will be blocked out of the Soul's life. Again, this is how the lessons and intentions reflected in the North Node in Taurus in the 10th house will be consciously actualized.

We have now described in all its totality the main/evolutionary karmic dynamic in the birth chart. This is the foundation of the house, so to speak, or the foundation upon which all other contributing factors in the birth chart will be interpreted and given meaning. Remember that Pluto, the South Node, and its planetary ruler correlate with the trinity of the past. Pluto's polarity point, the North Node and its planetary ruler correlate with the trinity of the future. Another insightful correlation with the planetary rulers of the Nodes is that the planetary rulers symbolize archetypes within consciousness that are emphasized in any Soul. For example, if an individual has the nodal axis in Gemini and Sagittarius, then the archetypes of Jupiter and of Mercury are highly developed and dominant within that Soul's consciousness.

6. Sun

The Sun (by house and sign position, and aspects it is making to others' planets) correlates to the manner in which this entire dynamic described so far, or this entire process, will be creatively actualized. Creative actualization of the special purpose is linked with the integration of the evolutionary intentions of the life. Thus, the natal position of the Sun correlates with the purpose that any Soul will have for the current life. It symbolizes how the current special purpose is integrated, and creatively actualized throughout the lifetime.

Again, the key in the planetary method of chart interpretation is to analyze the planets in the context of an existing structure, or the totality of the dynamics and processes that are described as we discuss each planet in a sequential order. In other words, the planets are to be interpreted in the proper context, and the sequential order of the planets determine that context. We can now understand, from an evolutionary point of view, why an individual has chosen a specific natal position for the Sun in any given life. The position of the Sun, as well as all the other planets in the birth chart, is chosen to support the evolutionary intentions and requirements for the life.

Let's put the Sun in Leo in the 1st house, building upon the current example to demonstrate how this method operates. How would the entire main/evolutionary karmic dynamic in the chart be creatively actualized and integrated? What specific purpose will the Soul have in this life? How will the Soul integrate the main/evolutionary karmic dynamic?

The need to develop the intrinsic identity separate and independent from anybody, or anything else, will be essential to the creative actualization process. The integration of the purpose for the life will revolve around the need for freedom and independence to generate whatever experiences are deemed necessary for the self-discovery process to be acted upon. Creative actualization of the special purpose and destiny will be linked with the development and expression of an independent voice. The individual's creative energy will be used to develop and express his or her own identity. The evolutionary intentions and requirements for the life will be integrated, and given meaning in this context.

7. Moon

The Moon correlates with the Soul's current egocentric structure and self-image. The Moon, by house and sign locality, symbolizes how the current evolutionary intentions are given a personal form (self-image), and consciously integrated and actualized on a daily basis. Emotional security is established through developing a specific self-image and personal form, in order to consciously actualize the evolutionary intentions for the life. The Moon will symbolize how the transition from the past to the future takes place in the present moment in time, relative to pre-existing emotional security patterns.

Let's put the Moon in Cancer in the 12th house. What specific dynamics will constitute the Soul's current egocentric structure, and self-image? The Soul will have a hypersensitive emotional body, and desire to unite emotionally with the Creator. The individual will desire to establish ultimate meaning through a connection to the Source. The individual will naturally desire to establish nurturing emotional connections with those with whom he or she forms personal and intimate relationships.

However, insecurities related to the family environment in the context of expressing the Soul's need to be nurtured, and personal emotional needs must be dissolved. The Soul must learn to internalize emotional security, and express his or her true emotional needs. A common problem symbolized by this Moon position is emotional withdrawal in the context of an ability to truly relate to others on an emotional level. With the Moon in the 12th house, the individual could potentially attempt to escape or avoid emotional reality through withdrawing into him- or herself, culminating in prior patterns of emotional insecurities, and a negative self-image must occur.

The 12th house Moon symbolizes delusions and illusions in the context of seeking emotional security in the external environment. Any person who appears to offer such emotional nurturing and security will be turned into the ultimate partner, or ultimate other. With the Moon in Cancer, seeking emotional nurturing and ultimate security within the family environment, and in close or intimate relationships will most commonly occur.

The Soul will integrate the evolutionary intentions in the current moment through the emotional body in general (Moon in Cancer) in the ways that have just been described. There must be an alignment with timeless universal truths that create a direct connection with the Source. Change can be made if the Soul has internalized emotional security, learned to nurture itself from within, and developed a conscious connection to the Source in order to create internal emotional security. Timeless, universal laws will be the basis upon which change is integrated. The

Soul's egocentric structure and self-image will be founded upon a connection to the Creator. The individual will be secure within change itself as these dynamics are developed, and the necessary past patterns of insecurities and a negative self-image are brought to culmination.

How would the Moon support the evolutionary intentions for the life, and creative actualization process symbolized by the Sun? Simply stated, as the Soul learns to internalize security, and align with timeless, universal laws through developing a connection to the Source, the negative emotional patterns of the past will be brought to culmination. The Soul's self-image will then become positive, and reflect its connection to the Source. The necessary evolution that must occur (Pluto's polarity point and the North Node), and the creative actualization of the special purpose (Sun) will manifest through a self-image of this nature on a daily basis.

8. Mercury

Mercury correlates with the nature of our intellectual framework, or structure, and the nature of the information that we collect. Mercury has a corulership of Virgo and Gemini. Generally speaking, the process of gathering information and ideas, and communicating these ideas and facts to others is reflected in Gemini. Gemini is the outer nature, or side, of Mercury. The process of organizing and analyzing all the facts, information, and ideas that we collect is reflected in Virgo. Virgo symbolizes the inner nature or side of Mercury.

Simply stated, our inner thought process, intellectual structure, and how we communicate with others is described by the house and sign position of Mercury, and aspects it makes to other planets. Mercury is deductive, linear, and empirically oriented, which is the reason it correlates with the left brain. One function of Mercury within consciousness is to give labels and classifications to the physical environment (i.e., we label or term a chair, a spoon, or a desk).

This planet, then, correlates with how we intellectually understand the entire process, or dynamics, that has been described up until this point. Again, Mercury correlates to how we mentally organize the world around us, and evolutionary reasons for doing that organizing in a specific manner. For example, there will be a vast difference between the mental organization, thought process, and nature of communication of a Soul with Mercury in the 8th house, and a Soul who has Mercury in the 1st house.

For example, let's put Mercury in Virgo in the 2nd house and interpret how an individual with Mercury in this house and sign will mentally organize the environment, the type of information that he or she will collect, the manner in which the individual communicates, and his or her inner thought process. The individual will collect information that is relevant to his or her evolutionary purpose and intentions (Mercury in the 2nd house). The only information that the individual will be interested in is information that he or she can personally relate to, that reflects his or her values, and which they can use to sustain ongoing survival on an emotional and physical level. The Soul will naturally think in terms of effecting self-reliance, and will gather information that reflects this need.

A common problem that will occur is that information and viewpoints that do not support the Soul's pre-existing notions or ideas of what is true and what is false will be rejected. In other words, problems will occur if the individual's limited viewpoints and intellectual understanding of life in general create a situation where he or she will not receive information that undermines, or threatens, the existing intellectual structure. For example, in a distorted expression of Mercury in the 2nd house the Soul will value materials, possessions, and wealth in order to feel self-reliant. Any information that does not reflect this orientation and value system will be tuned out, and criticized.

With Mercury in Virgo, the individual will be very analytical, and orientated to a left-brain type of mental processing and organization. The individual will naturally analyze the deficiencies and lacks in his or her own ideas, thoughts, and information that is collected even if this is not outwardly expressed. The Soul will be interested in information that promotes self-healing, self-improvement, and is oriented toward service to others in society.

Crisis (Mercury in Virgo) will be experienced when the individual can no longer relate to (Mercury in the 2nd house) the information that he or she has taken in from the environment that was previously perceived as relevant and accurate. The information will now be understood as lacking, or deficient, in some manner, which triggers a crisis because it no longer is of value. The intention of the crisis is to lead to self-analysis of what needs to be adjusted within the individual's intellectual structure. In the case of a Soul who has gravitated to material possessions and wealth in order to create self-reliance, there will come a point in time where the individual will no longer be able to relate to values of this nature. The crisis that is then triggered revolves around the need to adjust the mental structure to identify the individual's inherent resources and capacities in order to achieve true self-reliance from within. The individual will then be able to discern his or her true values, and establish self-reliance through the form of service to society.

The Soul must be inwardly secure within his or her mental capacities and viewpoints. The tendency to adopt, or live through, and thus become a vicarious extension of the viewpoints and opinions of others, must be overcome (Mercury in the 2nd house). Information that promotes the capacity to be self-reliant will then be combined with information that revolves around the need for self-improvement, and to be of service. Criticism of others who do not agree with the individual's points of view and values will most commonly manifest. Victimization and a sadist or masochistic pathology must be eliminated from the mental structure.

We can now put these core correlations of Mercury in Virgo in the 2nd house in the context of the entire evolutionary dynamics or processes, we have discussed up until this point. For example, how would Mercury in Virgo in the 2nd house mentally analyze and intellectually understand the main evolutionary/karmic dynamics and processes described so far?

Simply stated, the individual will analyze this process in a linear and deductive manner. The decencies, flaws, or lacks within this entire process will be improved upon through such mental analysis. The need for self-improvement and self-perfection creates the ongoing need for inner adjustment of whatever is analyzed as deficient, lacking, or flawed. Critical, negative, and undermining messages must be eliminated. Again, only information that the individual perceives as relevant to his or her evolutionary purpose will be absorbed into the intellectual structure.

9. Venus

Venus correlates with our inner relationship with ourselves, and the external relationships we form with others. Our external relationships are a reflection of our inner relationship. In other words, Venus has an inner nature reflected in our inner relationship, and an outer nature reflected in our external relationships. Venus has a corulership of Libra and Taurus. The two sides of Venus are reflected in these archetypes. Our inner relationship correlates with Taurus, and the inner side of Venus.

Our inner relationship creates our inner vibration, or inner magnetism, which then becomes the causative factor that attracts others. Our external relationships correlate with Libra, and the outer side of Venus. Our values, and the resulting meaning that we give to our life is symbolized in this planet in the archetype of Taurus.

Extremities of all sorts correlate to Venus relative to Libra. Thus, dynamics that are operating in extremity, and need to be brought into balance are symbolized by Venus. As described earlier, Libra correlates to the process of evaluating our identity, or individuality, through comparison and contrast with others. The need to be needed in relationships most commonly creates a situation wherein the individual will try on many different ways of being, values, beliefs, etc., that does not truly reflect the identity of the Soul. This dynamic creates a perpetual fluxuation from one psychological extreme to the next.

Venus also symbolizes how we are listening to ourselves (our inner dialogue), which is reflected in Taurus. Our inner dialogue is the determinant to how we listen to others. If we are only listening to our partner from the prism of our own filter, or our own inner dialogue, then we are not truly hearing what the other is communicating in an objective manner. The nature of projected needs and expectations in relationships is reflected in the natal position of Venus. The nature of the relationships that the Soul forms is symbolized by the house and sign position of Venus. Essential needs within relationships are symbolized by Venus. This includes the sexual values and needs of the Soul.

When we put all of the dynamics that correlate to Venus in the context of the entire evolutionary/karmic dynamics, or processes, we now understand why the Soul has created a specific inner relationship, and external relationship patterns. Again, the individual's values and inner relationship is the determinant to how he or she will relate to other people, and form relationships.

In our example, Venus is in Virgo in the 3rd house (not conjunct Pluto), and the planetary ruler of the North Node. We can clearly understand that Venus plays a very significant role in this Soul's evolution. Venus being the planetary ruler of the North Node symbolizes that the Soul's relationships will serve to evolve the Soul out of past conditions that are creating a non-growth situation.

10. Mars

Mars is the lower octave of Pluto. A lower octave is a denser expression of a higher vibration. The desires that emanate from Pluto are transmitted to Mars in order for the desires to be consciously acted upon. In other words, Mars is the conscious embodiment of Pluto. Mars correlates to the subjective desires we all have, and how we act upon, or out, those desires. Mars is the planetary ruler of Aries.

This planet symbolizes the need for freedom and independence in order to act upon our conscious desires. A continual state of becoming, and of self-discovery is reflected in Mars. The natal house and sign position of Mars, and aspects it is making to other planets, will symbolize the nature of the subjective and conscious desires of the individual, and how those desires are acted upon. In addition, Mars symbolizes the nature of our fears and anger. Anger is triggered when restriction to personal freedom in the context of self-discovery and growth occurs. When we put these correlations in the context of the entire process that has come before this point, we now understand how these dynamics, or processes, will be continually acted upon, or acted out, and thus given continual motion.

For example, let's put Mars in Cancer in the 11th house. What will be the underlying, or core, subjective desires of the Soul? How will the entire dynamics, or process, of the birth chart be acted upon?

The 11th house Mars desires to liberate and decondition from all past conditioning patterns that have inhibited, or restricted, the ability to express its own unique individuality. Any aspect within the Soul that is outdated, crystallized, and preventing further growth will be liberated from, or severed, on an ongoing basis. The Soul will desire to initiate actions that allow deconditioning and liberation from past conditioning patterns that restrict the expression of its unique individuality.

There will be a need to generate experiences that allow the discovery and expression of this individuality to occur. The 11th house Mars also symbolizes a fear of individualist expression relative to past experiences of trauma. A fear of being ostracized by society is also reflected by Mars in the 11th house. A very likely scenario is one wherein the Soul attempted to express individuality, but was traumatized by others in society who demanded conformity, and feared anybody who is different. The fear of individualist expression being restricted by others in mainstream society who demand conformity was then manifested. The Soul could have also been the recipient of many wounding projections by those in the mainstream society. Of course, the Soul will have also projected onto others in the same way. In all cases, trauma must be resolved in order to liberate from the negative influence of traumatic events in the present moment.

Mars in Cancer correlates with the desire to create internal security, and to nurture oneself from within through establishing an independent voice. The self-image must be positive. The individual will naturally desire to initiate experiences and actions that will serve as a vehicle through which internal security, and a positive self-image will be created.

Most commonly, the Soul will have a fear of being vulnerable, and of expressing its true emotional needs (Mars in Cancer). Emotional immaturity will manifest if the Soul has not learned to nurture itself from within, and expects others to provide emotional security. In addition, if internalized emotional security has not been actively developed, emotional anger will manifest if the individual is not receiving the emotional nurturing that he or she expects. Projected anger based on displaced emotions from childhood will manifest as well. With Mars in Cancer in the 11th house, the Soul will instinctually desire to create emotional connections with others who are also in the process of liberating, and are of like mind (of course, the evolutionary condition of the Soul will determine the nature of these like-minded individuals). There is a need to objectify the Soul's desire nature and emotional dynamics in order for the necessary liberation and deconditioning process to manifest. In addition, unresolved emotional anger relative to past traumas will create a detachment from the emotional body. Anger and frustration results because the Soul desires to connect, or embrace, the emotional body. Again, trauma would most likely have been experienced whenever the Soul attempted to express its own unique identity. These past traumatic experiences create fear in the context of expressing individuality in the present moment. This is a central dynamic from which the Soul intends to liberate.

How will Mars in Cancer in the 11th house act upon the entire evolutionary process? The desire to liberate from past conditioning patterns that are preventing growth and have become crystallized and outdated will be a central dynamic that Soul acts upon, in order to actualize the current evolutionary intentions. The desire to create internal emotional security based on a positive self-image is now linked with, or expressed through, the liberation process. These core dynamics are the foundation upon which the entire evolutionary/karmic process which has been interpreted thus far will be consciously acted upon. As mentioned before, Mars operates as a vehicle through which continual growth occurs relative to the entire evolutionary process throughout life.

11. Jupiter

Jupiter correlates to the belief system, or structure, of the Soul. Beliefs are the determinate to how we interpret life itself. Jupiter symbolizes the philosophical/metaphysical or cosmological context which it gives to life. This planet reflects a continual expansion within consciousness. Jupiter is the planetary ruler of Sagittarius. Jupiter correlates with the issue of truth, or honesty, and the need to realize truth from a philosophical/metaphysical context. This leads to an awareness of natural law. There are natural laws that explain the existence and operation of creation by the sheer fact that creation exists in the first place. Thus, natural law is a very deep correlation of this planetary archetype. Jupiter, then, by house and sign locality, will describe the Soul's belief system, or structure, and the resulting philosophical/metaphysical meaning that an individual has in life. Thus, how the individual is interpreting life will be described by the natal position of Jupiter and aspects it makes to other planets. Similarly, Jupiter correlates with the manner in which the entire process and dynamics are given a philosophical meaning and interpreted.

For example, let's put Jupiter in Scorpio in the 4th house (not conjunct the South Node). What philosophical meaning and orientation will correlate with this placement of Jupiter? How will the Soul interpret life? The 4th house Jupiter symbolizes that the individual will create a belief system that revolves around the need to be emotionally secure from a subjective point of view, establish internal security, and promote a positive self-image. With Jupiter in Scorpio, the Soul will have to be able to directly perceive the validity of the belief system. The individual will interpret life from an emotional and psychological level.

Jupiter in the 4th house symbolizes that the family environment will have a dramatic impact on the development of the individual's belief system. The individual will, most likely, compensate because of insecurities in the context of expressing his or her own true beliefs. Commonly, the individual will adopt the beliefs of his or her parents, and early childhood environment.

In addition, in a negative expression of this natal Jupiter, the Soul could unconsciously attempt to manipulate the beliefs of others in order to receive emotional nurturing, and to feel emotionally secure. This will occur specifically within the family environment, or from others with whom the individual is in a close, or personal relationship. Manipulation will manifest in the context of not being emotionally honest, and trying to convince and convert others. Emotional security is linked with the pre-existing belief system. Again, most commonly, the individual's belief system is an extension of the family, and early childhood environment.

Clearly, the act of compensation creates stagnation and nongrowth. Yet, Jupiter in Scorpio symbolizes that the Soul desires to purge any beliefs that are creating stagnation, and to merge with natural law through direct perception, or experience. In addition, the Soul will desire to psychologically penetrate to the bottom line of all the limitations within the existing belief system. The dynamic of compensation will be eliminated as this penetration occurs.

The belief system must allow a metamorphosis of the Soul's self-image to occur. All insecurities and dependencies upon the external environment to provide emotional nurturing and security relative to the belief system will be purged as emotional security is internalized. Any beliefs that are preventing growth, and that promote dependencies upon the external environment in general must be transmuted in order for a positive self-image to be created, and internal security to manifest. The individual will then transmute the need for others in his or her family, and close environment to know what beliefs are true and what are not. Positively expressed, the Soul will use natural law as a source of emotional empowerment and emotional security.

We can now interpret this symbol in the context of the entire birth chart or sequence that we have described so far. In other words, by understanding Jupiter in this way, we now understand how the entire process or dynamics in the birth chart are going to be given a philosophical meaning and context—the belief structure that the Soul will utilize. The belief structure of the Soul determines how this entire process will be interpreted.

12. Saturn

Saturn correlates with the structural order, or definition, of consciousness. Saturn describes the structure of consciousness itself. It symbolizes the totality of our conscious awareness, or what we are aware of consciously, at any moment in time. Saturn describes by house and sign locality and aspects that it makes to other planets, the structure of consciousness within any Soul.

A simple analogy that has been used to describe how Saturn operates within consciousness is the cup, or container, that holds water. The water takes the form of the cup, or container, that it is placed into. In this analogy, consciousness (Neptune correlates with the phenomena of consciousness) is represented by the water, and Saturn is represented by the container. This planet symbolizes how every other function (planet) within the birth chart will be conditioned relative to the structure of consciousness. Saturn also correlates to the nature of our cultural/societal conditioning, which is why it reflects the nature of not only our current inner and outer reality in general, but the past, as well. The need to actualize and establish our own voice of personal authority is symbolized by this planet. This, of course, manifests through the career, or a sociological role. Emotional maturity is learned through accepting the responsibility in our own actions.

Let's put Saturn in Scorpio in the 3rd house (not conjunct Pluto). What is the structure of consciousness within the Soul? Saturn in the 3rd house correlates to a consciousness that is structured to collect a diversity of information from the external environment in order to logically and empirically explain our connection, or place, in the world. With Saturn in Scorpio, the Soul will collect information that is psychological in nature, and allows a transmutation of all intellectual limitations to occur. The Soul will gravitate to information of a deeply metamorphic nature that promotes re-empowerment.

Negatively expressed, the Soul will attempt to manipulate the intellectual formation of another, and compulsively rationalize negative psychological dynamics that are blocking further growth. The individual will refuse to absorb information that does not support the existing structure of his or her own consciousness in the context of his or her viewpoints, ideas, and notions of what is true and what is false. Authority within society will be expressed by overpowering and manipulating others in order to be in a position of power and control. Positively expressed, the Soul will use information as a source of empowerment, and to create a transmutation of any psychological aspect within consciousness that is preventing further growth. The consciousness structure of the Soul will be in a constant state of metamorphosis as intellectual limitations and psychological penetration of the individual's intellectual structure occurs. The Soul's voice of authority within society will be based on psychological knowledge, and an ability to communicate this knowledge to others.

Again, Saturn, by house and sign locality, will condition the expression of every other planet in the birth chart. The entire process will be defined, structured, and ordered relative to the house and sign position of Saturn, and aspects it makes to other planets.

13. Uranus

Uranus correlates to the transformative impulse within the Soul. It correlates with the need to liberate and decondition from the conditioning patterns symbolized by Saturn. Uranus is forever knocking on Saturn's door in the context of the need to transform the existing structure of consciousness. This occurs because nongrowth and stagnation manifests whenever the existing structure of consciousness becomes crystallized, and outdated. Liberation from these past conditions promotes accelerated growth by radically altering the existing structure of consciousness.

Uranus symbolizes the desire to express the Soul's unique individuality—free from the conditioning patterns of the past ,which are linked to the society or culture of birth. The impulse to liberate and individuate triggers the psychology of rebellion against the consensus, mainstream society. Uranus, by house and sign position and the aspects it makes with other planets, symbolizes how the structure of consciousness within the Soul will be transformed throughout the current life.

Uranus symbolizes the individuated unconscious. The individuated unconscious contains content that is unique to an individual (this includes past-life memories). This content is progressively released into conscious awareness as the behavioral patterns that are preventing further growth are actively transformed, and liberation occurs. In other words, the individuated unconscious is activated through the act of individuation and liberation.

To demonstrate these principles, let's put Uranus in Sagittarius in the 5th house. What specific dynamics will the Soul need to liberate from in order for evolution to occur? What dynamics will create a transformation of the structure of consciousness throughout the life? What areas, or dynamics, will the Soul use to express its own unique individuality?

With Uranus in the 5th house, past patterns of excessive subjective focus which lead to an essentially narcissistic orientation to life in general must be eliminated. In other words, liberation from a pyramid reality structure must occur. The creative actualization process must be transformed. This will be done by linking the special purpose with a socially relevant need. Delusions of grandeur are another dynamic which must be severed in order for liberation to manifest, and the unique individuality of the Soul to be expressed. Most commonly, the Soul will be overly identified with his or her creative purpose and special destiny from an egocentric point of view. Uranus in the 5th house symbolizes that the Soul's creative actualization process will be a vehicle through which de-conditioning and liberation will occur. The Soul can express its unique individuality through creative actualization of the special purpose that is linked with a socially relevant need.

With Uranus in Sagittarius, the Soul will liberate through the belief system. The Soul must liberate from all man-made beliefs and doctrines that condition and repress the expression of individuality. Natural law must become the guiding light for the individuation and liberation process to occur positively. The need to convince and convert others to the belief system that the Soul is oriented to must be eliminated. Any generalizations of these beliefs (one size fit all) must be purged as well. Any pattern of emotional dishonesty must be eliminated. There is an emphasized need to align with a belief system that supports the development and actualization of individuality. The Soul will have very unique teaching abilities, which can be a potential capacity to creative self-actualize because it is linked with a socially relevant need.

The areas symbolized by Saturn that have become crystallized and outdated will be transformed through the liberation impulse of Uranus. In this case, the limitations of the Soul's consciousness structure relative to its intellectual framework (Saturn in Scorpio in the 3rd house) will be transformed through aligning with a belief system that is founded on natural law, and supports the actualization of the unique individuality (Uranus in Sagittarius in the 5th house). The special purpose or destiny of the Soul, and creative actualization process will allow the necessary patterns of behavior that are preventing growth symbolized by Saturn to be transformed. We can now put these core correlations in the context of the entire evolutionary dynamics described so far in the planetary sequence.

14. Neptune

Neptune correlates to the transcendent impulse within consciousness, and the need to establish a direct and conscious connection to the Creator. Neptune symbolizes the ultimate meaning that we create for our life. It symbolizes how we understand our life's intentions from a spiritual point of view (our spiritual purpose). Thus, the house and sign position of Neptune and the aspects it makes to other planets symbolizes the Soul's ultimate meaning in life, and where the Soul is naturally meant to spiritually develop.

Neptune is the planetary ruler of the archetype of Pisces. This planet symbolizes the process of culmination, and dissolution of an entire cycle of evolution. Thus, every unresolved dynamic must now be resolved, or brought to resolution, in order for a new evolutionary cycle to begin. The process of culmination, or completion, allows a brand-new cycle of evolution to begin (this is symbolized by Mars/Aries/1st house).

Negatively expressed, the areas symbolized by the natal position of Neptune will manifest as meaninglessness, emptiness, and disintegration. Neptune correlates to where any of us are most susceptible to delusions, yet simultaneously where we can become divinely inspired, and our connection to the Source can be consciously experienced.

The critical point is that delusions are created whenever ultimate meaning is projected outward in whatever area of life. This dynamic is based on our separating desires that have not been brought to culmination, and purged from the Soul. Disillusionment occurs as the Soul realizes these dreams and illusions for what they are: dreams. This occurs as the Soul actualizes illusions, only to experience them as something less than had been expected. The core realization that must manifest is that ultimate meaning can only be found within the Soul through developing a direct and conscious merging with the Creator.

Neptune correlates with the collective unconscious, or the totality of all the thoughts and vibrations on the planet from all forms of life at any moment in time. The response to the collective need occurs through the house and sign position of Neptune because, via this function within consciousness, we are all tuned into the collective unconsciousness.

To illustrate these principles, let's put Neptune in Sagittarius in the 6th house. What dynamics are being brought to culmination? Where is the Soul naturally meant to develop spiritually? What spiritual purpose and ultimate meaning will the Soul have in life? Where is the Soul most susceptible to delusions and illusions?

With Neptune in the 6th house, the Soul will naturally desire to be of service to others as a method to develop spiritually. This will occur through the individual's work function. The need to align with a work function that reflects the Soul's spiritual purpose (Karma Yoga) is essential.

With Neptune in the 6th house, the individual will most commonly seek some mundane form of service that does not truly reflect his or her spiritual identity, or capacity. This occurs because of constant self-undermining activity that has not been brought to an end. The individual is always making excuses as to why he or she will do what must be done when it is the proper time to act. The individual never feels good enough or ready enough to do what he or she is being directed to do on behalf of the Source. Thus, self-doubt and feelings of lack and inferiority will create a reality in which the Soul does not fully develop its spiritual capacity. This creates yet another source if guilt.

The Soul must dissolve past patterns of projecting this negative, critical attitude in the external environment in general. A pathology of masochism or sadism (or both) will be operative within the Soul. This distortion, of course, will be reflected in the individual's spiritual orientation, and the form of service (work function) that is performed until these dynamics are brought to culmination, and purged from the Soul. Victimization, and behavior that is linked to denial and avoidance, must be ended in order for a new evolutionary cycle to begin.

A mundane form of work will be gravitated to until the proper discrimination (6th house Neptune) of the Soul's intended work manifests. In addition, until the individual realizes that his or her first priority is to develop a connection to the Creator, then the busy-bee syndrome (where there is always another external obligation) will occur. The feelings of aloneness that create a deep existential void must be eliminated through spiritual development. Until these feelings of aloneness are resolved, the Soul will avoid/deny these feelings through attempting to fill the void with never-ending, external obligations, and work activity.

Neptune in Sagittarius symbolizes that man-made conditioned beliefs (indoctrination) must be dissolved in order for an alignment with natural law to occur. The Soul must discriminate (6th house) and eliminate all conditioned beliefs that create feelings of inferiority, lack, and doubt, and promote a masochistic/sadistic psychology.

The Soul's work function will be based upon its beliefs system. The individual's spiritual purpose will be linked with these beliefs, and the need to align with natural law. Natural law must become the foundation upon which a healthy discrimination between which beliefs to take in and which not to is developed. The Soul can then create a reality in which its true spiritual capacities or abilities are actualized through the service that is performed. Natural law will then be expressed through the individual's work function.

These are the core dynamics that must be brought to culmination, and where the Soul is naturally meant to develop spiritually. As the necessary dynamics are resolved, a new cycle of evolution can begin.

Now that we have described and illustrated the planetary method in a detailed, step by step analysis, we can more fully understand how this method graphically describes reoccurring themes, and how to synthesize all the isolated symbols in the birth chart into a holistic interpretation. A full analysis of the birth chart has been created as we determined the main evolutionary/karmic dynamic in the chart, and interpreted every other planet in the chart, based upon the understanding of the main evolutionary/karmic dynamic. How the planets in the birth chart interrelate and support the main evolutionary/karmic dynamic has been illustrated as this method was applied.

The House System of Chart Interpretation

The planetary method described a linear sequence of all the planets in the birth chart. Again, the planetary method creates a holistic interpretation of the natal chart through deductive analysis. The house method of chart interpretation is used to further understand the personal applications and unique expression of the natal birth chart. In other words, the house method provides a very deep understanding of how any natal birth chart is uniquely conditioned and expressed. This method is described in Jeffery Wolf Green's Evolutionary Astrology correspondence course (103–104).

This method is based upon the analysis of how each house cusp is conditioned, which is determined by an analysis of the planetary ruler of each house cusp. In the case of a planet in the house that is being analyzed, look at the house position of the sign that rules the planet. All of these factors, or elements, will provide additional information, and deepen our understanding of how any house in the birth chart is conditioned and will be uniquely expressed within consciousness. Clearly, we are describing layers when we use this method.

To illustrate how this method works, let's use an example of Pisces in the first house (Pisces ascendant). We must determine how this house will be conditioned through an analysis of the planetary ruler, Neptune, by house and sign position. We must also include aspects this planet makes to other planets. Let's put Neptune in Libra in the 8th house for our example.

1. The first layer is the archetypical meaning of the house that we are analyzing (the 1st house in our example).

2. The next layer is the sign on the house cusp (Pisces in our example). The sign will describe how the archetype of the house is conditioned, or expressed.

3. The next layer is the planetary ruler of the sign on the house cusp that is being analyzed by house and sign position (in our example Neptune in the 8th house).

4. In the case of a planet in the house under consideration (in our example it is the 1st house), the next layer is to condition that house with the planetary archetype of the planet in the house that is being analyzed. In our example, we will use Jupiter.

5 The next layer: locate the house position of the sign that is ruled by the planet in the house under analysis (in our example, Jupiter). Sagittarius will be in the 10th house in our example.

We will demonstrate all of these principles in a simple example. These layers describe core, fundamental and reoccurring themes within the birth chart that will be continually referenced during counseling work. When the two methods of chart interpretation are combined, and then used in conjunction with the Pluto methodology, we achieve an in-depth, thorough, and precise interpretation of the natal birth chart.

Applying the House System of Chart Interpretation

In our example, we will use Pisces on the 1st house cusp, and Neptune in Libra in the 8th house. We will put Jupiter in Pisces in the 1st house, and Sagittarius in the 10th house.

The first layer is to interpret the 1st house. The 1st house correlates with the need for freedom and independence in order for self-discovery and development of identity to occur. Experience is a vehicle through which self-discovery and development of the identity is realized. Thus, relative to the sign on the 1st house cusp, this house symbolizes an area in which the Soul will demand freedom to generate whatever experiences are necessary in order for self-discovery to occur. In this example, Pisces is on the first house cusp (Pisces ascendant).

The archetype of Pisces, then, will condition the 1st house, and how the Soul acts upon the need for self-discovery, and the development of the identity. We can now determine that this Soul will understand its own intrinsic identity in a universal manner, and through action upon spiritual development. This will occur instinctually, relative to the first house. The Soul will desire to initiate experiences in which universal, timeless, and transcendent principles can be used as a foundation to develop the identity.

Pisces correlates to the need to establish ultimate meaning in life, and to purge all delusions and illusions from the Soul. Merging with the Creator will create a clear reflection point in the context of developing the intrinsic identity. A connection with the Creator will allow delusions and illusions to be purged from the Soul.

The next layer to include is the planetary ruler of Pisces, which is Neptune in Libra in the 8th house. What additional archetypes will condition the 1st house relative to the development of the identity, and process of self-discovery?

For the sake of simplicity, we will start only with the house Neptune is in, and then add the sign. The 8th house Neptune symbolizes that a deep psychological penetration of its motivations, intentions, and desires will occur. The Soul will penetrate others in the same way. This psychological penetration and resulting metamorphosis of limitations will be used in order to develop the identity, and to get to the bottom line of all delusions and egocentric barriers that are preventing a direct and conscious merging with the Creator.

Disillusionment will have been experienced relative to projecting ultimate meaning within whatever spiritual activity the Soul had initiated (Pisces in the first house, Neptune in the 8th house). The rug of emotional security had been pulled from underneath the feet. The resulting fears of abandonment, betrayal, manipulation, and loss must now be brought to culmination. Culmination allows a brand-new cycle of becoming to manifest in the context of spiritual development, and how this impacts the formation of the identity. The Soul will be asking the 8th house question "why did these experiences occur?"

Neptune in Libra symbolizes that the Soul will have experienced abandonment, betrayal, and loss within relationships. The desire is to deeply merge with another at a Soul level (Neptune in Libra in the 8th house). Forming deep, committed relationships will be part of the process of developing identity and spiritual development (Pisces in the 1st house).

However, deep emotional expectations will be an intense source of conflict within relationships. The core dynamic that creates such conflicts is expecting another to provide the ultimate meaning in life that has not been found within (Pisces in the 1st house, Neptune in Libra in the 8th house). The Soul could then potentially feel betrayed, and project rage at the partner who is not fulfilling these projected needs.

These dynamics must be brought to culmination in order for positive and healthy relationships to be established. The development of the identity and process of spiritual development can then manifest in a positive and healthy manner as well. The instinctual awareness of the individual's and other people's motivations and intentions will manifest as the necessary patterns just described are brought to culmination (Neptune in Libra in the 8th house, Pisces in the 1st house).

The next step to include is the planetary archetype of Jupiter because it lands in the 1st house. Jupiter correlates with the belief system of the Soul, and how we understand our connection to the universe in a metaphysical, cosmological, and philosophical context. Our beliefs determine how any of us will interpret life, itself.

This core archetype will be an additional conditioning element in the context of the expression of the 1st house relative to the development of the identity, and the process of self-discovery. Jupiter conjunct the ascendant symbolizes that the Soul will desire to align with natural laws in order to develop his or her identity, and to provide ultimate meaning in his or her life. The development and understanding of the Soul's identity will occur in a metaphysical and philosophical context. This creates the need to merge with natural laws.

Relative to Neptune in the 8th house, the individual's psychological penetration will be given a metaphysical bottom line and interpretation.

The next layer, or step, to include is the house that the sign Sagittarius (archetype ruled by Jupiter) occupies. In this case, Sagittarius is in the 10th house. The 10th house symbolizes what the development of the identity, and spiritual development will need to express in society. The Soul will express its personal voice of authority within society through a career that reflects his or her identity, and need to spiritually develop. There is a potential for willful assertion of the individual's beliefs, and spiritual domination in the context of the beliefs with which the Soul has aligned, or is oriented to (Pisces in the 1st house, Jupiter conjunct the ascendant, Sagittarius in the 10th house). The evolutionary state, or condition, of the Soul will determine what beliefs the Soul will gravitate to, and how the spiritual component will be developed. In a negative expression, The need to convince and convert others to these beliefs will be instinctual, and is clearly a central dynamic that must be resolved in the present moment in time. In addition, falling prey to spiritual teacher types who want to control the individual is very likely in the context of Jupiter in Pisces in the 1st house conjunct the ascendant, Sagittarius in the 10th house, and Neptune in Libra in the 8th house.

This simple example is meant to apply the principles of the house method of chart interpretation. Again, we can analyze each house in the birth chart in this manner, in order to arrive at a very detailed and accurate interpretation of any natal horoscope. We must use this method in combination with the planetary method of chart interpretation, and the Pluto methodology, in order to fully interpret the birth chart.

Also by The Wessex Astrologer - www.wessexastrologer.com

Patterns of the Past
Karmic Connections
Good Vibrations
The Soulmate Myth: A Dream Come True or Your Worst Nightmare?
The Book of Why
Judy Hall

The Essentials of Vedic Astrology
Lunar Nodes - Crisis and Redemption
Personal Panchanga and the Five Sources of Light
Komilla Sutton

Astrolocality Astrology
From Here to There
Martin Davis

The Consultation Chart
Introduction to Medical Astrology
Wanda Sellar

The Betz Placidus Table of Houses
Martha Betz

Astrology and Meditation
Greg Bogart

The Book of World Horoscopes
Nicholas Campion

Life After Grief : An Astrological Guide to Dealing with Loss
AstroGraphology: The Hidden Link between your Horoscope and your Handwriting
Darrelyn Gunzburg

The Houses: Temples of the Sky
Deborah Houlding

Through the Looking Glass
The Magic Thread
Richard Idemon

Temperament: Astrology's Forgotten Key
Dorian Geiseler Greenbaum

Nativity of the Late King Charles
John Gadbury

Declination - The Steps of the Sun
Luna - The Book of the Moon
Paul F. Newman

Tapestry of Planetary Phases:
Weaving the Threads of Purpose and Meaning in Your Life
Christina Rose

Lightning Source UK Ltd.
Milton Keynes UK
UKHW021829191121
394181UK00007B/187